# Reading the animal text
# in the landscape of the
# damned

# Reading the animal text in the landscape of the damned

**Les Mitchell**

NiSC

First edition 2019

Text and the work copyright © Les Mitchell 2019

Published in South Africa on behalf of the author by
NISC (Pty) Ltd, PO Box 377, Grahamstown, 6140, South Africa


ISBN 978-1-920033-60-6 (print)
ISBN 978-1-920033-61-3 (PDF)
ISBN 978-1-920033-62-0 (ePub)




Design, typesetting and layout: NISC (Pty) Ltd
Proofreading: Peter Lague
Cover design: Advanced Design Group
Photographs: ©The Author
Printed by Digital Action (Pty) Ltd

*Do we recognise the suffering imposed upon billions of nonhuman animals by human animals in the flesh and milk industry; in vivisection laboratories; in using them for power and entertainment and in the taking of their natural habitat? Given that nonhuman animals are utterly powerless to resist this oppression how is our Society called to act?*

Central and Southern Africa Yearly Meeting of the Religious
Society of Friends (Quakers)
Heronbridge, South Africa 2006

## Acknowledgements

In so many ways countless people have contributed to this book and I am grateful to all of them and my thanks go to Mike and the staff at NISC for their professionalism and expertise in being able to put all of this together.

Special thanks go to Olive and Bob for guidance and the timeless advice to always "think for yourself", to Emma and Ruth for their belief and encouragement and to Pauline for endless patience as well as discussions, ideas, reading this work and for inspirational coffee and breadsticks. Thank you to Rachel for allowing me the privilege of using many of her words in re telling the story of herself and Jerom. And a loving, thank you to all of our special nonhuman animal companions, for joy over the years and through diverse countries. Truly we have crossed many rivers together.

# Contents

# Introduction

*As human beings we have the most extraordinary capacity for evil. We can perpetrate some of the most horrendous atrocities.*

Desmond Tutu[1]

THIS BOOK IS about reading the landscape of our world with its texts of normalised violence against nonhuman animals and seeking to understand how this mass violence can go on. While the writing may be on the wall, there is no doubt that these texts are absolutely everywhere, yet so common that for the most part we don't even recognise that they exist. But whether we recognise them or not they influence our thoughts and actions and prove devastating for those beings with whom we share this planet. Insidiously and in multiple ways, they are able to reach deeply into our psychology to uncouple our normal feelings of responsibility and culpability from the actions we carry out or support.

This book falls into three sections. First, we examine the problem of mass violence against animals and then go on to look at texts, discourses, ideologies and the power of language to socially construct the world including identities. In the next section we use these concepts for our broad analysis of a number of texts, both physical and language based, drawn from a wide variety of contexts but particularly relating to farming and animal experimentation. In the final section we examine what is required in order to carry out mass violence and we investigate the power of ideology and discourses to switch off our normal moral accountability so that we can be a party to, or support, the most hideous acts of violation.

Some of the areas we touch on are animal farming, animal experimentation, slavery, racism, history, language, discourses, power, government documents, guidance from medical authorities, war trials, advertising, scientific journals, mass human – human violence, social psychology, the struggle for women's rights, economic exploitation and alternative discourses.

I have tried to plot a direct and logical journey in these pages but as often happens with expeditions, there are always interesting side tracks to explore. So, I am afraid, at times we wander off here and there, although we always do so with intent. I trust you will find these diversions interesting and informative.

This book is a working document, hopefully contributing to our improved understanding in this field and offering useful tools for additional enquiry. It is a limited investigation which can be amplified by readers as they use what is in these pages and more, to make their own enquiries in their different countries, cultures, faiths, identities, disciplines and languages by reading the animal text and interpreting it for others.

At its core the book is about liberation and I do not believe that we as humans can separate our own paths to liberation from those of our nonhuman kin; our story is theirs and theirs is ours and we have been walking this path of life together, in our different forms, for the past 3.8 billion years.

Our first chapter begins with the paradox which is ourselves; we have both the capacity for profound compassion and self-sacrifice and the capacity for unconscionable cruelty, and as a species we exercise both.

# A world divided

*Full moon is falling through the sky*
*Cranes fly through the clouds*
*Wolves howl*
*I cannot find rest*
*Because I am powerless*
*To amend a broken world.*

Du Fu[1]

## Buried feelings

GREAT ORTON AIRFIELD lies in undulating English countryside with the town of Carlisle to its east and the river Eden to its north. Used in the Second World War by aircraft of the Royal Air Force and later for the storage of ammunition, the facility was closed in August 1952 and is now classified as disused.[2] The site continues to be of interest not only because of its war history but also because it is now an important conservation reserve. And there is one other, extraordinary reason – it is the location of a mass grave. Buried here, many metres below the surface in walled trenches, with a reticulation of pipes and pumps to remove seeping fluids, lie the bodies of nearly half a million individuals.[3] Some were young, others a bit older, although few would be described as old, and there are both sexes lying amongst the dead. What they all have in common is that they were killed on the orders of the British government.

While the killings deeply traumatised many people, there was little they could do.[4] Allender's *Fields of Fire* is a collection of prose, poems and postings from an online discussion group of the time, made up of people from all walks of life, and these along with other writings of the time make distressing reading.[5] We hear the voices of people who are deeply angry and feel overwhelmed by what is happening; they describe the incompetence of the killers, the smell of rotting corpses, the distress of the victims and the sight of great pyres burning in the land. There is an outpouring of love for those who suffered and lost their lives, as if they were family members – mothers, fathers and children.

This was the time of the foot-and-mouth epidemic of 2001 and the victims were the result of a massive killing strategy implemented by the government and designed to halt the spread of the epidemic. Although foot-and-mouth disease has a low mortality rate and relatively few animals were actually infected, in the end somewhere between six and ten million individuals had their lives violently extinguished.[6]

The site of the grave is now a nature reserve named "Watchtree", the construction of which was funded by the British environmental agency DEFRA. At its entrance stands a large stone carrying a plaque which reads:

> The Watchtree Stone
> taken from this ground
> A Symbol
> To the birth of the Watchtree Nature Reserve
> Dedicated on this day on the 7 May 2003,
> the second anniversary of the final burial
> A Memorial
> To 448,508 sheep, 12,085 cattle, 5,719 pigs
> buried here during the
> Foot and Mouth outbreak of 2001
> "The tree of everlasting life takes the goodness
> from the soil to sustain new beginnings"[7]

Here we have, as well as a memorial to those animals whose lives were taken, a tangible symbol of the pain, loss and perhaps culpability felt by people.

Perhaps we should not be surprised by this grief. Many people love animals and enjoy their company as companions, not only in Britain but in most places around the world, and being cruel to them is usually seen as a reprehensible act. In a European Union survey, most people said they thought farmed animal welfare was very important and "over four in five EU citizens declared that we have a duty to protect animal rights regardless [of] the cost."[8, 9] The American Veterinary Association reports that in 2011 there were 70 million pet dogs and 74.1 million pet cats in the US and that 63.2% of the pet owners considered their pets to be members of the family.[10]

Although pets cannot be described as blood members of our families, companion animals may be counted as fictive kin in the same way as godparents or non-related "aunties" or "uncles".[11] When pets die this can have a significant emotional effect on many guardians which can be made worse because there is often no acceptable way in society to properly grieve for these special loved ones, and also because such grief might not be understood by those around them.[12] Some people are so deeply traumatised that recovery is protracted, and in some cases they have feelings of personal responsibility for the animal's death and suffer from deep depression. In addition, not only is there the physical loss of a family member, or at least a very close companion, but the loss of shared activities in daily life.[13]

When our pets die, they may be commemorated with symbols, particularly tombstones which are frequently religious in nature, but local bylaws often prohibit pets from actually being buried in the same graves as their guardians. However, this is changing and mixed cemeteries are becoming more common, recovering a practice dating back to prehistoric times.[14,15] If not interred in a cemetery or cremated, beloved animal companions are often buried very close to home and family – something which seldom happens in industrialised countries to their human counterparts.

Our deep attachment to animals means they are often included as important beings in our spiritual or religious belief systems, and this is not just a recent phenomenon but extends back many thousands of years. Rod Preece says the following about some well-known people of our recent past:

> ...there were numerous others of prominence who believed in immortal animal souls. The moralist Abraham Tucker, the vegetarian physician George Cheyne, the poet Anna Seward, the parliamentarian Soame Jenyns, the revolutionary leveler Richard Overton, the academic Thomas Brown, the Anglican Bishop of Durham Joseph Butler, the Swiss naturalist Charles Bonnet, and the evangelist John Wesley were among those who proclaimed eternal life for the animal.[16]

In children's books, as in our mythologies as well as in many of the old stories, animals are characters; some good, some bad and some plain mischievous, but they are individuals just like us with lives and families, wishes and needs, who feel pain, love and loss.

Animals are, and always have been, significant parts of our social, cultural and spiritual worlds.[17] And of course heroic acts to save animals are a much-loved item on news broadcasts, usually towards the end of the bulletin.

But our loving relationship with animals is only one side of this story; there is another side which is so bleak and dark it is difficult to countenance, even to imagine that this is the same world.

## On the other side of the fence

As I write this, I am staying in a backpackers at the end of a dusty track on the coast of the Eastern Cape province of South Africa. To one side of me is the Addo Elephant National Park where the coastal bushveld is thick and lush, stretching over rolling hills to join with towering sand dunes plunging down to meet the Indian Ocean. The glare of the bright sunshine is mixed with deep greens and the cool shade of the forest, and the scents of wild flowers mix with the smell of the ocean.

On the other side, the coastal forest has been destroyed and the rolling hills are covered in grass except for the occasional pocket of trees. The terrain is crisscrossed with fences marking out camps for the cattle who are held captive here and the deeply eroded tracks tell the story of their monotonous daily routines. These creatures are the descendants of free-living aurochs, riverine-dwelling creatures that once roamed over large areas of the globe, the last free-living member of their group being killed in Poland in 1627.[18]

There is a network of buildings, food stores and mechanical equipment which, together with the land, is what we know as a "dairy farm". The older cows are herded together in large numbers; many of them are heavily pregnant while others have recently given birth. Some very young calves are loaded onto a trailer and tractor which then moves off down a track and large, heavy mothers panic and hurry after it, trying to keep their young ones in view. But today this is just a ploy to induce them to go to the milking shed and their babies are not going to be taken away. Well not today anyway, that will happen on another day, and soon. But the tanker will come in later today, as it does every day of the year, to take away their mother's milk.

Recently I watched a mother on this farm with her very young calf as they stayed close together and wandered around beneath a few lonely trees. While the mother grazed, her baby would suddenly go running for a few steps and bouncing around, before they came together once again and ambled slowly on. It was impossible not to smile at such a delightful scene. But the next day her baby was gone, and this mother stood alone beneath those same trees. She stared fixedly into the distance and bellowed towards the young calves far away; she dug in the ground in her frustration, throwing up clouds of sandy soil – she was clearly very distressed. But the fence prevented her from going anywhere and from ever meeting again the one she had given birth to just days before and who, for a few brief hours, had been her family.

It has now been four days since that happened and she still stands and watches over the fence and cries for her child. How many times has this happened to her, I wonder, how much grief has she suffered? How long will it be, how many more pregnancies will she go through, before they decide she is no longer economical and they come for her body as well?

In this industry, despite the bucolic setting, the animals are repeatedly made pregnant but have their babies taken away time and time again. Their male children are removed and killed after a few days or weeks, possibly being confined during that time and fed a restricted diet so that their muscles become soft, weak and pale and then their bodies can be sold as "veal". If the baby is female, she may be forced into the same system of exploitation as her mother.

When the effects of repeated pregnancies and the daily production of vast amounts of milk begins to take its toll on her young body, the mother's milk producing ability starts to falter and she is of no further use to those who are "farming" her. She will then be taken for slaughter, although by this time her body may be so damaged that she will be unable even to walk off the truck to the killing floor and will be hauled there by men using ropes to drag her frail body on its final journey. This industry is just one example of the numerous ways in which we inflict violent abuse on nonhuman animals as a routine practice and on a daily basis.

Animals in some form or other are ever-present in our daily lives, although mostly in the shadows. Merchandise made from the dead and exploited bodies of nonhuman animals fills our shops, working places and homes. Animal flesh is on sale in multiple forms; animal "products" such as milk, yoghurt, eggs, cheese, butter and gelatin are ubiquitous and even the paper we write on probably has an animal-based size spread upon its surface to change its absorption characteristics. Wise describes the uses made of a cow's body:

> For example, the blood of a slaughtered cow is used to manufacture plywood adhesives, fertilizer, fire extinguisher foam, and dyes. Her fat helps make plastic, tires, crayons, cosmetics, lubricants, soap, detergents, cough syrup, contraceptive jellies and creams, ink, shaving cream, fabric softeners, synthetic rubber, jet engine lubricants, textiles, corrosion inhibitors and metal-machine lubricants. Her collagen is found in pie crusts,

yogurts, matches, bank notes, paper, cardboard glue; her intestines are used for strings for musical instruments and racquets; her bones in charcoal ash for refining sugar, in ceramics, and in cleaning and polishing.[19]

Billions of animals are used in agriculture and untold millions in experimentation, while countless others spend their lives providing power, as in personal transport, carrying loads, ploughing and pulling vehicles. Others are used for various forms of "entertainment" as in "performing animals" or in "trophy hunting".[20]

## Legal abuse

Our daily use of animals has become routine and it is hard to think of it as being anything remarkable at all. But how can we best describe this phenomenon, how can we characterise our practice of coercing other living beings to serve our purposes? The law seems a reasonable place to turn for help but unfortunately, we find very little to assist us in its tomes. Certainly, there are laws pertaining to animals and their treatment at our hands, but legislation relating to the protection of animals, particularly those used by humans, is usually weak, vague, ambiguous, and at its core, serves the desires of those in society who wish to use animals.[21] Here is an example of some legislation concerning animals, taken from the Ohio statute 959.13:

> A) No person shall:
> (1) Torture an animal, deprive one of necessary sustenance, unnecessarily or cruelly beat, needlessly mutilate or kill, or impound or confine an animal without supplying it during such confinement with a sufficient quantity of good wholesome food and water;...

and

> (4) Keep animals other than cattle, poultry or fowl, swine, sheep, or goats in an enclosure without wholesome exercise and change of air, *nor or feed cows on food that produces impure or unwholesome milk;...[22]

Many questions arise from these few sentences. What is meant by to *unnecessarily or cruelly beat* or *needlessly mutilate or kill?*\* Beating describes a violent assault, so is it possible to beat another being in a non-cruel way? And under what circumstances can beating be deemed to be necessary and who is it necessary for and with what goals in mind? What does it mean to needlessly mutilate or needlessly kill an individual? When is mutilation and/or killing deemed to be needed, who is it needed for and what would be an acceptable rationale for these odious acts?

Paragraph 4 describes how it is not acceptable to keep certain animals in an enclosure *without wholesome exercise and change of air* because this constitutes cruelty, but for other

---

\*  There are times when I want to emphasise a particular word or phrase but it also happens to be part of a quotation. For the sake of clarity, in such cases I have used italics for emphasis but left out the inverted commas, trusting that the reading will be smoother and the meaning will still be clear.

animals, surprisingly it does not. How can it be possible that cattle, poultry, fowl, swine, sheep and goats do not need exercise and to breathe fresh air?

To be fair, the Ohio legislation is only one example and is far from being unusual. In South Africa the Animal Protection Act speaks of *cruelly beats* and *confines, chains, tethers or secures any animal unnecessarily or under such conditions or in such a manner or a position as to cause that animal unnecessary suffering...(c) unnecessarily starves or under-feeds or denies food or water to any animal...* [23]

Karen Davis notes that, "Farmed animals are excluded even from the definition of 'animals' under the Federal Laboratory Animal Welfare Act of the United States,...[24] Overall, animal related laws have little to do with the wellbeing of the animals but are carefully crafted to protect human desires and our right to use animals.

If this claim seems a little harsh, consider how many legal systems in the world ban the forcing of a piece of metal into an animal's mouth so that humans can control her or him, how many outlaw the taking away from animals of their young, or outlaw killing them or riding them or using them for a whole range of things? How many systems have improved any animal's legal standing by revoking their status as human property?

Given this ubiquitous semantic deceit in legislation, it is hardly surprising that it is extremely difficult to find definitions for terms such as cruelty or abuse, which when applied to animals, are free from societal, cultural or financial influences.[25] However, Robert Agnew does offer one such definition for abuse, which in essence could just as easily apply to humans as nonhumans. Very importantly, it is based on recognising the actions the victim is subjected to rather than the desires and power of the perpetrator who is carrying out those actions. Abuse of an animal is described as;

> ...any act that contributes to the pain or death of an animal or that otherwise threatens the welfare of an animal. Such abuse may be physical (including sexual) or mental, may involve active maltreatment or passive neglect, may be direct or indirect, intentional or unintentional, socially approved or condemned, and/or necessary or unnecessary (however defined).[26]

This definition is reasonable, impartial, clear and rigorous. However, when we apply it in the context of the exploitation of animals by humans, we reach two inescapable conclusions. Firstly, these animals are abused and secondly, we, directly or indirectly, are their abusers. This might seem outrageous, but that is probably only because we have been doing it for so long and we were born into a world where it is understood to be normal and expected.

This is the definition of abuse I will use from now on.

## Minds in the balance

Considering our love and concern for animals on the one hand and our immense abuse of them on the other, we are faced with a paradox; one which has far reaching implications for the lives of nonhuman animals and which comes into stark focus at the mass grave with which we began this chapter. All of the individuals commemorated on the Watchtree Stone were going to be killed anyway, simply as raw materials for the UK "food supply chain". Almost a million nonhumans meet their deaths in that country's highly organised transportation, killing and dismembering machine every single year, but not one of those deaths will be commemorated with a plaque or words of hope for the future; their suffering is hidden; the taking of their lives just part of a daily industrial routine. [27] As Rudkus, the character in Upton Sinclair's book *The Jungle,* says when he sees the mechanised killing in the Boston stockyards of 1904:

> They had done nothing to deserve it; and it was adding insult to injury, as the thing was done here, swinging them up in this cold-blooded, impersonal way, without a pretense at apology, without the homage of a tear. Now and then a visitor wept, to be sure; but this slaughtering-machine ran on, visitors or no visitors. It was like some horrible crime committed in a dungeon, all unseen and unheeded, buried out of sight and out of memory.[28]

It is this paradox – love and abuse, compassion and cruelty – which lies at the heart of this book. The question is a simple one; how can good, kind, caring people, continue to support the mass institutionalised abuse of nonhuman animals in its many forms? We must also include here many of those wonderful organisations which are deeply committed to social change of various kinds. Almost without fail, the plight of animals is simply missing from struggle agendas on the environment, sexism, racism, xenophobia, workers' rights and so on. Calls for justice, peace, equality, reconciliation and an end to violence and oppression are not meant to include animals. Their pain and suffering are invisible or discountable or simply transformed into non-existence in the incandescent light of human self-interest.

No doubt there is not merely a single answer to this puzzle. I hope at least to show that language and ideology play central roles in hiding, excusing, reinforcing, justifying, morally disengaging and thereby perpetuating this mass abuse; and importantly, that the abuse of animals does not stand in isolation, but is part of a matrix of abuse which is perpetrated against both human and nonhuman animals in numerous ways.

Given that this misery cannot happen without our human agency, our journey must begin with ourselves and in particular with how we understand the world.

## CHAPTER 2

# Reality, truth and the devil's rope

*Reality leaves a lot to the imagination.*

John Lennon[1]

## Tool kit

WITHOUT US AND our ideas about the world, the mass abuse of animals simply does not exist, so we must start by looking at ourselves. In order to do this, we will need some tools, and the ones we are going to find especially useful are the concepts of *social practices, ideology, power, texts* and *discourses*. We will look at these in the next few pages before setting out on our investigations into the Animal Text.

## Social practices

Social practices are things we do regularly, such as teaching, buying, selling, playing sport, doing research, carrying out rituals and so on. Each social practice has some reasoning behind it to explain and justify what we are doing. But not all social practices are equitable. Some are based on unequal power relations and are prejudicial and exploitive to one or more of the parties concerned. I will refer to these, unsurprisingly, as *exploitive social practices*. These practices especially need the support of a rationalisation to justify what is being done, because the rationalisation plays the role of legitimising in people's minds, the oppressive power relations.[2]

I will use the term *ideology* very specifically in these pages to refer to such rationales and to mean a corrupt construction of reality which justifies and normalises power inequality and exploitation. So, an exploitive social practice draws on an ideology to legitimise its unequal and abusive power relations.

At the core of this is *power* and it is the party with the power which commands the practice and whose version of what is going on, the ideology, is the dominant and perhaps the only explanation of events.

In short, one party has the *power* to initiate and control the *exploitive social practice*, which it justifies by drawing upon an *ideology*. Or in other words, I have the power, I exploit you and I have a good story to tell about why it's okay for me to do that.

## Selling lives

Let's look at an example of a seemingly unremarkable, yet exploitive social practice involving a farmer and a local butcher:

**Butcher:** Have you got any weaners?
**Farmer:** Plenty, how many do you need?
**Butcher:** Twenty
**Farmer:** Come inside and we can work out a price

Although this appears to be about two individuals, there are really three parties involved; the farmer who has taken the pigs from their mothers, the butcher who wants to kill them and sell their bodies, and the piglets, who presumably wish to live and return to their mums. The social practice is the buying, selling and eventual killing of individuals (baby pigs), benefiting both the farmer and butcher.

The farmer and the butcher both have power. They have social power for three reasons; they have status because they are humans; they have recognised and generally respected occupations, and the law allows them to do what they do. They both have economic power and additionally they have the physical power to coerce the pigs. The pigs on the other hand have no power, social, economic or physical with which to influence events, but they have the most to lose by being deprived of their families and their lives.

The verbal exchange never mentions their suffering and death or their loss of family and their family's loss of them, but only deals with what is important to those who have power. The ideological assumptions are that we humans have a right to do this to animals and that the "weaners" are just objects for sale. The exchange is portrayed as a simple transaction where items are bought and sold.

If the pigs' interests were actually considered it would seem to many people laughable or perhaps outrageous, though not because it is either of these things but because it challenges the dominant ideology being used. The ideology which claims that doing this to animals is normal and natural and we have the right to do it. Any opposing views are seen as aberrant.

## Common sense

Many ideologies are so familiar and deep-rooted that we no longer perceive them for what they really are – particular constructions of reality in the service of power. We simply think of them as everyday common sense, for which the linguist Norman Fairclough uses the term *ideological common sense*. Other views seem unthinkable and other worlds impossible, which as Bourdieu points out, leads to the, "... recognition of legitimacy through the misrecognition of arbitrariness."[3]

Such oppressive constructions appear in beliefs such as, sexism, racism, homophobia, slavery and speciesism. Andrew Sayer notes that systems of domination

> ...are maintained not only through the appropriation, control and allocation of essential material requirements by the dominant class, race or gender but also through the reproduction of particular systems of meaning which support them...[4]

We are born into a world where many of these exploitive social practices with their component ideologies already exist and we become socialised into accepting them. The institutionalised nature of many of these practices gives them immense power and at the same time the capacity to evade scrutiny because of their apparent normality and universality. Fairclough points out that ideological power is "...the power to project one's practices as universal and 'common sense'..."[5] Those who refuse this dominance, who question or reject it, become portrayed as outsiders, dissidents, troublemakers and extremists.

And this dominance has long been fused into the fundamental structures of our societies and as linguist Teun van Dijk points out:

> Power and dominance are usually organized and institutionalized. The social dominance of groups is thus not merely enacted, individually, by its group members, as is the case in many forms of everyday racism or sexual harassment. It may also be supported or condoned by other group members, sanctioned by the courts, legitimated by laws, enforced by the police, and ideologically sustained and reproduced by the media or textbooks.[6]

How apt are these words when we consider our domination and exploitation of billions of nonhuman animals?

## Texts – transmitting meaning
Meaning is something which is a bit difficult to define, but we understand it as the transmission of such things as information, concepts and feelings. Perhaps the most obvious way we transmit meaning is through language, but we can also do it in other ways as well by such things as our appearance, body language, music, paintings, dance, rituals, touch, and facial expressions. Artefacts such as buildings, weapons or even rubbish dumps can also tell us something. If it is able to transmit meaning we can describe it as a *text*. A text is anything which is semiotic.

Of course, texts can be interpreted differently and we need to be aware that there may be multiple perspectives or layers which could be examined. If we look at a large dam it might be considered as a triumph of the human spirit and a monument to technological ingenuity. Conversely, it could be understood as an invasion from outsiders, a violation which robbed nonhuman and human communities of their ancient homes and land, leaving them outcasts. Much depends upon from whose perspective we are looking at it and, as with most things, it is usually the perspective of those with the greatest power which holds centre stage.

We will look at a whole range of texts from a wide variety of sources including newspapers, legal documents, websites, scientific organisations, government reports, journal articles, physical texts in our environment, historical descriptions of events and exchanges, activism and so on. Some of these might be examined in detail while others will allow for a more general reflection and consideration by the reader.

## Reading minds
Off the north-east coast of Scotland lies a small group of islands called the Shetlands and

on these are found a large number of stone circles and other constructions. They were created by people who lived around 5000 years ago, long before the great pyramids of Egypt were built, and they were used for many hundreds of years after their creation. These stone monuments are physical manifestations of how those ancient people understood their world and what was important to them. They had their genesis all those years ago in ancient minds and the traces of their thinking remain today literally set in stone. It must have taken great application, planning and sacrifice to carry out this work, so it was certainly seen as important, at least to some in that population. Much of the meaning of these texts has been lost to us, but archaeologists are trying to piece it together, drawing upon what is at these sites and what is known of similar locations. These stones are texts which speak to us, however imperfectly, across millennia.

On a less grand scale, consider a whip which is used on donkeys. It is made for a purpose and is employed during the activity of using a donkey cart for carrying goods and people around – certainly an exploitive practice. The whip's genesis, including the planning of how it was going to be made, the size, the materials and so on, began in a human mind. But also, in that mind was the ideology which justified its making and the use to which it would eventually be put – beating donkeys to control them and to get more work from them. The ideology is implicit in the text (the whip), as is the exploitive practice, indeed they are the reason the text exists at all. Once again, the text represents in physical form, processes of the human mind.

If we look around right now, we will see numerous texts flooding our world and many of these, if we read them deeply, will tell stories of our violence, especially against animals. Examining today's artefacts, we have a luxury which archaeologists do not have, in that we know the contexts, uses and makers of these artefacts and can relatively easily trace their origins, but on the other hand we also have the disadvantage that these things are so familiar that it is difficult to really "see" them for what they are, to stand back and read them. They are too commonplace and we are up too close.

In order to help us out with this we can ask specific questions about artefacts we are interested in, as if we are tourists from another world. This can be an interesting and often rather disturbing experience. We can use questions such as, what is this thing designed to do, who made it, where did it originate, is there anything special about the design, are there similar objects in other places, what was sacrificed/destroyed/used to make it, who does it benefit, who does it harm, is there a system of thought, practice or ideology behind it? Asking these and similar questions offers us some distance on our subject and helps us to see it as if for the first time, hopefully resulting in a better understanding of the meanings it can communicate.

There will always be room for different interpretations, but this does not mean that any analysis is valueless or cannot be rigorous and insightful. Anyway, let's try this out.

## Cowboy country

Here is a pretty mundane example – barbed wire. Hardly what we might think of as an in-depth semiotic resource, but this spiky stuff has a story to tell. We would commonly encounter it as part of a fence around a field of animals so let's use that picture. Nothing out of the ordinary, a tranquil rural scene reproduced billions of times all over the world. Now for a closer look.

Barbed wire or "the devils rope" was developed in the 19th century and although there were a number of versions around, it was Joseph Glidden of DeKalb, Illinois who, on 24 November 1874, was awarded the patent for his barbed wire design which was named with great confidence, "The Winner". This invention turned out to be very popular, DeKalb became known as the Father of Barbed Wire and along with Isaac Ellwood, another barbed wire enthusiast, went on to form a business named "The Barb Fence Company".[7]

The wire was popular and allowed homesteaders on the plains to keep animals, not *in* their fields but *out* of their fields. At that time, the plains were open and in Kansas, for example, there was a law which allowed cattle to graze freely, which meant a cropper (farmer growing crops) had to fence out the animals or risk losing all of his crops and months of hard work.[8] But if his fence was breached by the animals, the law said he was entitled to compensation from their "owner". This of course is the classic confrontation often depicted in cowboy films where farmers and cowboys battle over land.[9] The 1940s musical *Oklahoma* even has the famous "Farmer and Cowman" song with this first verse

Oh, the farmer and the cowman should be friends,
Oh, the farmer and the cowman should be friends.
One man likes to push a plough,
The other likes to chase a cow,
But that's no reason why they cain't be friends.[10]

This clash is not just a modern conflict but goes back thousands of years, at least to Roman times and almost certainly earlier.[11]

When the railroads arrived on these plains, the rail companies were obliged to fence any parts of the track going through already legally fenced homesteads. But they found they had a problem because their fences would disappear and end up being used elsewhere. It was difficult to prove that any particular wire had actually been stolen from the railways because one bit of barbed wire looks pretty much like another, so "The Barb Fence Company" developed a special form of barbed wire for the railways, with a square strand so that their wire could be identified as belonging to them.[12]

Over time, as the plains became more occupied, the main use of barbed wire went from keeping animals out to keeping them in and it was only years later that its use to confine animals was extended to use in human conflicts for restricting, delaying and injuring combatants as well as for confining human prisoners.

Now, back to our field, where we can ask a few questions to help us to gain a bit of clarity. Remember, we need to imagine that the questioner (ourselves) has no idea about this history and has previously been totally unfamiliar with fields enclosed by barbed wire.

Here are examples of some questions we might ask, along with possible answers:

**Q.** *What is this wire designed to do?* **A.** Firstly, to confine and control nonhuman animals who are described as the possessions of humans. Secondly, to keep out other nonhuman animals who might wish to go on to this land to consume some of the food there and to access available water, or to make a home. The wire is made in such a way as to restrict movement and cause pain and minor injury although it may cause death to wild living animals, directly as they try to migrate, or indirectly by restriction of access to water or food.

Q. *Who made it?* A. Humans.

Q. *What materials is the wire made from?* A. Steel; and the poles from wood or metal.

Q. *Is it widely used?* A. Yes, it is used in this way in numerous places all over the world.

Q. *What was sacrificed, destroyed or used up to produce it?* A. To make the steel, iron ore was mined and then heated using coke derived from coal. These processes caused damage to land, water and the air. Some nonhuman communities were destroyed. In addition, natural vegetation was cleared and replaced by plantations to provide trees for use as poles.

Q. *Who does it benefit?* A. The wire allows large numbers of humans to make money in various ways from exploiting the bodies of nonhuman animals and some humans make money directly from the sale of the wire itself. The land it demarcates is also viewed as a commodity and is bought and sold to the benefit of some humans.

Q. *Who does it harm?* A. The animals who are confined and exploited, the humans who may have been forced off the land, and the animals who are kept out of the area and are unable to gain access to food and water.

Q. *Who has the power in this situation?* A. Power resides only with the humans but more especially with certain groups of powerful humans

Q. *Is there a system of thought or practice behind this?* A. Animals are legally defined by humans as property and as such can be used however the "owner" sees fit. Animals, it is understood, are viewed as less than humans, which it is claimed, gives humans the right to use them for their own purposes. Land is also defined as property in this ideology and is something which can be owned, bought and sold.

*Semiosis.* Our barbed wire field tells us of a world where living beings and the land can be owned, and are commodities to be exploited, bought and sold. The wire is important to some people, and resources used to make the barbed wire result in some environmental destruction and pollution. The exclusion of others from the land causes them hardship and possibly death.

Power resides only with humans and particularly with some humans. The exploitive social practice is animal farming and the ideology of human elitism justifies and normalises what is done. The barbed wire fence erected around this field is a semiotic artefact of this practice and its ideology.

Of course, your questions and answers might be different from mine, but doing this type of exercise can be very useful in helping to uncover ideologies and exploitive social practices which are embedded in the physical terrain of our everyday world.

## Landscapes of the damned

Once we begin to read our environment in this way, it can be a revelation – and a pretty depressing one at that. Our world shifts as we begin to really see and interpret the artefacts of our cruel past and our current violent exploitation of animals. Body parts in supermarkets, ingredients in food, cattle trucks, food manufacturing plants, boxes of eggs, pest killers in a garden shop, a bridle and bit, a leather sofa, cartons of milk, slabs of cheese, woollen garments, whips, zoos, pet shops, fox hunting, horse racing, birds in cages, animal rugs, gelatine products, pharmaceutical products tested on animals and so on. There are countless texts all around us, large and small, telling the story of our institutionalised violence.

Stand with me on a pebbly beach in north Wales and look east to see a little harbour with small fishing craft and beyond it, low hills, giving way to higher ground and eventually the mountains of the Snowdonia National Park. Dry stone walls meander all over the lower slopes while clusters of stone buildings with slate roofs are scattered about and look out over bright green fields. The stone walls, buildings, fences and gates seem to grow organically out of the soil as if they have been here forever. It is all incredibly beautiful.

Attractive though it is, this is a landscape steeped in a history of suffering. The fields were once thick forests, home to living beings of all kinds, but were cleared to provide grazing for captive animals; the drystone walls were built to prevent the movement of those captives and protect the wealth which their bodies promised. The clusters of buildings today house the equipment, supplies, food and people who make their livelihood from exploiting the bodies of these nonhumans.

Benign though the view appears, it is, like so many others, actually a landscape of the damned. The ideology of human minds is manifested here through physical changes made to the world, which facilitate the practice of the exploitation of animal's bodies – a practice which has been carried out for many thousands of years, It is so normalised today that justifications are seldom offered; it is has simply become ideological common sense.

Before we leave this scene, we must not forget that the little picturesque harbour and the colourful boats mentioned earlier are also everyday artefacts of another of our longstanding and bloody pursuits.

Even a scenic English canal with its canal boats and tow paths is a text which tells a history of hours of monotonous work carried out by horses pulling large boats hour after hour, day after day. The canal boats were big, normally 17 ft (5.2 m) wide and 100-plus ft (30 m) long.

> The loads themselves could weigh anywhere between 40 and 80 tons. Once the loading was accomplished, the rest of the work was then turned over to the mule and the horse: who had the ominous task of having to tow these sizable barges.[13]

Often, they would be hauling coal which had been dragged out of the pit by "pit ponies" who were really small horses, exploited for the purpose and who seldom saw the light of day, living lives of terrible hardship.

It was not only horses but mules, donkeys, oxen, dogs and sheep who were forced into work of all kinds and humans were also part of this story with many people being exploited relentlessly from their early childhood and in the same vicious economic system.

But there would come a time when emancipation for humans would begin, using the collective strength of the workers through the trade unions and via political action. This struggle continues to this day but for the animals there has been no liberation and sadly the political left, with a few notable exceptions, seems unable or unwilling to make the obvious comparisons and calls for serious action.

On the outskirts of many cities and towns we see the silos packed with "animal food" as part of complexes of buildings housing thousands of nonhumans in intensive farming units (factory farms). We might also see feed lots, fenced areas of barren, trampled, earth with crowds of animals being intensively fed to increase their weight before slaughter. These are common sights and therefore easily missed but such corpse fuelled engines surround our conurbations, relentlessly pouring animal body parts and "products" into the many human mouths waiting expectantly in their hinterland.

The physical texts of our world are a gigantic library for us to read. Dams, cities, factories, shopping malls, car parks, dried up rivers, polluted air and the list goes on. There are some photographs of physical texts which might be of interest in the appendix and I have made a few observations about them but you will surely have your own to make.

Visual representations are also important texts. Old paintings, for example, often show hunting scenes, animals pulling great heavy wagons or dogs being beaten. In advertising, photographs are deliberately designed to portray messages regarding their products. Milk, cheese and yoghurt may be sold in packaging portraying happy cows in rolling green meadows, leaping around and bearing contented grins. Even more bizarrely, packages of the body parts of dead cows may show a satisfied living animal and there is one pork sausage wrapper which shows a pig standing upright on two legs with arms folded and a cheeky smirk. A short wander around the aisles of a supermarket is an object lesson in how to tell visual lies and mock the dead at the same time. It is an education in itself.

Photographs posed by trophy hunters are also a revealing field of study. Blood, open wounds, spilled entrails and shattered bones are carefully hidden in the sanitised portrayals. The hunter is often placed above the animal in some way, holding her, sitting on her, looking down upon her, projecting the message of power and dominance over the victim. In addition, the weapon, often a rifle or crossbow, is given prominence and there has naturally been speculation about whether this is in fact a form of phallic symbol. And then there is the "look how clever I have been", grin of self adulation without which no trophy hunting photograph would be complete.

Having a photograph taken with a corpse is not something that is a common social custom. Neither is commemorating the killing with the amputation of a body part such as an ear, tail, foot or head to keep as souvenirs nor giving a sexualised dimension to bloodshed. Taking pleasure in serial killing and pimping for those who wish to do it, must surely give us cause for concern on many levels.

Whatever our interpretations might be, there is no doubt that we are surrounded by animal texts of numerous kinds and whether we realise it or not they do exert an influence upon us. For the animals, this is the landscape of the damned. As Elisabeth Costello says in Coetzee's novel *The lives of animals*:

> Let me say it openly: we are surrounded by an enterprise of degradation, cruelty, and
> killing which rivals anything that the Third Reich was capable of, indeed dwarfs it, in
> that ours is an enterprise without end, self-regenerating, bringing rabbits, rats, poultry,
> livestock ceaselessly into the world for the purpose of killing them.[14]

Next, we turn to look at that which is our most powerful tool in building and sustaining ideologies and the key to exposing and changing them – our use of language.

## CHAPTER 3

# Saying more than we think

*The basic tool for the manipulation of reality is the manipulation of words. If you can control the meaning of words, you can control the people who must use the words.*

Philip K. Dick[1]

## The language we use

OUR LIVES ARE saturated with language and it has enormous inherent power as great writers and orators have always known. It is in the texts of language that we construct, conserve or remake our understandings about our world.

Language use appears deceptively simple, often understood as just a tool for communication and employed every day in many different ways. But the language we use is far from neutral, containing such things as embedded ideas, hidden assumptions, implied norms and power differentials. It is with our language that we craft new ideas about the world and change existing ones, we construct identities, assign values, dispute over causes and effects and do many other things.

Language in use is a contested space where opposing views vie for dominance and those who dominate wield significant power. To control and manipulate language is to define what is normal, what is truth, what is reality. It is no accident that when a coup d'état takes place, one of the first institutions seized is the national broadcaster.

## The communication processes

When we communicate, the person who is sending the message draws upon their language competency, background, culture, experiences and outlook to produce the message which they send. These things are described by Fairclough as "member's resources".[2] The person receiving the communication draws on their own "member's resources" to make sense of that message. Naturally this means that not every message is interpreted in exactly the way the sender expected and much depends upon the sender knowing something about their receiver in order to get the message across. Politicians and corporations are skilled at doing this on a large scale but we also do it ourselves on a micro level in general conversation – we know our audience and speak accordingly.

Knowing our receivers means we often use short cuts and do not have to clarify all the things we say. People who are racists, believing they are speaking to another person who shares their views, may simply refer to people of another "race" with third person pronouns such as "The problem with *them* is that *they* do this and *they* think that…". They speak in this way because they expect the receiver to share their outlook and interpret their words automatically, understanding exactly who *them* and *they* are.

Sometimes a text will be silent about a particular aspect of what is being discussed. For example, on a web site offering hunting safaris in South Africa we can find descriptions of things such as the veld and the animals, accommodation options and celebrations of hunts and kills. However, the website is completely silent about the suffering and deaths of the animals and how their bodies are shattered by the ammunition, and it is also silent about any right to carry out this carnage. In the first case, the suffering and mutilation of the victims are essentially understood as irrelevant and in the second, the right to kill is expected to be taken for granted by the reader. No discussion is deemed to be needed on these subjects and so the text is silent about them. It seems a strange thing, but what is not included in a text, can be enormously revealing. Sometimes the silence can tell us much more than the words.

## Hidden meanings

It is surprising how much information even a small section of language can transmit, because we will draw upon our "member's resources" to interpret it. For example, we know when we hear the expression *birds of a feather flock together* or read that *it takes two to tango* that the former is not about ornithology nor the latter about ballroom dancing, but there are other meanings in these words which it is expected we will understand.

An interesting illustration of this process concerns a bumper sticker and this is how it works. You ask a group of people to imagine a sticker on a university student's old car which reads, "Nobody is ugly at 2 a.m." Then ask them to consider, individually or in pairs, what this means – and some surprisingly consistent answers are usually returned. Most people interpret it as being to do with going out in the evening to have a good time and in the process consuming alcohol, probably large amounts. Then towards the end of the night's drinking, around 2 a.m., members of the opposite or same sex (as preference dictates) all begin to look very attractive indeed.

The interesting thing however is that this interpretation is made despite the fact that this one, very short, sentence never mentions going out, drinking alcohol, the significance of 2 a.m. or searching for prospective sexual partners. People making these interpretations are drawing upon their own experience, collective knowledge, culture and ideas about students and social life to understand the meaning. The writer of course expects them to do exactly this and to have member's resources in common with her/him in order to get the joke.

But not everyone interprets it this way. Some people are simply confused by the words, some "understand" only part of the sentence and when I was discussing this with one group, one of the members interpreted the sticker as meaning that at 2 a.m., in the dark, everybody in the world is beautiful. What a lovely thought.

## Discourses

We regularly come across sections of text which construct the world in a particular way or from a particular perspective and these we can describe as *discourses*. A scientific discourse would, for example, draw on the ideas of science and perhaps use scientific terms such as mass, acceleration, momentum and solubility, and possibly use numbers in various ways. A military discourse might utilise ideas such as strategic objectives, firepower, logistics, assets and intelligence. We can have a sexist discourse, a racist discourse a right wing discourse, a football discourse, a religious discourse and so on. Often, we come across discourses which don't seem to fit into any familiar category so we can tag these with a name which we feel best expresses their representations.

For example, it is quite common to see articles about certain foods which can make us stronger, cure diseases, increase mental acuity, make us lose weight, help us to run faster or whatever. In short, miracle foods. So, if we came across something of this nature, we might call it a *miracle food* discourse or perhaps a *superfood* discourse.

Some discourses portray and promote ideological views, where exploitive and oppressive practices and relations of power are normalised and justified. This important aspect of language and its power to shape events was emphasised during the South African Truth and Reconciliation Commission hearings which received testimony about atrocities committed under the apartheid regime including murders, torture, harassment and other forms of extreme violence. The Commission's report says this about language:

> It is common place to treat language as mere words, not deeds, therefore language is taken to play a minimal role in understanding violence. The Commission wishes to take a different view here. Language, discourse and rhetoric does things: it constructs social categories, it gives orders, it persuades us, it justifies, it explains, gives reasons, excuses. It constructs reality. It moves certain people against other people.[3]

And we can certainly say that language moves people against animals.

The critical analysis of language plays a very important role when it comes to oppressive discourses because it can help to expose the underlying ideologies being drawn upon and in so doing open them up to rigorous examination. Ideologies are often buried deep in our minds and integrated into our societies, which means that while they are still active in building and justifying particular views, they remain shielded from critical scrutiny.

When specific discourses are used repeatedly, they reinforce the ideology upon which they draw. The more we say something and hear others say it, the more confident we are that it is true and the more normal and common sense it becomes.

## Linguistic forensics

When we critically examine what is said or written it's a bit like looking at a crime scene. We go searching for clues, tracing back links, identifying where specific word choices come from, finding similarities with other texts and so on until a coherent picture begins to emerge of the messages underlying what the words say.

One method of doing this which I will draw upon is called Critical Discourse Analysis (CDA). This is what van Dijk says about CDA,

> Critical discourse analysis (CDA) is a type of discourse analytical research that primarily studies the way social power abuse, dominance, and inequality are enacted, reproduced, and resisted by text and talk in the social and political context. With such dissident research, critical discourse analysts take explicit position, and thus want to understand, expose, and ultimately resist social inequality. This does not mean that we are unable make good, worthwhile, valid and rigorous analyses of texts but that to do it well we need to be aware of the presence of the researcher in all of this.[4]

There are many ways of doing CDA and it is possible to analyse relatively short lengths of texts in great detail or look at much larger ones in a more generalised way.[5] But as we did earlier with physical texts, we need to give ourselves some distance from the texts and one way of doing this is by reading and re-reading them and asking questions as we go.[6] I will draw on methods described by Norman Fairclough and other researchers to outline some things we can consider in carrying out our analysis and trying to understand how the text portrays reality.

## Examining the text

Here are some questions we can ask to help focus our analysis;[7]

**Discourse vocabulary.** Are there any special words or a particular vocabulary being used? Such words can alert us to the presence of particular discourses.

**Lexicalisation.** Do word choices suggest anything? Examples are; using *terrorist* instead of *freedom fighter*, *fireman* instead of *firefighter* or *lower animals* instead of *other animals*. Terms such as *whore, prostitute* or *sex worker* used to describe a woman would alert us to the likelihood of very different ideological positions being held by the speaker in each case.

**Euphemism.** Are euphemisms used or some other way of avoiding describing what happens or of obscuring it? What is it which is being hidden? What other words could be used to describe it?

**Metaphors.** Are metaphors used and do they tell us anything about the world view being portrayed?

**Agency.** Who has agency and who does not? One identity might be portrayed as passive or helpless while another is portrayed as active, capable and able to change the world around them. This, for example, is the way in which women and men have been differently portrayed in the past.

**Status.** Who is valuable and who is not? Whose lives might be disposable or less important, who is given more consideration and who less?

**Power.** Who or what has the power? Are the power relations unequal? Who gets to "speak" and who does not? Who gets to act and who is constrained? Who is treated equitably and who is not?

**Identities.** How are the identities of the different agents constructed? How are they portrayed?

**Silence.** Is there silence in the text about anything? Is there somewhere where we might normally have expected a discussion, description, explanation, outrage or some other reaction but there is nothing? Are some things simply missing from the account? The silence of the text can be so important because it signals what is understood as obvious and accepted or sometimes what is seen as utterly irrelevant. Often, this is where we will uncover ideological common sense.

**Ideology**. How do the discourses construct the world? Do they appear to draw on any particular ideology or ideas about the world? How does the ideology have the potential to bring about harm?

**Saying it differently**. What is the text actually saying? Can we describe it in another way, can we recontextualise it and in so doing give the ordinary and routine a very different perspective and raise important questions?

**Switching places.** One thing which can sometimes help us to see texts better is by reversing the roles of the agents in them.[8] An adult lecturing a child might seem very serious but the opposite could be hilarious, a woman smacking a man on the head with a frying pan might be quite funny but the opposite rather ominous. In texts where animals are present, exchanging places between humans and nonhuman animals often produces hideous and frightening scenarios, even when considering some very ordinary, everyday texts.

These are just a few of the ways we can interrogate a text and here is a short example using a short text about animal traction.

## Nice words

This extract is from a "resource book" promoting "animal traction" and at the first reading it all sounds very positive and appears to be portraying a win-win situation. It is often worth reading the text through a few times to start with:

> Animal power is a natural, renewable energy source. It is ecologically sustainable as animals consume locally available feed and reproduce themselves. Draft animals cause less pollution and environmental damage than motorised alternatives. Animal power is widely available and is generally affordable by rural communities. Work animals aid productive crop-livestock integration. They eat (and transport) crop residues and produce (and transport) organic manure.[9]

## Analysis

**Discourse vocabulary.** Are there any special words phrases or a special vocabulary being used?

The words *natural, renewable energy, ecologically sustainable, locally available, less pollution and environmental damage,* and *organic manure* alert us to the presence of what we can call an environmental discourse. Broadly speaking, this draws on the idea of some form of environmentalism and sustainability.

**Lexicalisation.** Do particular word choices suggest anything?

The terms *Draft animals* and *Work animals* describe living beings as classes of things. In addition, the names make it clear that the animals' reason for existing is to carry out work for humans.

The term *Animal power* classes animals as a form of energy resource such as oil, coal or gas. This is further emphasised by describing animal power as a *renewable energy source,* by claiming it causes *less pollution and environmental damage* and by comparing it to *motorised alternatives.*

**Euphemism.** Are euphemisms used or some other way of avoiding describing what happens?

The text says that "Work animals aid productive crop-livestock integration." suggesting that the animals are willing participants. The term "aid" is a euphemism for the animals being coerced into work.

**Agency.** Who has agency and who does not?

All of the agency is with humans, the animals have no agency whatsoever and are forced into this system.

**Status.** Who is valuable or special and who is not?

This is all about benefit for humans, who are understood as the only ones worthy of consideration. Any benefit which might accrue to the animals is either incidental or a way of making them more useful to humans. The animals are tools used for the benefit of humans.

**Power.** Who or what has the power in the text?

The text is written by humans and this power is used to create an anthropocentric perspective and portray a benign system beneficial to humans and nonhuman animals. In the physical world all of the power also resides with humans.

**Identities.** How are the identities of the different agents constructed?

The animals are portrayed as living machines which provide power and manure. They are not portrayed as sentient beings or as having lives of their own to lead. While humans are not directly referred to at all, except for "rural communities", it is clear that humans are the instigators and controllers of everything proposed here. They are in total charge and actions are taken for their benefit.

**Silence.** Is there silence in the text about anything?

There is complete silence about the lives of the animals, their loss of freedom and their coercion to work for the benefit of humans. It is understood as common sense, ideological common sense, that humans have a right to treat animals in this way and therefore it does not have to even be stated.

**Ideology.** How do the discourses construct the world?

There is an ideology drawn upon which takes for granted the right to exploit animals in order to achieve human desires. Achieving anthropocentrically identified environmental goals is also used to justify this exploitation and is incorporated into the ideology.

## What is the text actually saying?

The text describes how these nonhuman animals can be effectively coerced and their bodies used to benefit rural humans in what is claimed as an environmentally friendly manner.

In the chapters which follow, there are many excerpts drawn from a wide range of sources and these make fascinating subjects for analysis, although we will only be able to look at most of them quite briefly. However, there are a huge number of everyday texts all around us which we can examine and which will be able to provide us with important and often surprising insights. We certainly have no shortage of material.

## Animals and language

While a great deal of work has been done regarding discourses and ideology in relation to gender, class, race, economics, advertising and the like, research specifically related to nonhuman animals has been scarce until relatively recently. But how we think of nonhuman animals is critically important; it is literally a matter of life or death and as Lawrence observes, "... social constructs determine the fate of animals."[10]

We are reminded once again by the South African TRC, of the power embedded in words when the Commission points out that some people did terrible things under the Apartheid system yet believed that what they were doing was right – that it was, indeed, their moral duty.

> In the South African context it is important to understand how multiple discourses combined, intersected and intertwined to create climates of violence. In this respect the ideologies of racism, patriarchy, religions, capitalism, apartheid and militarism all intertwined to "manufacture" people capable of violence. Ideologies in these sorts of combinations provide the means and grounds for people to act violently and yet, ironically, believe they are acting in terms of worthy, noble and morally righteous principles.[11]

This is particularly significant for our enquiry as we will see later.

Now we begin our survey of this landscape by looking in more detail at language, old and new, relating to humans and animals and what better place to start than with the lie in this sentence?

## CHAPTER 4

# Violent language

*In the olden days the voice of man, raised in reason, was confronted by the roar of the lion, the bellow of the bull. Man went to war with the lion and the bull, and after many generations won that war definitively. Today these creatures have no more power. Animals have only their silence left with which to confront us. Generation after generation our captives, heroically, refuse to speak to us.*

J. M. Coetzee[1]

## Calling names

JOAN DUNAYER who writes extensively on language relating to animals, claims that

> [s]peciesism can't survive without lies...Linguistically the lies take many forms, from euphemism to false definition. We lie with our word choices. We lie with our syntax. We even lie with our punctuation.[2]

The closing sentence of the last chapter referred to humans *and* animals which is probably the commonest lie we tell regarding other animals. It underscores that dividing line, fashioned in human minds, which we employ to make an imaginary partition between ourselves and other animals. Despite the fact that we *are* animals, referring to humans *and* animals places us in a fantasy category producing a false dichotomy of humans on the one hand and every other animal in existence on the other. It is similar to speaking of seagulls and birds, or Zimbabweans and Africans – the first term is part of the second and so the phrase does not make any sense. However, we are very attached to this strategy; we like it because it serves our elitism.

We also see this alleged hierarchy in the sequence in which we use certain nouns; we say, *humans and animals* which sounds easier on the ear than *animals and humans* and talk about *a man and his dog*. We also have a habit of doing something similar to this with the sexes, speaking of *a man and his wife* or *husband and wife* although we do have *the bride and groom* on the day of their wedding.

So deep in our minds is this imagined division between animals and humans that we do not have suitable non-prejudicial nouns or noun phrases with which to describe animals who are not human animals. *Nonhuman animals* is a term which goes some way towards helping but unfortunately it automatically makes humans the reference point.

Another possibility is *other than human animals* although this has a similar problem as does using *humans and other animals*. The word *anymal* has even been proposed as a term to refer to any animal species other than the species of the animal "speaking".[3]

But for many, perhaps most, people the word *animal* simply does not convey the understanding that it also includes humans, and when we use the term animal, we usually mean nonhuman animal and automatically exclude humans. If we do not have suitable words to describe something it means it is either an extremely abstract concept, which in this case it is not, or it is not important to us and/or represents something which we would prefer not to acknowledge. In these pages, for ease of reading, I will use the terms *animal* and *nonhuman animal* as equivalent, trusting that the particular context will make the meaning clear.

And what about how we use the word *animal* in everyday language? Certainly, we use it when talking about dogs or cats or sheep, but calling someone *an animal* although scientifically correct is, in most cultures, a severe insult. This abusive nature is captured in English phrases such as; *acted like an animal; is an animal; looks like an animal; attacked like an animal; behaved like an animal; was eating like an animal* and so on. It is understood that animals are just not up to the standards of humans; they are uncontrolled, unkempt, have no social graces, behave badly and are extremely prone to random violence.

Sometimes we actually go so far as to name the animal concerned such as calling a person *a cart horse, an elephant, a monkey, baboon, dog, cockroach, rat* or *mouse*. Each of these is abusive in its own right and in its own special way. On the other hand, when we look at the word human and the positive qualities ostensibly attached to it the bells ring and the choirs burst into song. We say such things as *what it means to be truly human; a great human being; our shared humanity* and laud a person for being *a humanist*. When we are *humane* it means we are kind, gentle, wise, giving and compassionate and we can even use humane as an adjective in the term *humane slaughter* to describe the killing of nonhuman animals, which makes it sound like a good thing for everyone including those who are the victims.

At times we do acknowledge, rather grudgingly, that we have something of the animal about us and talk of our *animal nature, animal passions, animal desires* and *animal needs* where these are usually euphemistic for taboo subjects relating to our bodies, particularly sex. But there is always an implicit understanding that we have something more to us which transcends our "animal nature" and that it is this animal part of us which so often holds us back or leads us astray, often into the most licentious behaviour.

Perhaps our attitude towards nonhuman animals is most poignantly summed up in our description *only animals*. Animals are clearly things which do not warrant any priority or care, they are unimportant, peripheral, even disposable. Professor Andrew Linzey, the Oxford theologian who has spent most of his academic life working in the field of animal theology and ethics, recalls this from his student days;

> "I don't know why you're spending all your time on this. They're only animals – for heaven's sake!" That was the reaction of one of my fellow students at King's College. London, when I was studying theology in the 1970s. It was not, it has to be said, an uncommon reaction.[4]

In such phrases as, *I was treated like an animal, we were packed in like animals, you can't treat people like animals, our accommodation was only fit for animals*, we recognise that our treatment of animals is routinely expected to be poor; that in some way this is the norm for animals and therefore it is entirely acceptable. And of course, nobody wants to be in *the dog house.*

Animals are always below humans and humans deserve better standards of treatment. Treating a person *like an animal* is understood to be a terrible thing to do. A dog sleeps outside in the cold because that is what dogs do or more truthfully, that is what we want them to do.

We are also very good at subtly placing our own attributes onto animals. We describe a person's behaviour as *chickening out* or as being *asinine* and the media are forever reporting *brutal* attacks and *brutal* regimes. But brutes are seldom, if ever, gratuitously violent and the most lethal animal on the planet is *Homo sapiens sapiens* – a fact which seldom seems to penetrate our hubris. On an average day in in the country where I live, South Africa, around fifty people will be murdered, forty-five attempted murders will take place and a hundred-and-ten rapes will be reported (multiply by a factor of somewhere between four and nine for actual rape figures) yet attacks by shark or lion, which are extremely rare events, is guaranteed to provoke banner headlines and fill the local and international news media for many days.[5, 6]

## Pigs and porky pies

Arron Stibbe examined our use of the word "pig" by looking at the British National Corpus, which is a collection of over a hundred million words currently in use in Britain and collected from sources such as newspapers, TV, magazines, books, etc. He found that although there are many animal words and phrases in the corpus there are an awful lot relating to pigs – names, metaphors, similes and idiomatic expressions, in fact, more than any other nonhuman animal.[7] Overwhelmingly these terms are negative and construct pigs as fat, greedy, dirty, murderous, lying, patronising, ignorant and so on. This might come as no surprise and work by Leach (1964) suggests that this degrading of pigs in English comes from the time when many people kept pigs and lived very close to them.[8] From the day of the pig's birth they would begin to know the little creatures and would care for them, feed them and quite likely have them in the house in winter. But in the end, they were going to kill them. This is a difficult thing for most people to do; to know and care for another being and then take her/his life. But by continually denigrating the animal and creating a distance from her/him, the killing seems in some way acceptable, reasonable and in the end justified.

In some cases, the derogatory expressions about pigs which Stibbe found, refer to an apparent belief that negative attributes such as *greedy, fat,* and *dirty* are actually true about real pigs and that these are their natural attributes. Leaving aside the veracity of this dubious belief, there are other cases where the expressions are extremely unlikely to be true – for example, *devious, thieving, lying* and *abusive* surely cannot apply to real pigs. But here is the clever bit. If, for example, we call a person *a lying pig*, we are saying that they are a pig (insult) but also that they are a liar (further insult) and in doing so we manage to get two insults for the price of one.

In yet other cases, there are no specific descriptions of supposedly negative pig attributes actually made, but it is sufficiently insulting only to say that the person is *like a pig* in some way or other such as, *acting like a pig, behaving like a pig, being like a pig.* The mechanism operating here is that we delve into what can be described as our cultural model of pigs in order to find all of the derogatory attributes which supposedly relate to them.[9] We then, probably unconsciously, choose from this list (ugly, dirty, uncouth, fat, lazy, lying, etc. ) to fill in the blanks about the person being insulted. In this process, we not only send or receive the required message (insult) but continue to reinforce the negative cultural construction of pigs upon which we are drawing. This is a mechanism we use, not only to oppress other animals but other humans as well. As Stibbe points out:

> While the cultural model bears little relation to actual pigs, it bears all the hallmarks of cultural models in other areas, such as racism or sexism. Members of the dominant group base their feelings of superiority and self-worth on the supposed shortcomings of another group,...[10]

While this psychological gulf separating ourselves from other animals seems like a gaping fissure it has probably not always been this way in our own lives. Freud, writing in 1917, observes the following about children and animals:

> A child can see no difference between his own nature and that of animals. He is not astonished at animals thinking and talking in fairy-tales; he will transfer an emotion of fear which he feels for his human father onto a dog or a horse, without intending any derogation of his father by it. Not until he is grown up does he become so far estranged from animals as to use their names in vilification of human beings.[11]

Many of the old stories about the beginning of the world record a time when humans lived with animals and spoke the same language. In the book of Genesis which is common to Jewish, Muslim and Christian faiths, all creatures in paradise, including humans, co-exist peacefully and all of them are vegan.

## Violent words and victims' lives

It is surprising how many "animal" words and phrases we can find once we start looking. For example, there are jobs such as *shepherd, herd boy, gamekeeper, jockey, stable boy, animal technician* and *butcher;* places such as a *tannery, meat packing plant, abattoir, zoo, cowshed, farm, rendering plant*; specialised equipment as in a *steak knife, meat grinder, tenderiser, weaning ring, castrator, milking machine, electroejaculator, artificial vagina, cattle ship, sausage maker* and even areas of study such as *dairy science, poultry science, meat science, fresh meat processing* and the list goes on. And just to illustrate the point here is a very tacky paragraph using a few common animal terms.

*Don't spare the horses* because we cannot wait *until the cows come home* because we have been feeling rather *cooped up* recently and want to *get back in the saddle* although we should *reign in* our impatience a little and not *unleash* our frustration to *get the bit between our teeth* but eventually *take the bull by the horns*. Of course, we could do some *horse trading* here and there to *spur* things along and maybe *kill two birds with one stone* and then we will see who's in the *cockpit* although all this might seem a bit too much like *going the whole hog*. It is as if we have been *wearing blinkers* all along and should not have got involved with a *warren* of *hare brained, pig in a poke* schemes with those *vermin* with their *piggy eyes* who have made everything into a *dog's breakfast*. But soon they will be *eating out of our hands* so we must stop *bleating about things* or being *sheepish* and no longer remain *cowed*. It will be *like a red rag to a bull* but we will go on and *bring home the bacon* and afterwards *return to the fold*.

My sincere apologies to sensitive readers for this gross abuse of the English language but I believe it is in a good cause.

## History

Our long history of abusive treatment towards nonhuman animals is ingrained deep into the English language, although much of it goes unnoticed, obscured by the dust of time and everyday use. We have expressions such as *flogging a dead horse, the straw that broke the camel's back, going on a wild goose chase* and *there are more ways than one way to skin a cat*.

This last expression seems to date back to a debate about actually skinning cats and whether this is done when they are alive or dead.[12] An excerpt from the House of Commons, *Minutes of Evidence Taken Before Committee on Bill for Prevention of Cruelty to Animals, 1832* records the following exchange;

> 138.  And if I understand you, you saw this man skinning this cat alive? – Yes.

> 139.  You are perfectly satisfied that those cats were skinned alive? – I should think so[13]

However, a contrary view is reflected over forty years later in the magazine *The Leisure Hour* of 1879:

> The Dutch cat-killers have a most peculiar and clever way of killing their cats. It is a fallacy to suppose that cats are skinned alive. In the first place, to skin a cat when alive would be utterly impossible; and, secondly, it does not make any difference to the quality of the skin. The origin of the fallacy is probably that a cat is easier skinned immediately after death than if allowed to become rigid.[14]

What this "peculiar and clever way of killing their cats" is we do not find out but presumably the "Dutch cat-killers" did what they did for profit because cat fur was used at the time to adorn women's clothing. Similar versions of this phrase are, *there are more ways of killing a cat than choking it with butter (or with cream)* and *more ways to kill a dog than choking with pudding (or by hanging)*.

Treating people *with kid gloves* is another expression with an unpleasant history. It means to handle something or someone very gently, but there is mention of real kid gloves from as long ago as the 1730s.[15] The gloves would be very soft and while some were  made of the skin of baby goats others were made from the skin of lambs.[16] Wearing kid gloves was a sign of wealth, elegance and aristocratic idleness. One notable wearer in the 19th century was a man with a long name, William Pole-Tylney-Long-Wellesley, the fourth Earl of Mornington, but he did his reputation no good at all when he apparently made the fashion blunder of wearing his gloves for riding – which as everyone knows is a calamitous choice.[17]

Although they were seen as items of finery and admired by some, others thought them ostentatious and later the term kid gloves came to be used in a derogatory way. Here is a bit of hard hitting stuff from the Leicester Chronicle of 1842:

> This contraband system of political allusions appears to suit the taste and nerves of the cautious, gentlemanly, kid-gloved Conservatism, which cannot endure the shock of attending a public meeting.[18]

While the body parts of goats have been used for many things living goats were also used for something quite unusual. They were employed as wet nurses in the 18th and 19th century in Europe as also, on some occasions, were donkeys.

> Children in foundling hospitals fared slightly differently. Carefully selected cow's milk was a better food for infants if breastfeeding was not possible. The safest method was direct feeding from the udder of a goat or ass. Alphonse Leroy described his success at the foundling hospital at Aix in 1775: "Each goat which comes to feed enters bleating and goes to hunt the infant which has been given to it, pushes back the covering with its horns and straddles the crib to give suck to the infant. Since that time they have raised very large numbers in that hospital."[19]

Another common skin used is the *chamois leather*, much loved by those who enjoy cleaning motor cars and windows and which is made from the skins of small goat-like animals who live in the mountainous areas stretching from southern Europe to the Caucasus.[20] Sheepskin may now be used as a substitute or possibly even a synthetic product. However, the hunger for "soft skin" has not gone away and recent reports suggest that some cows are sent to slaughter while pregnant so that the skin of their foetuses can be used to make especially soft leather.

## A deadly mess

When there is a complete mess, a real disaster, we might use the word *shambles* as in, *it was a complete shambles* but this is a word with a long and sinister history. In the UK there are many places with names related to the word shambles with one particularly famous example simply called *The Shambles*. This is an old street in the northern English city of York and is a famous tourist attraction, once being voted Britain's most picturesque street.[21] The present buildings were erected in the 15th century although the location was mentioned much earlier in the Doomsday Book and so it must be considerably older as a site of business and settlement.

This street was the place where animals would be brought to be killed and butchered and their body parts sold to customers. It would have been a site of blood, bones, body fluids, tissues, the sounds of pain and the smell of death – an horrific mess in so many ways. The name *shambles*, derives from *shamel* meaning booth or bench (table? or shelf?)

and it was also known as *fleshshamel* as flesh was sold on its tables and shelves (the word *tol* also means a fee levied for selling flesh).[22] In 1872 there were 26 butchers shops operating in the street. A tourist guide offers this unpleasant, chatty little titbit about some of the architecture;

> It is also interesting to notice the way the pavements on either side of the street are raised up, this was done to create a channel which the butchers would wash away their waste through; offal and blood would gush down Shambles twice weekly.[23]

Another place called *The Shambles,* although not quite so famous, is in the small settlement of Chesterfield in Derbyshire.[24] Names which have been used for this location over the last 700 years include; Flescheharneles (1365), Bocheria (1420, 1421), Fleshamulz (1473), the Bochery (1502), le Fleshe Shambles (1559), le Shambles (1560) and The Shambles (present day).[25] The names tell us that killing and dismembering animals at this site has a very long history; it is an intergenerational convention and reflects what has happened here again and again. Behind this story, all but invisible, stand the countless lives lost and the terrible suffering which must have been endured here. We see in action over hundreds of years, an ideology which justifies violence against nonhuman animals and sanctions the right to use any animal's body for human desires.

## Bodies of no further use

In colloquial English *I am knackered* is a humorous phrase and means to be extremely tired with the related phrase, *to be sent to the knacker's yard* also used humorously and meaning to be disposed of as being no longer of any further use. But these and similar terms are far from funny and concern the practice of disposing of animals who are no longer wanted and who have outlived their usefulness to human beings. The knacker's yard was a place where old and injured animals, particularly horses, were sent to be killed and their bodies used for various things such as their skin for leather, bones for fertiliser and boiled up joints and feet to make glue. Historically, "working animals" had a very hard time in Britain and in many cases, horses were worked to death or close to it, on the roads and in the mills and factories as industrialisation increased. So, a final bit of profit for the "owner" could be squeezed out from the animal's bodies by selling them to the knacker's yard.

Related to this industry is *rendering*. It is a term used in the visual and performing arts meaning to present or interpret a work, but while this use dates from around 1862 it has an earlier meaning from at least 1792 which is the extracting or melting of fat.[26] The bodies of animals who are killed in farming and other industries are routinely subjected to rendering and it is a term now in wide use. A Food and Agricultural Agency (FAO) document on slaughterhouses explains:

> Rendering is a heating process for meat industry waste products through which fats are separated from water and protein residues for the production of edible lards and dried protein residues. Commonly it includes the production of a range of products of meat meal, meat-cum-bone meal, bone meal and fat from animal tissues.[27]

Rendering in its broad industrial sense today means to take everything usable from an animal's body and turn it into a wide range of "products". There are around two hundred and fifty rendering facilities in North America alone and this excerpt describes their "raw materials";

> The U.S. currently produces, slaughters, and processes approximately 100 million hogs, 35 million cattle, and eight billion chickens annually. By-products include hides, skins, hair, feathers, hoofs, horns, feet, heads, bones, toe nails, blood, organs, glands, intestines, muscle and fat tissues, shells, and whole carcasses. These by-product materials have been utilized for centuries for many significant uses.[28]

Note the production discourse here. We are told, the US *produces* and *processes* hogs, cattle and chickens with *by-products* from this process of *glands, blood, intestines, toe nails, feet, heads,* etc. The animals and their body parts are portrayed as just materials which are both produced and used in a massive and diverse production processes.

One big industry organisation is the National Renderers Association or NRA, not to be mistaken for another organisation with the same acronym and also associated with large scale violence against animals. It has representation internationally and produces a magazine titled, rather blandly, *Render; The International Magazine of Rendering*.[29] Its website informs the reader that, "The National Renderers Association does not discriminate on the basis of race, colour, national origin, sex, religion, age, disability, political beliefs, sexual orientation or marital/family status."[30] However, it clearly does discriminate on the basis of species.

And there is a bit of money to be had in this grizzly business if the 82nd National Rendering Association Annual Convention of October 2015 held at the Ritz-Carlton Hotel at Dana Point, California is anything to go by.[31] Companies with attendees at this event make an interesting list with names which include; Gelita, Darling Ingredients Inc, Big Heart Pet Brands, Valley Proteins Inc, Tallowman, West Coast Reduction Inc, Pilgrims Pride Corp, Farmers Union Industries, Tyson Foods Inc, Sustainable Sourcing, Guangdong Haid Group Co., Ltd, Zhejiang Biomass Solutions Co. Ltd. Smithfield Foods, K-Pro GMBH, Kusters Water, and Clemson University.[32]

## Domestication or deception?

Although as humans we think of the pleasure of some form of cosy existence with a happy family around us as domestication, the word has terrible connotations when applied to animals. Our domestication of animals began around 10 000 years ago with sheep and goats the first to be "farmed" then cattle and pigs following.[33] The animals were no longer allowed to roam and seek food naturally and live as they had done previously. These early incarcerations were almost certainly brought about by violence, perhaps killing the parents and taking in the young ones who were left helpless. Research suggests that those animals kept in captivity were often far from healthy with evidence of poor diet, stress, gum disease and physical trauma.[34] As time went by, domesticated animals came under increasing human control with almost every aspect of their lives subject to human wishes and whims, enforced by the use of instruments such as whips, chains, collars, harnesses, thorns in the nasal septum, mutilation, castration, hobbling and other forms of violence.[35] Castration not only controlled the breeding of the animals but made them more pliable and easier to dominate. Ownership was denoted by burning marks into the flesh or other forms of mutilation and still is today.

With every individual captured and confined in this way or what I will refer to as each *domestication event*, the nonhuman individual was swallowed into the great control and reification machine and from that day on the lives of all of her descendants, would be utterly devastated. From that single event, at a distant moment in time, all of her lineage would be marked for a life of incarceration rather than their birth right of freedom. They would be born into a world where they would be owned, manipulated, mutilated, their families destroyed and their bodies used; they would have few if any choices and most would be destined to die young and violently. All would take their first and last breaths as hostages to our desires as they still do today. At her domestication event when those cruel restraints were inflicted upon her, they also reached through time to her many descendants and in that instant also bound those as yet unborn into a life of slavery.

All of this is a far cry from the domestication of animals which is often portrayed today as a mutually beneficial contract between humans and animals. This is a belief which is very popular and in the following extract from a history web page, it is described as follows,

> The domestication of animals is based on an ancient contract, with benefits on both sides, between man and the ancestors of the breeds familiar to us today.[36]

No it isn't. In relation to the animals who are used by humans it is a one sided, ongoing violent and exploitive assault. If this fictional contract is a supposed benefit to animals it is without doubt a benefit they would happily do without.

Spencer observes that the control over every aspect of another's life gives the "owner" a sense of power and "owners" may have many animals, giving them an even greater sense of power and status.[37] The word cattle is derived from *catel* meaning personal goods or a principal sum of money and came to be applied to moveable property and particularly to animals who are "owned" and who are today referred to as livestock.[38] *Chattel* is a related word which now means personal possessions and was, at times, applied to slaves.[39] The word *capital* relates to the head (*capitas*), as in "head of cattle" and came to refer to a principal sum of money.[40]

### Animals, women and words

Some time ago the sociologist Linda Kaloff noted that a consistent research finding is that women are more concerned about animals than are men:

> While substantial differences in attitudes toward animals have been found by age, region, race and education (Kellert, 1980), one of the most consistent findings in the literature is the tendency for women to be more concerned than men about animals.[41]

She argues that this gender differences may be shaped by social structure and women's experiences, "[t]hus, the experience of oppression may produce empathy for other oppressed groups and egalitarian worldviews."[42]

Mason describes our hierarchical thinking with respect to women and animals and suggests that the domestication of animals may have gone hand in hand with the loss of status for women and their subsequent repression:

> On the dominionist ladder or hierarchy of being, women of one's own group are a step down. They have been regarded as "near the animal state" according to Sir Keith Thomas in his survey of European attitudes in Man and the Natural World. Other writers have explained how the subjugation of women under patriarchy began with animal-domesticating, animal-herding tribes of the ancient Middle East. These first male supremacists rewrote creation stories and other myths, destroyed goddess cults, introduced misogyny into poetry and myths and ultimately reduced the status of women.[43]

Women, like animals were, and still are in some cases, seen as possessions. Sometimes this is implied and subtle while at other times wholly overt. One such example occurred in a court case a number of years ago in Cameroon and concerned a woman who wished to inherit her deceased husband's property. The presiding judge first made the statement that "Women are property" and followed this by asking the rather tricky question, "How can property own property?"[44]

When a woman is said to be "making herself cheap", perhaps by having a number of sexual partners or doing something else which is disapproved of by some in society, it implies that she must have had a price to begin with and therefore could be purchased.

Nature is often given a female persona in which can be peaceful, nurturing and fertile as well as wild, chaotic and dangerous and Merchant, from an historical perspective, notes that "disorderly women, like chaotic nature, needed to be controlled."[45] She describes how Francis Bacon (1561–1626) reduces the image of female Nature to a resource to be exploited for production:

> Sensitive to the same social transformations that had already begun to reduce women to psychic and reproductive resources, Bacon developed the power of language as a political instrument in reducing female nature to a resource for economic production. Female imagery became a tool in adapting scientific knowledge and method to a new form of human power over nature.[46]

In this paradigm, female Nature must be "bound into service", enslaved, "put in constraints" and moulded. Much of Bacon's imagery for describing his scientific methods and objectives is derived from the courtroom and he "...treats nature as a female to be tortured through mechanical inventions..."[47]

Carol J Adams writes extensively about women and animals and has shown the similarities present in the objectification of both. In her book *The Sexual Politics of Meat* she famously politicised the concept of *the absent referent* where the once-living being whose body is consumed does not exist to the consumer of that flesh.[48] She writes that

> Behind every meal of meat is an absence: the death of the animal whose place the meat takes. This is the "absent referent." The absent referent functions to cloak the violence

inherent to meat eating, to protect the conscience of the meat eater and render the idea of individual animals as immaterial to anyone's selfish desires.[49]

She draws the parallel between animals' and women's bodies; the bodies of animals being physically butchered into parts and women's bodies being dissected culturally with the goal in both cases being consumption which is disconnected from the sentient individual.[50] Adams makes great use of the examination of advertisements to show the play between the sexualisation of dead animals' bodies and the objectification of women.

Images using animals and animal flesh are common in relation to sex. For example, meat is used generally to describe the sexual organs of both men and women with phrases such as *meat and two veg* used to describe the male genitals as well as the *mutton dagger*, the *pork sword* and the *pork dagger* used to describe the penis. The term *polony* is used to describe a girl or young woman and *pussy* to describe the female genitals as well as women in general when it is used as a mass noun.[51] The terms *meat injection* and *porking* are used to describe sexual intercourse, *milkers* and *puppies* are used for women's breasts and the phrase *mutton dressed as lamb* used to denote a woman dressing in fashions usually worn by women younger than her age.[52] In vernacular usage, *pulling a pig* denotes the seduction of a person deemed ugly and is sometimes played as a cruel game.[53]

Nick Fiddes also points out that there are strong links between the language system of meat and that used to describe women in normal discourse and in pornography.[54] Women are referred to as *cats, chicks, dogs, cows* and as a *filly, minx, sex kitten, bunny girl* and many other animal forms. Men *hunt* them and they may be *ridden* and men have *trophy wives*.[55] Women can be *tasty*, *juicy* and *succulent* with a young woman who has recently reached the age of sexual consent being described as *fresh meat*.[56] This is the language of masculine power and Fiddes observes that, Nature and women have been characterized as twin threats to this supremacy.[57]

Many of the attitudes towards animals and women, and the social constructions of their identities, signal a specific view of reality which is the belief in a world composed of a hierarchy of beings. This belief, in its many forms, exercises immense power and can have terrible consequences. It is important that we recognise and understand it because its employment as an ideological justification for violence and oppression is common. One of the earliest statements of this world view is found in ancient Greece, which is where we turn next.

## CHAPTER 5

# Chained minds

*The dominant cultures of our world are as convinced of the superiority of our species over others and of our right to rule the planet as most South Africans once were about their right to oppress other South Africans.*

Cormack Cullinan[1]

## Aristotle, chains and ladders

THE IDEA THAT the whole of existence is a complex world composed of greater and lesser beings has held a central position in Western thought for centuries and has a history which stretches back at least 2300 years to the Ancient Greeks.[2] While there are a number of variations, the grand version of The Great Chain of Being describes a world which is hierarchically arranged from the greatest to the least. It begins with the highest beings, the wholly spiritual god or gods and works its way down via the angels, to man, women, animals, plants, the soil and minerals. From the spiritual down to the earthly – and man is seen as having a bit of both in him. There might be many subdivisions within each group depending upon the version being used and for example, Greek men were seen as higher than Greek women because it was believed that women were not as good at reasoning as men and didn't have as sound a sense of justice. In addition, some women and men, it was claimed, could not reason for themselves at all but could only appreciate the reason of others and these were deemed natural slaves.[3]

One of the major thinkers about this chain or ladder, is Aristotle and he outlines in his *Politics* some ideas about the nature of existence as he understands it. Below we examine three excerpts. The first concerns the inherent hierarchy of the world. He begins by posing and then answering a question about slavery:

> But is there any one thus intended by nature to be a slave, and for whom such a condition is expedient and right, or rather is not all slavery a violation of nature? There is no difficulty in answering this question, on grounds both of reason and of fact. For that some should rule and others be ruled is a thing not only necessary, but expedient; from the hour of their birth, some are marked out for subjection, others for rule.[4]

He declares that some are born to rule and others to be ruled over and this is just the way of the world.

In the next excerpt, the idea of purpose or teleology is proposed and linked to hierarchy:

> In like manner we may infer that, after the birth of animals, plants exist for their sake, and that the other animals exist for the sake of man, the tame for use and food, the wild, if not all at least the greater part of them, for food, and for the provision of clothing and various instruments. Now if nature makes nothing incomplete, and nothing in vain, the inference must be that she has made all animals for the sake of man.[5]

Everything that exists serves a purpose and animals, although they may provide different things, exist for "the sake of man."

The final section differentiates animals even further, dealing with "domesticated" and free-living animals:

> The same holds good of animals in relation to men; for tame animals have a better nature than wild, and all tame animals are better off when they are ruled by man; for then they are preserved. Again, the male is by nature superior, and the female inferior; and the one rules, and the other is ruled; this principle, of necessity, extends to all mankind.[6]

In the first sentence the mythical ancient contract between man and animals is echoed and control by humans portrayed as being beneficial. The "better nature" of the tame animals referred to is because they have been coerced into submission and those with less than a good nature killed off or not allowed to reproduce.

The extract also tells us that men are superior to women and therefore must rule over them which means men must rule over both women and animals.

Despite all the above, Preece points out that Aristotle was not without sympathy for animals, having respect for them and believing that men and animals had some psychical qualities in common.[7] Unfortunately, not all of those who came after him would have such inclusive views.

## Long chain running

The philosophers, Zeno, Cleanthese and Chrysippus lived after Aristotle and followed the Stoic philosophy which had slightly different views about these matters. Although it did allow for a greater degree of equality amongst humans, it was business as usual for the animals and they were still for the use of man.[8] Cicero explains;

> In fact there is nothing else beside the world that has nothing wanting, but is fully equipped and complete and perfect in all its details and parts. For as Chrysippus cleverly puts it, just as a shield-case is made for the sake of a shield and a sheath for the sake of a sword, so everything else except the world was created for the sake of some other thing; thus the corn and fruits produced by the earth were created for the sake of animals, and animals for the sake of man: for example the horse for riding, the ox for ploughing, the dog for hunting and keeping guard; man himself however came into existence for the purpose of contemplating and imitating the world...[9]

Here again is the idea of one thing existing in order to be used by another and although this was alluded to in a general way in previous extracts, we have here a much more explicit concept of specific purposes for the lives of animals. They have defined purposes for their lives and these purposes all relate to what they can do for humans. However fanciful or laughable this may seem when stated so plainly, the basic ideology is very much alive and flourishing today as we shall see later.

Overall, things possibly got worse with the Stoics because animals were seen by them as having little mental capacity, being unable to remember the past, anticipate the future or communicate by voice.[10] As such they were shifted even further away from human lives and any previously acknowledged sentience was degraded.

Nearly one and a half thousand years after Aristotle, the idea of the Great Chain was solidly entrenched in Western thinking as shown by this rather notorious section of the writings of St Thomas Aquinas (1225–1274);

> ...for his disobedience to God, man was punished by the disobedience of those creatures which should be subject to him. Therefore in the state of innocence, before man had disobeyed, nothing disobeyed him that was naturally subject to him. Now all animals are naturally subject to man. This can be proved in three ways. First, from the order observed by nature; for just as in the generation of things we perceive a certain order of procession of the perfect from the imperfect (thus matter is for the sake of form; and the imperfect form, for the sake of the perfect), so also is there order in the use of natural things; thus the imperfect are for the use of the perfect; as the plants make use of the earth for their nourishment, and animals make use of plants, and man makes use of both plants and animals. Therefore it is in keeping with the order of nature, that man should be master over animals.[11]

Aquinas believes that there was a time when all creatures were obedient to man but this was lost with the fall from grace. However, they are still subject to man and the ladder of perfection still exists with the imperfect for use by the perfect which means that both animals and plants are meant for the use of man.

But not all interpretations of the Great Chain have been negative towards animals. Some describe a kinship of beings or alert us to those who are seen as more vulnerable, and who need our care and protection. Priscilla Wakefield, a Quaker, wrote of our responsibilities to other creatures, John Lock of the closeness of humans and animals in reason and knowledge and Johann Wolfgang von Goethe that each animal is an end in itself.[12]

However, for many, the elitist and oppressive version of the Great Chain seems to exercise an inexorable attraction. Francis Bacon (1561-1626), seen as one of the founders of modern scientific method, writes of the myth of Prometheus, "This fable carries in it many true and grave speculations" and he makes these interpretations:

> The chief aim of the parable appears to be, that Man, if we look to final causes, may be regarded as the centre of the world; insomuch that if man were taken away from the world, the rest would seem to be all astray, without aim or purpose, to be like a besom without a binding, as the saying is, and to be leading to nothing. For the whole world

works together in the service of man; and there is nothing from which he does not derive use and fruit.[13]

The phrase, "...the whole world works together in the service of man..." rather succinctly encapsulates the whole belief of purpose in the world and that purpose for animals always being to serve man.

## Racializing science

As the 17th century moved into the 18th, science starting to challenge many long-held assumptions including those related to the living world. In 1735 Linnaeus published his work, Systema Naturae, a system of classification for animals, plants and minerals although at that time there was still a belief that species did not change but were immutable and so evolutionary theory was not a part of his book. By 1858 Rudolf Virchow had shown that cells only arise from other cells and in 1859 Alfred Wallace and Charles Darwin both published work on the evolution of species. Gregor Mendel followed this with his work on inheritance in 1865.

It is perhaps worth pausing at this point to note a few other important things which had been going on in the world. In 1402 Spain began its colonial endeavors by invading the Canary Islands and in 1415 Portugal followed suit by invading Morocco. By 1441 the first slaves arrived in Lisbon and in the same year Pope Nicholas issued the papal bull Dum Diversas which gave permission to invade lands, subjugate and capture Saracens, pagans unbelievers and enemies of Christ, in other words just about anyone you felt like, and make them into perpetual slaves. The formation of the Dutch East India Company took place in 1602 and by 1607 there was a British settlement in Jamestown, Virginia with the first slaves arriving by 1652. In 1798 France invaded Egypt.

While slavery and the slave trade was widespread and viewed by many as being important to prosperity, there was a significant social movement against it which culminated in Britain passing the Slave Trade Act in 1807 making the slave trade illegal anywhere in the British Empire (slavery was already illegal in Britain). This did not end slavery and slaves could still be held and used, but then the Slavery Abolition Act (1833) put an end to that and by 1834 all slaves in British territories had been emancipated. Many other slave trading countries followed a similar path.

The employment of scientific method and its continually expanding world view brought new understanding into many spheres but the hierarchy of the Great Chain wasn't going away. Many people still believed humans to be above other animals, certain human groups to be above others and men to be above women. There were some scientists who wanted to prove these ideas and one such example concerns a researcher who was trying to do some scientific work on beauty but had his results hijacked by racists.

The Dutch physician and scientist, Petrus Camper (1722–1789) was interested in an amazingly wide variety of things but this concerns his research in the areas of aesthetics and comparative anatomy and he was apparently accomplished in both spheres. However, he was about to inadvertently amble into one of the great debates of his time. One of the things which interested people was why "races" looked different from each other and what caused those differences. For example, it was suggested by some that variations in the thickness of lips or the shape of eyes was caused by the manipulation of babies by midwives or mothers shortly after birth and one explanation about African's people's noses being "flattened" in relation to European noses, was put forward by George Buffon who claimed it was caused by babies bumping against their mother's backs while being carried.[14]

At this time, at least in the Western world, Ancient Greece was looked upon as having been the pinnacle of civilisation and the Greek people as the epitome of beauty but after the demise of that civilisation it was believed things had all rather fallen apart and gone downhill. Camper, being interested in beauty, decided to look at the various angles he could measure in the faces of humans and nonhumans using ancient Greek faces as the reference by which to judge all of the others. He took all kinds of measurements and one of the angles he employed shows the way the face slopes from the forehead downwards to the jaw and this came to be known as the facial angle or *Camper's angle*. He inspected a range of skulls both human and nonhuman and among other things noted how the angle varied:

> The angle that Camper outlined ascended through the profile of a tailed monkey (42°), through a small orangutan, on which he had published the first monograph, (58°), the Kalmuck Asian and the Angolan African (both 70°), and the European's near-vertical (80°) angle. This peak could be surpassed "by the rules of art alone," as in the classical sculpture of the Apollo Belvedere which stood at the head of Camper's sequence (100°).[15]

This is fine because Camper was only interested in beauty as understood in relation to his chosen ideal and his results are drawings of skulls and the various angles which he had measured. Of course, we might query whether the Ancient Greeks actually are the pinnacle of beauty and certainly an orangutan, for example, might completely disagree, which seems fair enough, so naturally this would be open to some discussion. However, it is the interpretations others made of his work combined with their distortion of the theory of evolution, which is what turned out to be the major problem.

Up to that time the belief about all living beings was that God created them just as they are and that they did not change over generations. Despite the Great Chain being a popular idea, it would be a bit difficult to claim any hierarchy of "races" because God had simply made people that way. And the other living beings too.

However, given Darwin's new ideas regarding evolution, an argument could erroneously be made, that some beings are "primitive" or "less evolved" and therefore inferior while others are "advanced" and "more evolved" and therefore superior or to put it another way, some groups got left behind in the evolutionary race. Arranging Camper's results to represent a progression, supposedly from "primitive" to "advanced", meant that humans were superior to animals and that some "races" were superior to others.[16] Martin Kemp, writing in the journal *Nature* explains;

> Camper's "negro" could be stigmatized as evolutionarily more primitive. The nineteenth-century campaigns of craniological measurement and ethnographic

photography, together with huge collections of skull types, provided great banks of data that could be exploited to detect those races that stood closest to the animal origins of man.[17]

Camper's work said nothing of the sort but Kemp notes how it was built into a racist and anthropocentric "proof" of a hierarchy ranging from birds though to Caucasians:

> In conjunction with the voguish physiognomics of Johann Kaspar Lavater, this diagnostic move was readily made, not least in Charles White's "An Account of the Regular Gradations in Man and in Different Kinds of Animals and Vegetables" of 1799, in which profile drawings of heads were arranged in ascending succession from a long-beaked bird (literally bird-brained) to the noble profile of an exemplary Caucasian. However, Camper himself was not prepared to make this move.[18]

And later,

> The progressive misuse of Camper's non-racist characterizations is a salutary reminder of what can happen to apparently "neutral" results when a climate of belief is radically transformed. Place his observations together with Lavater's diagnostic physiognomics and Darwin's Descent of Man in the same social cooking-pot, and we can see how an ugly dish can result.[19]

It is evident that, science or no science, we were not willing to abandon our love of the Great Chain in some form or other.

## Evolving nonsense and real kinship

According to Marjorie Spiegel, whereas previously the view that "civilised Christians" were above all other people had served as a reason for the exploitation of other races and nonhuman animals, with the advent of Social Darwinism the, "unmitigated violence towards the 'lower' animals and the enslavement of black 'savages' in Africa" were looked at as expressions of an evolutionary birthright.[20]

Our popular portrayals of evolution today – even those in many scientific textbooks, betray our desire to be seen as above every other creature. Stephen Jay Gould describes how the way we represent human evolution, including the classic representations where early man goes from being some kind of monkey walking on all fours right through by stages to an upright, tall human male striding away at the head of the line is simply not supported by the evidence.[21]

He ridicules the idea of some type of ascending evolution and particularly human superiority saying "...the familiar iconographies of evolution are all directed – sometimes crudely sometimes subtly – towards reinforcing a comfortable view of human inevitability and superiority."[22] Evolution is not a series of steps which are climbed one by one by different creatures with the highly evolved beings at the top and the laggards lower down. Evolution is about two things, survival and reproduction and to be successful you have to be good at both, whatever the prevailing conditions. Gould suggests that evolution can be better depicted as a much-branched bush with many of the branches and twigs ending in extinction and only a relatively few surviving.

He also points out that there are many very successful groups such as bats or antelopes who have numerous members, but that we humans are the last survivors of our group, yet we use this very fact for our self-aggrandisement;

> I need hardly remind everybody that at least one other mammalian lineage, preeminent among all in our attention and concern, shares with horses the sorry state of reduction from a formally luxuriant bush to a single surviving twig – the very property of tenuousness that permits us to build a ladder reaching only to the heart of our own folly and hubris.[23]

Nee writing in the journal *Nature* suggests that from our various anthropocentric representations of evolution, always with humans at the top, it appears we might have, "some deep psychological need to see ourselves as the culmination of creation."[24]

But understanding humans as one of a huge number of living beings, each special in its own way, does not belittle the achievements of human societies or the efforts of individuals. Evolution offers us a dazzling view of the world, stressing as it does, our deep kinship with all other life. David Baltimore writing at the time of the release of the first draft of the results from the human genome project says this about what it revealed:

> First, it confirms something obvious and expected, yet controversial: our genes look much like those of fruit flies, worms and even plants…the genome shows that we all descended from the same humble beginnings and that the connections are written in our genes.[25]

When it comes to our near relatives, work has shown how similar are the genomes of chimpanzees, bonobos, humans and gorillas:

> The genomes of all three species are, in any case, highly similar: humans and chimpanzees share more than 98% of their genes, while humans and gorillas share more than 96%.[26]

And:

> It is known that whereas DNA sequences in humans diverged from those in bonobos and chimpanzees five to seven million years ago, DNA sequences in bonobos diverged from those in chimpanzees around two million years ago. Bonobos are thus closely related to chimpanzees.[27]

The morphological and genetic evidence suggests that humans, chimpanzees and bonobos all come from a common ancestor and that gorillas might have branched off from this line at an earlier stage but are still, genetically, very close to us. I find it deeply moving that we share this common history with our sisters and brothers of the forest; that in a very real, biological and historical sense, they are us and we are them.

When the findings about chimpanzees and humans were first released it caused a lot of interest about our kinship and shared ancestry. However, a number of commentators went to great lengths to focus only on the two per cent difference rather than the 98% in common and to claim that this few per cent is so very important and that it is this which makes us human; which makes us so very special. They could just as easily have argued from the other angle that it is the few per cent difference which makes chimpanzees who they are and equally makes them so very special but nobody seemed interested in making this particular point. What is evident in such anthropocentric attitudes is our desperate craving to be the universal reference point, the default calculous by which all beings must be measured and must inevitably fall short.

For many years this has been the position taken almost exclusively in scientific research relating to animals. The question is asked again and again, how do *they* compare with humans; human problem solving, social skills, tool use, communication and so on. We continually theorise and debate about how and why animals are less than us.

Even the vocabulary of science, written in textbooks and heard in lectures, still contains phrases suggesting hierarchy such as *higher animals, lower vertebrates, higher primates, primitive animals* and from time to time *more evolved* or *less evolved* might slip through. As Carol J. Adams points out, "Conditions for violence flourish when we structure our world hierarchically, in a false Darwinian progression that places humans at the top" and later makes the crucial observation, "The further down the great chain of being one is placed, the less the barriers to violence." In the 21st century, The Great Chain is alive and well and in relation to animals those barriers to violence are paper thin.

With Adam's prophetic words we will shortly turn to look at language relating to farmed nonhumans and the ideology standing in the shadows behind it. But before we do this, I want to briefly explore two areas; first, the ideology of purpose and its very good friend eugenics, and then, consideration of whether animals can be viewed as slaves.

## CHAPTER 6

# Lives with purposes and other lies

*No science is immune to the infection of politics and the corruption of power.*

Jacob Bronowski[1]

## Good breeding?

OUR ABIDING LOVE affair with the ideas of the Great Chain appear in many guises but a popular one is breeding. We can *have breeding*; *breed* other beings and *breed* in our own right. Some people will tell you that breeding is very important and when they say this they might be talking about people, animals or both.

Breeding is also an activity people *do* to a variety of animals: sheep, goats, cattle, horses, dogs, cats, rabbits, hamsters and so on. Breeds are unnatural in the sense that they are not found in situations where animals are allowed to live freely. Certainly, some animals may share particular characteristics in a given environment but that is not the same as a breed. Breeds are caused by genetic manipulation and are the result of human interference in the natural reproductive processes of a group – and that interference is usually violent and protracted.

Some breeds of dog are now so genetically damaged that the animals face a shortened life of pain and discomfort – and all this in order to look "good" to human eyes. In some cases, the inbreeding can be so severe that many animals are born dead, an effect known as an inbreeding depression.

There are big companies who do it, small concerns and individuals and there are clubs, special societies, strict regulations, registration processes and so on and perhaps nowhere is this love of breeds and breeding more obvious than in the farming of nonhuman animals. But before we take a look at this aspect let's just have a look at human breeding and see what we think about that.

## Eugenics for all

Eugenics can be traced back to the work of Sir Francis Galton, who coined the term in 1883 and claimed, amongst other things, that leadership qualities are inherited and that this explained why the British ruling class was in the position which it was in – ruling the country.[2,3] This is a very convenient argument especially if you can get those who are not part of the ruling class to believe it. But it was also understood that good breeding could be destroyed by something called degeneracy and that this was the cause of the various disorders of inheritance such as early death or madness and that one of the chief causes of degeneracy was masturbation.[4]

In 1899 this idea led Harry Clay Sharp, a prison physician at the Indiana State Reformatory, to carry out vasectomies on prisoners; at first doing this to boys in the institution in the hope of preventing them from masturbating but later realising the eugenic value of preventing their procreation.[5,6] From that time onwards they could not pass on their "bad" traits to future generations.

It was due to his advocacy and that of other physicians that in 1907 Indiana enacted a law requiring the sterilisation of "degenerates" which was the first eugenics law in the US although in 1887 castration had been used both as a punishment and in an effort to prevent further crime.[7,8] The general idea of the selective breeding of humans was gaining in popularity.

In the early 20th century the American Breeders Association (ABA) was interested in bringing science together with plant and animal breeding but it also turned its attention to questions about human "races"; their hereditary differences, selective breeding, the idea of superior stock, and the problem of "inferior types".[9,10] Charles B. Davenport, one of the eugenics movement's leading figures, wrote a book, published in 1910 titled, *Eugenics: The Science of Human Improvement through Better Breeding* and according to one commentator, the book had "a distinctly agricultural flavour" and proudly included Davenport's affiliation with the ABA on the title page.[11] Animal agriculture had been practising eugenics for thousands of years and as Carlson ominously notes:

> Agricultural genetics also provided the favored model for negative eugenics: human populations like agricultural breeds and varieties, had to be culled of their least productive members, with only the healthiest specimens used for breeding.[12]

Eugenics became an accepted part of America's progressive agenda, with California leading the way and by 1930 it had carried out more than sixty per cent of the country's 12 000 forced sterilizations. Selden writes that high school students in the US might, for example, see a film called *The Black Stork*, about eugenics and supporting sterilisation, attend a sermon on Sunday explaining how the best people should marry each other for the benefit of the future human race and on a field trip to a state fair they may be able to be evaluated at the "Fitter Families Exhibit", perhaps even winning a medal with the inscription "Yea I Have A Goodly Heritage".[13]

The United States was a model for other countries which also sought to sterilise their "defectives". In 1929 Denmark was the first European country to pass such laws, followed in rapid succession by other Scandinavian nations, with Germany passing its sterilisation law in 1933, shortly after the Nazis came to power.[14] The year before, in 1932, the Third International Conference of Eugenics had taken place in New York with the theme "A Decade of Progress in Eugenics".[15]

The concept of having and preserving a pure genetic population, whatever this is understood to be, means that the existing population must be both improved from within and defended from the danger of contamination from outside. In some ways everyone in the elite group needs to be, to use that much loved bureaucratic cliché, fit for purpose. Within this ideology the mass sterilisation of "defective" individuals is a logical step as is the control of immigration, a prohibition on intermarriage and the permanent removal of "defective" individuals or groups who are believed to constitute both a threat to the stock and to be a burden on resources. The American psychiatrist, Foster Kennedy publicly supported the idea of killing mentally challenged people.[16]

Today eugenics is viewed by most people as abhorrent and any suggestion of using its methods as unthinkable. But the ideas behind it have never gone away and were there long before the organised movement of the 1930s. The irony is that it is exactly these principles which we use every day in the breeding of animals for food, for experimentation and for all sorts of other purposes and which are celebrated in scientific journals, in breed societies, farming magazines, testing companies' catalogues, horse racing and animal shows as well as in our universities and colleges where we teach young people how to do eugenics.

## Lives for a purpose

The idea of a purpose for the lives of nonhuman animals is one of the strange things which arises from the ideology of the Great Chain of Being. If asked directly if they believed in the idea of animals having a purpose for their lives, my guess is that relatively few people would say yes, but the reality is that we draw on this ideological construction again and again and purposes for the lives of animals is a common portrayal in texts of all kinds.[17]

Let's look through a few texts from a farming magazine to help highlight the discourse. Some texts actually talk about purpose directly and here are three examples. This first is about a particular breed of cattle:

> The Pustertaler hails from the Puster Valley in the Tyrolean Alps where it has proven its value as a dual-purpose breed for milk and meat production.[18]

The Pustertaler, we are told has a *dual purpose*, which is producing meat and milk for humans. Then for sheep we have:

> This is the result of strict selection over the years for high wool quality, which complements a high level of reproduction and lamb-growth rate in the stud – true dual-purpose sheep.[19]

This is similar to the first example but now it is sheep who have the dual purposes, this time of producing babies and wool. Finally, for chickens there is:

> The heavier brown-egg strains are the closest thing to a dual-purpose breed.[20]

The chickens here have the dual purpose of producing eggs and flesh for human consumption.

On most occasions though, the claim of purpose is not explicitly stated but is built into the "name" of the animal – who are of course, named by us. Naming things is an important act and it is those who have power to name the world, who define reality.

In farming there are numerous examples of *purpose names* such as: *meat cattle, beef calves, beef animal, beef types, beef breeds, specialised beef herd, red beef animals, red beef cows, mutton breeds, broilers, wool sheep, layers brown, eggers, white-egg layers…*

It seems so obvious that a *beef animal* must exist to provide beef, what else could it possibly be for? In the same way *wool sheep* provide wool and *layers* give eggs. The name tells us that this is what they are, this is what they do, this is why they are here and this is how we should use them.[21]

Unsurprisingly, given the pervasive production discourse in farming, one common purpose for the lives of animals is the making of money for their "owners". We have *commercial Gelbvieh cattle, commercial Mutton Merino sheep, commercial herd, commercial boars, commercial cows, commercial animals, commercial breeding cows, commercial calves and commercial hybrids.*

Some animals find their purpose in different aspects of reproduction. It might be bearing babies, supplying semen for sale, bringing about conception or affecting another animal's hormones. So, we have *breeding cattle, stud cattle, breeding ewes, stud animals, breeding stock, breeding cows, stud goats, stud ram, breeding rams, stud animals, stud herd* and *commercial breeding cows.* Then there are *teaser rams* as opposed to *proper rams* each with their own specific "job" to do. And of course, there are *dairy herds, dairy calves and milking cows.*

This story becomes even more bizarre with descriptions such as *slaughter lambs, slaughter stock* and *prime slaughter lambs* – animals whose purpose in life is to be slaughtered. But purpose names serve an important function in that they neatly allow us to sidestep any ethical concerns about using and killing the animals concerned.

But we should not point fingers at the agricultural industry alone because we use this trick in our everyday thinking about all sorts of animals. You can easily make your own list but here are some of my examples of animal purpose names: *war horse, race horse, cart horse, dray horse, carriage horse, workhorse, pack mule, pit pony, lap dog, hunting dog, service dog, working dog, guard dog, herding dog, guide dog, house dog, pet cat, zoo animal, yard dog, sheep dog, game fish, sport fish, laboratory animals, laboratory rats, companion animals, beast of burden, truffle hog, cull hen, sled dog, cage bird, draft animals, game, circus animals, Christmas turkey, porker, Thanksgiving turkey, roaster, game birds, fur animals, fighting cocks, sleigh dog, pets* and *farm animals.*[22]

None of these actually exists of course. They are all fictitious beings, originating inside human heads and reflecting human desires.

We might argue that humans also have similar names which suggest a purpose – butcher, baker, referee, teacher and so on but we understand that these are roles freely chosen and that they in no way imply that this is the totality of the person or their reason for existence. Even when we say somebody was born to be a teacher it is understood that this is a complement to their special abilities in the role they choose to play. It is part of *who* they are, not *what* they are supposed to be used for and that is a big difference.

In almost every case the purpose names of animals objectify them, reifying them from the moment of their birth into instruments to an end. In addition, they are portrayed as bereft of agency, which in reality is physically and coercively denied them by our human domination.

In some cases we draw upon our "member's resources" to interpret purpose names, for example, *sled dogs,* we understand, are to be harnessed to a sled and forced to pull it. Some names are even shortened to one word such as *broiler* or *porker* but we still know what they are to be used for. A *dairy cow*, we recognise has the purpose of providing milk for us and we often say she *gives* milk, which obviously is a fiction but makes it seem as if she has some sort of choice and willingly contributes her milk for our consumption. And we say *laying hens* give eggs and *beef animals* provide beef and so on and once again we have the portrayal of this phony pseudo-benevolent relationship of domestication.

Overall the ideological concept of purpose allows us to believe that when we use animals for "their purpose" we are doing what is right, normal and expected. There is no ethical problem in using something for the purpose for which it exists. A Christmas Turkey is supposed to be slaughtered at Christmas, a draft animal to carry loads, farm animals should be on a farm, a cage bird naturally belongs in a cage and laboratory animals are for experimenting upon.

With all of this in mind let's have a look at a newspaper lifestyle article about food which draws on a range of discourses including that of purpose.

## The cow who died to teach

The article concerned is from the South African *Sunday Times* newspaper which appeared just before Heritage Day, a holiday when different groups in the country are called upon to celebrate and share their heritages. The article is about two things, a competition between trainee chefs who prepared different traditional dishes, and something the article calls "thoughtful consumption". We can just look at an extract, starting with the headline and the first few lines of the piece:

> **One Nguni cow turned into 400 plates of food to teach responsible eating**
> She died for a good cause – a single indigenous Nguni cow brings diverse groups
> together and provides a lesson in thoughtful consumption. Take one Nguni cow, one
> spring day in Soweto and 20 recipes, and you have a plateful of delicious reasons to
> think differently about food.[23]

In the headline a sentient individual euphemistically *turns into* plates of food to teach people something. There is no reference as to how this individual *turned into* plates of food, it just appears to happen. No description of her transportation, who took her life and how it was taken, her suffering, death and her family's loss of her presence. All are obscured by the bland phrase *turned into*. These things are not important to the article and the text's silence about them signifies this.

In the next sentence we are told *she died* although there is no agent involved or details given. She certainly did not die of natural causes but was killed intentionally by somebody, somewhere so that people could consume her body, but this remains unsaid and unimportant in the discourse. The text also claims that she *died for a good cause* implying she gave her life willingly as part of this project and that her death was some type of purposeful sacrifice. The good causes we discover *are bringing diverse groups together* and *providing a lesson in thoughtful consumption*. How nice. Human pastimes take precedence over her life but she is serving her purpose by contributing to the comradery and instruction of humans.

The next sentence is set out to read in the form of a recipe where the constituents are: her body, a spring day and twenty recipes. Now she is only an ingredient just as animals' bodies all over the world are understood as simply ingredients. The dish produced is a *plateful of delicious reasons to think differently about food.* This continues the discourse in which animals dutifully serve humans by giving their bodies and their lives to satisfy human endeavours – this time it is a lesson in thinking differently about food.

The "thinking differently about food" idea is quite similar to the discourse of *Respect* where it is claimed that the killers of an animal treat the animal with respect by doing such things as using every part of the body or giving it to others so that they can eat it or saying a respectful thank you to the animal or whatever. Indeed, later in the article we read, "The idea was to use as much of the carcass as possible – the nose to tail eating philosophy." Well, that sounds very laudable, unless it was you or a member of your family who was killed.

This article is an example of a social practice being legitimised by the ideology embedded in the discourses. There is also the unspoken ideological common sense which understands that humans have a right to do this to animals and an important part of the legitimising process is the idea of purposes for animal lives.

Considering what we have been looking at regarding purpose and remembering Aristotle's claim that some people are born to be slaves, a question which is often asked is, can animals who are used by us rightfully be described as slaves? It's an important question, let's consider it next.

## CHAPTER 7

# Bound together?

*I know why the caged bird sings, ah me,*
*When his wing is bruised and his bosom sore,—*
*When he beats his bars and he would be free;*
*It is not a carol of joy or glee,*
*But a prayer that he sends from his heart's deep core,*
*But a plea, that upward to Heaven he flings—*
*I know why the caged bird sings!*

Paul Laurence Dunbar[1]

## Slavery in our land?

MARJORIE SPIEGEL, IN her book *The Dreaded Comparison,* writes convincingly of the similarities between the way we make use of animals and what happens in slavery.[2] However, whether we can classify animals used by humans as slaves still remains a sensitive and controversial issue. We can try to answer this question by examining the social practice of slavery and the ideology relating to the practice and comparing these with our use of animals. I will focus mainly on farming for these comparisons but it is not difficult to extend much of what is said to other animal uses as well. This will necessarily be a relatively limited enquiry but I hope it will offer some valuable insights.

## Slavery as a social practice

Slavery has been around for a very long time and been practised in many places and in different ways. Sometimes it was the result of people being captured in war or having a debt to pay or even as a business run by the slavers. Some slavery has been incredibly harsh yet in other instances relatively benign with slaves eventually managing to gain their freedom. However, probably the greatest focus has been on the colonial slave trade.

The historian P. E. Lovejoy writing in *Slavery in the Context of Ideology* gives us the essence of slavery:

> First, slaves were property. As individuals they were owned, and while they were also recognized as human beings, their fundamental characteristic was that they were commodities. Slaves were outsiders by origin, who lacked kinship ties and who had been

denied their heritage through judicial or other sanctions. The relationship between slave and master was ultimately based on coercion, realized initially through the original, often violent, act of enslavement and maintained thereafter through the threat and occasional institution of physical force. Slaves were completely at the disposal of their masters: The labor power of slaves could be used however desired; even their sexuality and, by extension their reproductive capacities were not theirs by right.[3]

The paragraph describes not only the horror and hopelessness of human slavery but harshly illuminates the parallels between this practice and the practice of our use of animals. The word *slave* could easily be substituted with *animal* and the paragraph would still be just as accurate. Total ownership, freedom denied by judicial sanction, violent coercion, the continual threat of violence, being at the total behest of the master, forced physical labour and the ownership of the capacity for sexual reproduction – every single one of these is also true for animals who are used by humans.

The defining characteristic of slavery is first and foremost the ownership of one being by another. Slaves are possessions. The total ownership of animals by humans is a common sense assumption made clear in such farming phrases as *my sheep, my cattle, my goats, my calves, my milk* and even *my semen.* The bodies and the various powers of the animal's bodies and the "products" of those bodies from eggs to faeces are all owned by someone other than themselves. We also speak of racehorse owners, owners of donkeys, dog owners, cat owners and so on and free-living animals are not excluded from this but are also owned by the state or a "land owner".

A telling phrase in the above excerpt is, "who had been denied their heritage through judicial or other sanctions." This seems to echo Bentham and without any doubt the animals we use have all had their heritage stolen as well as their freedom denied and their ancestral lands taken away, but the law does not allow any challenge to this state of affairs because it declares them property and property has no rights. Justice stands impotent due to the legal objectification of these sentient individuals and their families.

Another example emphasises similar points, this time it concerns the Mangbetu people of north eastern Zaire and Hutereau writes:

> Slaves...are the absolute property of the master. He beats them, sells them, trades them, mutilates them, executes them...Slaves have no right to legal protection.[4]

And ownership does not only extend to the individual who has been enslaved but to their unborn children as well. Meillassoux observes this of women slaves:

> As a rule their children belonged to her master even when he was not the genitor. The male slave with whom she had these children was not the "father" and had, as a result, little or no interest in them.[5]

Then de Sardan, again focusing on women, writes of the Songhat-Zarma people of Mali and Niger and draws a telling farming comparison:

> The child of two slaves belonged to the master of the woman, just as the increase of a herd belonged to the owner of the cow.[6]

And similarly, from Allan, writing of slavery in north eastern Nigeria:

> ... any child born to a slave woman was a slave from birth, and could be sold or given away by its master as soon as it was old enough to leave its mother. Thus a female slave was regarded as a profitable investment, in the same way as a cow or a ewe is regarded at the present time.[7]

Families were not seen as important by those who wielded the power:

> A marital union between two slaves does not prevent the master from removing one of the two partners to conclude an exchange or endow a relative or client with a wife. [8]

Walvin writes about colonial slavery and the way in which slaves could be simply sold off and families shattered:

> It was at this point, when the young slaves had begun to work and had an economic value and potential of their own, that many of them were removed from their family home and placed in what their master thought was more appropriate labour.[9]

Here we are faced with the dreadful existential sentence handed down by chattel slavery. It not only imposed slavery upon an individual for a lifetime but was a sentence reaching deep into the future. Not only would the victim suffer and be denied her freedom but this would be the case for all of her children and her children's children in perpetuity. The parallel with the "domestication" of animals could not be more unambiguously drawn.

In some places, female slaves had few children, and often those who were born would have stood little chance of survival to adulthood, but in North America around 1750 and beyond, with a levelling out of the gender ratio and stable slave families emerging, a further exploitation of slave women emerged – as producers of new slaves:

> Thus slave reproduction became another form of exploitation for slave women, for they were not only expected to work and contribute to the well-being of family and community, but their owners came to expect them to produce future children to add to their stock of slaves.[10]

And coercion, often very violent, was an ever-present threat. In the following extract, William Beckford writing in 1790 draws striking comparisons regarding the coercion of both slaves and animals, observing that the whip was an

> ...instrument of correction in Jamaica, whether it be in the hands of the cart-man, the mule-boy or the negro-driver, [and] is heard in either case, to resound among the hills and upon the plains...[11]

In antebellum United States "troublesome" slaves were sent to "nigger breakers" to be "tamed" and made compliant.[12] Compliance in a slave was a much-prized commodity as it is in animals today from cattle to race horses to the elephants who are "broken" until they become compliant to our wishes.

Slaves were sold off at auction with the more impressive or useful commanding the best prices. They were inspected before purchase by slave owners and even medical personnel. During the slave trade a ship's surgeon would be on board ship and his work began:

> ...on the African coast when, alongside experienced traders, they carefully examined the new slaves (intimately and often publicly) before deciding if the slave would make a commercial investment.[13]

Slaves were transported in slave ships packed to carry as many people as possible with the slaves enduring severe hardship and health problems from the long and unpredictable sea journeys. Those who survived might be in very poor physical condition, weak and emaciated, but they were often fattened up in a slave yard before being offered for sale.[14] The export of living animals is common today and they are packed into ships and endure searing heat and stifling atmospheres, rank with airborne faecal matter and ammonia. Fattening up or "finishing" animals is a routine practice in farming and is carried out at special facilitates before slaughter or sale in order to obtain the best price.

These paragraphs briefly describe a practice which is so abhorrent, so heart-breaking, it is harrowing to even contemplate. Human slavery, quite rightly provokes nothing but utter revulsion, yet I think it is clear that the actual *practice* itself is so very similar to what happens to the animals whom we use, to describe this as something other than slavery would be unreasonable.

But what of the ideology which supported slavery for it surely could not have continued for so long without some justification, however flawed, however self serving the justification might have been?

## Slavery discourses and ideology

We get a glimpse of the ideology in use at the time from Walvin writing in *Black Ivory*:

> ...Europeans saw little reason to imagine that the slaves had left behind anything worthwhile in Africa. Though the more observant of the slave-traders (especially those who subsequently repented of their ways) acknowledged the grief displayed by the slaves, few thought that they had come from societies where family ties, with their resulting emotions and affections, played any significant role.[15]

It was convenient to draw on an ideology where relationships, love for family, love of home and love for the land did not matter to the slaves. It was expedient to believe that they did not have significant emotional lives and that they were losing nothing by being enslaved.

We believe similar things about the animals we use. For example, we tell ourselves that animals rapidly "get over" their grieving after we take away their babies although we have no way of knowing how long the pain really lasts; perhaps a lifetime but believing otherwise is expedient for us.

In a book published in 1860 with the mammoth title *Cotton is king, and pro-slavery arguments: comprising the writings of Hammond, Harper, Christy, Stringfellow, Hodge, Bledsoe, and Cartwright, on this important subject*, there are arguments, as the title plainly suggests, favouring slavery or at least opposing its immediate cessation. Moves to abolish slavery in nations throughout the world, as well as the American states, had been well under way for over a hundred years and so this book comes near to the end of colonial slavery. But that had not yet arrived and ominously the book's publication date is just one year prior to the outbreak of the American Civil War. It is a valuable source to help us get a feel for the explanations advanced to continue with slavery when the rest of the world had changed or was changing. It helps us to understand the ideologies being drawn upon.

The introduction to the book claims that the description of the practice of slavery which was being projected by its opponents was an error, claiming that it depicted what was done to slaves years ago and in other places but not what was actually practised in the Southern States. It suggests that perhaps this practice should not even be called slavery at all. Here is a longish extract but it helps to give a feel for the arguments:

> Such is not our labor system. Though we prefer the term slave, yet if this be its true definition, we must protest against its being applied to our system of African servitude, and insist that some other term shall be used. The true definition of the term, as applicable to the domestic institution in the Southern States, is as follows: Slavery is the duty and obligation of the slave to labor for the mutual benefit of both master and slave, under a warrant to the slave of protection, and a comfortable subsistence, under all circumstances. The person of the slave is not property, no matter what the fictions of the law may say; but the right to his labor is property, and may be transferred like any other property, or as the right to the services of a minor or an apprentice may be transferred. Nor is the labor of the slave "solely for the benefit of the master, but for the benefit of all concerned; for himself, to repay the advances made for his support in childhood, for present subsistence, and for guardianship and protection, and to accumulate a fund for sickness, disability, and old age.[16]

First we see the importance of naming the world, which is essential to constructing a preferred view of reality. This is why the argument about what to call this practice and these people taken from Africa is so important and not a minor, technical, linguistic, difference of opinion. They are not slaves in the normally understood meaning of the world it is claimed but just part of a "domestic institution". The description hides the true nature of the practice and provides an ideological prop with which to support it.

The claim that slaves are not property (which they clearly are under law) but only the right to their labour is property, again shows the importance of naming and in addition is an argument designed to obscure and confuse and in reality, it changes nothing. But this explanation does help religious supporters of slavery because to describe a fellow human being as property would be a significant problem if that person happens also to be a Christian sister or brother, which might then lead to their enslavement becoming unacceptable.

The explanation about how this *domestic institution* works is particularly revealing because it is almost exactly the same as our old friend the imaginary domestication contract between humans and animals. The slave labours for herself and her master but in return she will receive protection and sustenance. Her contributions, of whatever kind, are a form of payment in return for the master's care for her. It is portrayed as if this is actually an existing arrangement, a done deal of some kind and one which has been entered into willingly by both parties and is to their mutual benefit. This and the animal domestication contract are both lies but their ideologies supply suitable justifications for carrying out exploitation without the guilt.

Later on in this book it is argued that the north of the country was the home of slavery and that the Southern States slipped into it because this was the place which was much more geographically suited to the use of slaves and that over time slavery became part of the fabric of the society, a part which for the most part remained unexamined.

> They had never made the inquiry whether the system were fundamentally wrong, but they judged it by its fruits, which were beneficent to all. When therefore they were charged with upholding a moral, social, and political evil; and its immediate abolition was demanded, as a matter not only of policy, but also of justice and right, their reply was, we have never investigated the subject. Our fathers left it to us as a legacy, we have grown up with it; it has grown with our growth, and strengthened with our strength, until it is now incorporated with every fibre of our social and political existence.[17]

The passage is fascinating because while clearly trying to evade responsibility for this odious practice there is also a germ of truth here because it elucidates so accurately the insidious and covert operation of ideological common sense. The claim to have grown up in a world where doing this was normal, accepted and expected is almost certainly true. It would be part of the everyday world, the way things have always been done, acceptable to many, perhaps most, and those who thought differently would become outcasts. Being born into a world where violence and abuse is normalised and completely acceptable is something we share with those old slave-using communities. We grow up understanding that what we do to animals is normal and acceptable, even to be celebrated; that we have always done it and that we should do it.

Unsurprisingly we also find at some point that racism emerges and we read that "the negro is now an inferior species, or at least variety of the human race, is well established, and must, we think, be admitted by all." It claims that "the negro" needs the influence of the white man to "emerge from barbarism."[18] This is the old idea of a hierarchy of beings, in this case it is racism, with nonhuman animals we use speciesism.

In this very brief survey the similarities between the practice of slavery and the practice of humans using animals are compelling as are the similarities in the ideologies employed in both cases. We cannot claim that human slavery, with its diverse forms, and animal exploitation with its own multiple practices, are exactly the same. However, given the striking similarities of both in the physical practice used and the ideology employed, I believe that it is reasonable to conclude that the use of animals by humans can rightfully be described as a form of slavery.

## Objections

One objection to this conclusion might be that slaves are human and only humans can therefore be counted as slaves. But there seems no valid reason why the practice of slavery should have separate terms depending upon the species of the victims and I would argue that this is a form of anthropocentric argument.

Another objection might be that slavery can only apply to persons and that animals are not persons. It is true that only humans are legally described as persons at present but we should remember that slaves were not counted as persons either in ancient Greece or during the slave trade, which is why they were not able to be represented in court. Midgely points out that the Latin word *persona* was never applied to slaves because a *person* was an actor in the drama of life which slaves were not.[19] In Ancient Greece they were nonpersons and Aristotle makes this clear by saying, "so also an article of property is a tool for the purpose of life, and property generally is a collection of tools, and a slave is a live article of property."[20]

In 1879, Chief Standing Bear of the Ponca tribe was the first Native American to be recognised by an American court of law as a person. Nash records this chief's pertinent observation about keeping animals:

> Ownership of nature appeared in their eyes morally wrong, a form of slavery. Standing Bear made the connection explicit with regard to domesticating and keeping animals. It was better to hunt wild creatures, he wrote, because herding "enslaved the animal" and deprived it of its basic rights: the right to live, the right to multiply, the right to freedom.[21]

And now it's time to put on our wellies to go down on the farm and wade through some texts about farmed animals, along with our ideologies about them – and the animals are definitely not responsible for this manure.

## CHAPTER 8

# Bucolic facades

*Yoineh Meir thought that the Messiah Himself could not redeem the world as long as injustice was done to beasts. By rights, everything should rise from the dead: every calf, fish, gnat, butterfly. Even in the worm that crawls in the earth there glows a divine spark. When you slaughter a creature you slaughter God...*

Isaac Bashevis Singer[1]

## Down on the farm

RECENTLY SKY NEWS UK did a story about vegan protests at slaughterhouses in the UK. It was fairly balanced and had footage of trucks arriving and activists demonstrating but there was also this classic pronouncement from The British Meat Processors Association:

> Our members do have concerns that it is only a matter of time before someone is hurt as a result of this behaviour and we continue to work closely with local police forces in order to ensure everyone's safety.[2]

The behaviour they are refer to is protesting against animal slaughter but the ringing irony of the statement apparently went unnoticed. The whole point of the demonstrations was that violence was already taking place and that the demonstrators wanted it stopped. Apparently, the Meat Processors Association does not think anyone is getting hurt by what they do. Welcome to the flesh industry.

Much of what we will look at in this chapter relates to larger farmed animals, but of course there is much more than this. The chicken and egg industry for example is a whole bizarre world on its own and a shocking account of it can be found in Karen Davis's book *Prisoned chickens, poisoned eggs.*

What we describe as farming has been going on for thousands of years, but the word *farm* in English only dates from the 18th century, originally meaning to hire something out, but over time it came to mean a place where something is produced.[3] Whatever the name, keeping animals in restricted areas, be they large or small, takes place in almost every country of the world. Sometimes the animals are relatively free while in other systems they are more restricted and in yet other schemes the animals are highly confined, usually indoors, they do not stand on natural ground or experience direct sunlight and all food is brought in for them. Because of the similarity of this to an industrial production plant these sites are often called factory farms, although the official name is now Confined (or concentrated) Animal Feeding Operation or CAFO. Unfortunately, the nice name does not make the lives of its victims any better.

In their lifetimes, animals may have many "owners" and are bought and sold as economics dictate, living their lives on a conveyer belt which ends on the kill floor. Even when they are raised on open farms many will be sold to feed lots or finishers. Often these places are barren areas with no shelter from sun, rain, snow or wind and the animals are packed into them. The South African Feedlot Association tells us this is big business:

> Today the SA Feedlot industry is a flourishing industry that produces approximately
> 75% of all beef produced in South Africa which in real terms is in the region of
> 1,35 million head per annum with a one time standing total of +420 000 head.[4]

So, 1.35 million cattle go through feedlots each year, and on any given day in South Africa there are over 420 000 animals held in them.

But farms are just one part of a highly structured, institutionalised system of violence. The industry is complex with many players including farming operations, the purveyors of animal flesh in its many forms as well as "animal products" such as milk, eggs, cheese and yoghurt, the industrial complex which processes animal body parts, suppliers who offer such things as feed, scientific services, specialised vehicles, specialised equipment, transport services, refrigeration, public health assistance, veterinary health care, suppliers of semen, baby chicks, embryos and the list goes on and on. Governments support the system financially with subsidies and with expertise; parastatals promote it, colleges and universities teach how to do it, picture books tell children about the happy life of animals on farms and parents buy toy farms with animals and farmers for their children to play with. Hardly ever is this whole matrix represented as the highly structured system of violence and abuse for profit which in reality is what it is. The inescapable fact is that nonhuman animal farming, of whatever type, exploits the bodies of unwilling individuals in order to make money from them.

So, what are the ideologies supporting the exploitive social practice of animal farming? We mentioned earlier that discourses are sections of language which construct aspects of the world in a particular way and this is where we can look for clues to the ideology in use. The depictions of farming itself and how animals used in farming are portrayed can offer us vital insights.

## Production machines and raw materials

Farming, understood as a production process is a core discourse in farming literature.[5] A production discourse is characterised by words such as *input, output, profit, loss, productivity, re-stocking, sales, capital expenditure* and so on. We can think of it as similar to a car plant or chemical manufacturing operation where there are raw materials going in, machines to manufacture the product and product being produced. Animals might be constructed as inputs, production machines, outputs and quite often, more than one of these in the same system.

Here, from a farming magazine, is an unambiguous portrayal of cattle as both machines and product:

> [The farmer] is a great believer in the fact that cattle farmers are not simply raising beef, but are rather selling grass that has been converted into beef by their cattle.[6]

Grass goes into the machine and flesh is produced. The animal is both a grass converting machine and the product itself – flesh. *Raising beef* is a strange phrase because beef is the flesh of a dead animal and so the phrase literally describes bringing up or *raising*, dead flesh. In the USA it is common to use the term *beeves* as a description for cattle and even beeve as its singular.

It is not only farmers and farming journalists who might use this ideological construction of cattle. Neil deGrasse Tyson the celebrity astrophysicist and science educator, once infamously tweeted, "A cow is a biological machine invented by humans to turn grass into steak."[7]

Although there are frequent constructions of animals as production machines and farming as a production system these are easily missed because the language is so familiar. Phrases such as the *sheep enterprise, efficient feed converter* [about an animal], *game meat production, commercial flock, replacement ewes, milk production* and so on don't necessarily surprise us but once we consider them, it is clear they convey the ideology of animals being parts of production systems.

Here is a text about "Beefmaster" cattle, describing how they can be used for farming in the harsh conditions experienced in the Botswana bushveld:

> Cattle bred for the Botswanan veld have to be hardy, structurally efficient and fertile. They also have to produce good carcasses and meat of a high quality. [8]

In the first sentence there is a claim that the animals must be *hardy, structurally efficient and fertile*. The second term, *structurally efficient,* portrays a machine and the third term, *fertile,* alludes to another production activity – baby production. These babies will become part of the exploited group or be sold off or killed at an early age.

Regarding the meaning of *hardiness*, the Beefmaster website says this about what is supposed to be one of the prized attributes of Beefmasters:

> Hardiness is [a] genetic trait that can be measured by continued production and longevity. Hardy cattle has [sic] the ability to stay healthy and produce under veld conditions and in different climates with very little assistance. Individual animals that have the ability to carry on their relentless production assignment year after year with minimum assistance.
>
> A bull must remain attentive and fertile and be able to cover cows for several years. Cows must produce an acceptable calf each year.[9]

This is all about production. The hardiness trait, we learn, is measured by *continued production* and the cattle are able to "*produce* under veld conditions and in different climates", they have the "ability to carry on their *relentless production assignment* year after year" and cows must "*produce* an acceptable calf each year." What is meant by an acceptable calf is not made clear. The South African Livestock and Stud Book Association has this to say about Beefmasters, "[T]he Beefmaster is a meat machine. The more effective the better. Any other goals are merely for show."[10]

In the second sentence there is a claim that the responsibility allotted to these animals is "producing good carcasses and meat of a high quality." This is striking for two reasons, first, as in earlier examples, the animals are charged with the duty of growing their own bodies for consumption by humans and second is the idea that dead flesh has some form of measurable quality; that some dead flesh is better than other dead flesh. Human flesh apparently falls outside of this assessment – at least for most members of the population. This theoretical *quality* is instrumental in nature because it depends entirely upon what you wish to do with the flesh you have acquired from this fellow being and in some ways this is not dissimilar to the assessment of living human flesh in pornographic and sexist discourse.

It is also worth noting the choice of words (lexicalisation) in referring to the animal's dead bodies. We are unlikely to describe an eviscerated human corpse as a *carcass* but even if we did, we would never describe it as being *good*. A *good carcass* in this case refers to an estimate of the amount of money a human can receive by selling it to others for eventual consumption. In addition, we can also note that the animals are not described as being killed and dismembered but euphemistically simply *produce* carcasses, being themselves portrayed as the agents of that production.

The requirements referred to as well as the supposed qualities of the flesh are functions of dominant power. The implicit violence in the whole process is never mentioned and the text is silent about it because it is both taken for granted and understood as irrelevant.

Later in the same article the writer describes how the farmer (John) stops mating "his" cows when they reach the age of eleven. These are the cows who have been "producing" babies for years:

> At this age the mothers are allowed to wean their calves and regain body condition before they're slaughtered – so that John still gets a good price for them.[11]

For the mother, this birth will not be a time to retire and spend the years to come with her new offspring – all of her nine or ten other children having already been taken away from her. Not even with her final child can she have this special time together but she will be killed and butchered for the farmer's profit. The machine is worn out and it's time to trade it in for scrap. A cynical calculation is made; a tipping point of economic gain or loss is what determines if she lives or dies. Do I get more money by letting her live and exploiting her body one more time or is she worth more to me now dead? Family was never going to be an option for this mother or ever will be for the many billions like her.

## Quality control – science tests the products

Animals themselves are often treated as products and there are many so called products derived directly from them such as eggs, flesh, wool, milk and semen along with thousands of secondary products used in everything from sweets (gelatine) to soap (animal fat). In everyday industrial production, science plays a vital role in making the system more efficient, in fixing problems and in the quality control of the products – and animal farming is no different.

Here is a text about a company which sells pig semen for artificial insemination. The semen is "tapped" from boars, scientifically evaluated, stored, sold and then distributed:

> Every batch of semen in the Pig Gen lab is meticulously screened for mass motility, progressive movement of spermatozoa, percentage of live sperm and sperm concentration, as well as pH if this is necessary. Hence there should be no reason why better results cannot be achieved with AI relative to natural service. There is a high uniformity and consistency of performance and carcass quality in pigs from different units using the same source of seedstock.[12]

The scientific discourse is shown by terms such as *screened, mass motility, spermatozoa, percentage, pH, concentration* and so on. The product is checked scientifically using a range of criteria just as any industrial product would be, in order to make sure it comes up to the required specifications. The scientific discourse is a crucial part of the underlying claims regarding quality and trustworthiness. "Scientifically tested" is a well-worn cliché but it seems it does not get old – and numbers always look impressive. The lexical choices, *batches* of semen and *seedstock* suggest a production process.

The promise of *better results* than *natural service* (normal reproduction), is claiming a superior outcome compared to the opposition just as washing powder advertisements often do. Further selling points are *high uniformity, consistency of performance* and *carcass quality.*

But standing back for a moment from all of the scientific and industry jargon we can ask, what is really going on here? This is all about being able to efficiently make female pigs pregnant so that they produce standardised babies who at a predetermined stage of their lives will be killed and whose bodies will be eviscerated to provide carcasses which can be sold to make a good profit. Science will be ever present in this process to act as the match maker, quality control monitor, development expert and eventually the efficient undertaker.

The male pigs are production machines producing semen which is to be used on female pigs; the female pigs are production machines producing babies and their babies are the final product, which is sold. Eventually of course the male machines and female machines will also be sold and killed. While selling semen might seem to promote life, the real focus is always on death and the profits it will bring.

And just to show how scientific this can get, here is something from a paper given at the Forty-Ninth Annual North Carolina Pork Conference, which carried the chirpy logo, "We bring a lot to the table":

> It appears that the most frequent cause of suboptimal performance for farms using semen from boar studs was use of aged semen and poor water quality. In contrast, poor storage conditions were most prevalent for on-farm laboratories. Finally, problems associated with poor semen extender quality and dilution rates were common on both types of semen production facilities.[13]

So now we know.

## Producing producers

This next extract is also about producing animals but this time it concerns animals who are going to be used specifically for the purpose of reproduction. It comes from an article describing changes being made on a sheep farm by the farmer, Michael:

> Since they started the Swarco Dohne Stud, Michael has been determined to ensure the rams they supply are not only of superior genetic merit, but fertile, fit and ready to mate. To qualify to be offered on auction, rams have to pass a number of tests, which include a second fibre diameter test, a genital soundness test, and a libido and mating dexterity test carried out by a vet.
>
> "Rams that fail these tests are not put up for sale. That's part of the client service guarantee that we offer," says Michael.[14]

Lots to consider here but I just want to highlight a few things. The rams, we are told, must have *superior genetic merit* although what qualifies as merit depends upon who is setting the criteria and what is important and valuable to them. The *superior* in this case in no way concerns the wellbeing of the individual animal but only refers to the utility value of the animal's body to humans. Then, we have talk of rams passing tests. They have to pass a number of tests concerned with wool thickness and ability to mate successfully – including an intriguingly named *genital soundness and mating dexterity test* to be carried out by a recognised scientific expert – a vet.

Passing or failing makes it seem as if the animals themselves are striving for excellence and suggests some agency on their part. In reality their bodies are being accepted or rejected by humans and even though the animals have no agency whatsoever there are consequences to success or failure. Passing means they will be sold on to somebody else while failure is probably fatal.

In another text, describing a similar production operation, the violence is much more obvious:

> "We follow a strict selection regime with the rams," he says. "Just prior to shearing, at 12 months, rams are classed visually and almost half are culled. After final inspection, only the best are retained as breeding material to be offered on the various sales..."[15]

Not looking acceptable to human eyes and against human criteria even at the age of one year means the death sentence. Interestingly in this extract, the "best" animals transform into an amorphous commodity referred to by using the mass noun phrase, *breeding material* which will be offered for sale in the future.

## Breeds as brands

We touched on breeds in chapter six but we can take things a bit further here because one of the notable things about animal farming is the huge amount of interest shown in breeds. The industry just loves breeds. Farmers proudly display their allegiance to their breed on signs at the entrances to their farms and there are societies dedicated to breeds of all kinds. Cattle breeds include Beefmasters, Herford, Brangus, Gelbvieh, Romagnola, Beefalo, Bonsmara, Beef Shorthorn and Amerifax; sheep breeds are Merino, Dorper,

Barbados Blackbelly, Polypay, Montadale, Blackhead Persian, Swaledale and Bergamasca; with goats there are Boer goat, Toggenburg goat, British Alpine goat, Kalahari red, Sable Saanen and the Danish Landrace goat and for chickens there are Dorking, Dominique, Campine, Buckeye, Croad, Langshan and Rhode Island White. All of these animals are used in farming for specific purposes.

Breeds are like brands where enthusiasts and traders extol the virtues of their chosen merchandise, its uses and specifications. Some breeds are quite old, others new but they are all the result of genetic manipulation in some form. Today with large amounts of genetic data at hand for all sorts of parameters and new biological techniques, old breeds can be continually "improved" and new breeds can be "synthesised" to fill particular niches.

Earlier we looked at Beefmasters, and The Beefmaster Cattle Breeders' Society of South Africa explains that The Beefmaster is "...a synthetic breed that is genetically composed of ±50% Brahman, 25% Hereford and 25% Shorthorn blood."[16] The *meat machine* has been manufactured deliberately, a living machine constructed to fulfil a purpose.

## Breeding violence

Breeding is not a benign activity but systematised violence. On the Beefmaster Cattle Breeders Society of South Africa website there is a page titled "About the Beefmaster breed" which describes the animals and gives breeding advice. Here are some extracts from it with the subject area written in bold and then text concerning the breeding process following. It is a litany of relentless cruelty.

> **Developing the breed.** This was achieved after years of selective breeding, careful experiments and vicious culling of unwanted animals.
> **Fertility.** [The cow] should wean a good calf every year under natural veld conditions, if not, she should be culled.
> **Temperament.** Differences in temperament are already observed before weaning and calves with poor temperament are culled at weaning. After weaning temperament is constantly monitored and animals that show unacceptable behaviour are culled.
> **Conformation.** Bulls and cows that show any signs of structural defects such as problems with feet and legs are culled.
> **Weaning.** After the initial selection for weight gain females are not culled on their own weight, but for weaning a light-weight calf.
> **Milk production.** Weak calves as well as their mothers should be culled.[17]

The farmed animals we see in fields today are the lone survivors of a longstanding and systematic regime of mass murder. Behind each one stands many thousands of dead who were judged deficient and unworthy of life. They are living texts telling a story, both antique and contemporary, of our unrelenting savagery against our captives.

## Breed stories

But just to get an idea of how technical this can get and how the animals as sentient beings disappear in the scientific discourse, have a look at this piece from the American

Sheep Industry website describing some recent research about "ewe productivity":

> In cooperation with Virginia Tech and the U.S. Meat Animal Research Center, ewe
> lambs of the three-breed types were enrolled in a four-year project where the cumulative
> production of the ewes was measured in a rangeland, commercial-scale production
> system. The productivity of 212 Rambouillet, 236 Polypay and 231 Romanov-White
> Dorper × Rambouillet-crossbred ewes born in 2009, 2010 and 2011 was evaluated
> through four lambings. Beginning as lambs, study ewes were managed in a range-
> type production system, annually mated to terminal-sire type rams and evaluated for
> multiple measures of ewe productivity.[18]

The paragraph is dense with production and scientific lexicalisation including, *Virginia Tech, U.S. Meat Animal Research Center, breed types, cumulative production, measured, commercial-scale, production system, productivity, crossbred ewes, evaluated, study ewes, range-type production system, terminal-sire type rams, evaluated, multiple measures* and *ewe productivity*. The Research Center we are told specialises in what are called *meat animals* and there is no doubt about the supposed purpose of their existence.

We are also informed that the ewes were *enrolled* in a four year project making it seem as if they had some choice when in reality they were simply coerced into being used in an experiment. The animals are referred to only by breed names; *Rambouillet, Polypay and Romanov-White* and *Dorper x Rambouillet terminal-sire type rams* robbing them of any sentience or individuality.

Taking us deeper into this carnal world here is another extract, this time from "The Cattle Site" describing a scientific investigation into the flesh of Belgium Blue animals.

> In an extensive 3-year test, done by the USDA at the Meat Animal Research Center,
> Clay Center, Nebraska, the Belgian Blue crossbred cattle were tested with the industry
> standard Warner-Brazner shear test for tenderness. The Belgian Blue cattle had a
> lower shear value than the Hereford-Angus contemporary average, 12.8 versus 12.9,
> with comparable tenderness and flavor on the sensory panel. Belgian Blue cattle
> also exhibited less than half the fat cover, .21 inch cover versus .45 inch cover, a 53%
> reduction. Belgian Blue is on line for the new standards. The Belgian Blue also showed
> 16% less marbling and 14.2 more ribeye area than the average carcass.[19]

This describes the animals as if they are still alive when actually they are all dead. The *shear value* is a measure of how easy it is to chew their flesh and a special machine is used to find out how much force, known as the Warner-Bratzler shear force, is required to tear a sample of flesh apart. Yes, a dedicated, calibrated, scientific, flesh ripping machine and you can buy one for around 4 000 US dollars.

The sensory panel is made up of humans who assesses the flesh for such things as appearance, smell, taste, juiciness and texture. Marbling refers to fat in the muscles (intramuscular fat) and ribeye is flesh cut from the outer part of the ribs.

The results we are told lead to the conclusion that the "...Belgian Blue is on line for the new standards" in other words this living production machine will provide product (flesh), which will conform to the required specifications.

And finally, we visit a very big physical text, one written in steel and concrete, employees, fields, research labs and money; welcome to the US Meat Research Center.

## Carnal desires at the house of flesh

The center is situated in a place called Clay Center, Nabraska in the United States, a small town of around eight hundred people. It is on fifty-five square miles of land and was founded some 50 years ago to assist US animal farmers. Michael Moss writing in the New York Times explains what happens there:

> At a remote research center on the Nebraska plains, scientists are using surgery and breeding techniques to re-engineer the farm animal to fit the needs of the 21st-century meat industry.[20]

Just a few of the many current research projects which the centre lists on its website[21] are:

- Strategies to Optimize Meat Quality and Composition of Red Meat Animals;
- Improving Lifetime Productivity in Swine;
- Applying Developmental Programming to Improve Production Efficiency in Beef Cattle; Identifying Genomic Solutions to Improve Efficiency of Swine Production;
- Genetic Research to Enhance Efficient and Sustainable Production of Beef Cattle and Sheep;
- Characterizing the Relationship Between Early Postmortem Loin Quality Attributes with 14-Day Aged Loin Quality Attributes & Sensory Characteristics.

But all is far from well out here in the countryside. The New York Times article documents ongoing problems at this establishment over many years and in order to gather this information the newspaper carried out interviews with over twenty current and former employees and used the Freedom of Information Act to obtain thousands of pages of records.[22] What it discovered was a litany of cruelty and neglect which is hard to believe could ever have been allowed to happen. The driving force behind it all was to make better, more profitable, "meat animals".

The newspaper recounts how numerous projects were disastrous, such as breeding cattle to produce twins, making lean pigs with body fat so low they had difficulty getting pregnant, leaving lambs to die of exposure and predation in the open, operating on pig's brains to try to make them more fertile and so on. It is certainly a shocking account spanning many years and it is worth remembering that this facility is no back street slaughter yard but employs a large staff of well-qualified people. It also appears to enjoy a free pass when working on animals and it is outrageous what the staff are officially allowed to do:

> The center has about 30,000 animals, tended by about 44 scientists, 73 technicians and other support workers. The scientists, who do not have medical degrees, and their assistants euthanize and operate on livestock, sometimes doing two or more major surgical operations on the same animal.[23]

In the USA, animals used in agricultural experiments are not protected by the Animal Welfare Act and despite objections about the work and even considerable unhappiness from the meat industry itself, there have been few restraints exercised as the scientists pursued their goals, causing severe suffering to many animals in the process.

The nonhuman animals are ideologically simply objects of scientific investigation and manipulation with the goal being greater efficiency and higher profits for the animal exploitation industry. They are things to be used and then discarded.

The centre continues with its work of making "better meat animals" and in a recent report the New York Times details further problems which have been identified at MARC as well as a number of other US Department of Agriculture (USDA) facilities.[24] In 2017 the USDA suddenly removed inspection reports and other information from its website.[25]

## Conclusion

This has been the merest glance at a massive industry and examples such as those above can be found in abundance. In farming, the discourses of purpose, production, animals as machines, as raw materials, as product, as objects of scientific enquiry and manipulation interweave and combine seamlessly so that the animals as sentient beings are conceptualised out of existence. Behind all this stands an ideology which assumes the right to use animals to fulfil human desires although the exact nature of that ideological justification is seldom if ever articulated. Ideological common sense and the profit motive are apparently sufficient justifications in themselves for people's day-to-day actions.

But while the exploitive social practice of animal farming is deeply entrenched in our societies, on the odd occasion our routine obsession with flesh consumption can be disordered by events. This happened a few years ago in the UK and the results are revealing as we will see as we delve into the story of the Great Horsemeat Scandal.

# Horsemeat and bull

*...but for the sake of some little mouthful of flesh, we deprive a soul of the sun and light, and of that proportion of life and time it had been born into the world to enjoy.*

Plutarch[1]

## The drama begins

In 2013 FLESH from horses was discovered in some foods in the UK and other European countries which according to the labels were only supposed to contain the flesh of other nonhuman animals. This led to a public outcry, police action, mass testing, economic uncertainty, health fears and emergency government meetings and enquiries. In the end there were no outbreaks of infections, nobody was poisoned and in fact no humans were harmed at all but the horsemeat scandal, as it came to be known, loomed large in the media and the national psyche for many months and still does today.

The public story began in January 2013, providing the first inklings of the revelations to come:

> The problem was first picked up by Irish food inspectors who announced in mid-January 2013 that they had found *horse meat in frozen beef burgers*. Subsequently, the UK informed the Commission on 8 February 2013 that a UK company (Findus UK) had been selling beef lasagne supplied by a French company (Comigel-Tavola Luxembourg) which tests showed contained between 80-100% horse meat. (emphasis in original)[2]

From then on things really blew up with the story being explored from every conceivable angle as various government agencies, retailers, wholesalers and others were drawn into the gathering storm. Countries struggled to understand what had happened, how it had happened, the scope of the problem and any health threats which might exist. The credibility of government agencies was called into question, even governments themselves and retailers' reputations were on the line and falling like dominoes. In the UK, new revelations would appear almost daily; various authorities gave press briefings and tried to calm fears as new laboratory results were made public in a steady stream of reports.

In many ways, it was quite a strange affair, treated partly as a humorous distraction and partly as a deadly serious threat. What it offers us is an unusual opportunity to explore, however imperfectly, aspects of the relationship between people in the UK and the eating of the flesh of nonhuman animals. The events open a liminal space, uncomfortable with questions and contradictions, revealing underlying ideologies and paradoxical standpoints.

## Humans and horses – an abusive love affair
### Work

Humans have a long association with horses. Eight thousand years ago the migrating nomadic pastoralists of the Eurasian Steppes enslaved various animals including horses which they used for transport, as weapons of war and for milk, blood and flesh.[3]

Over thousands of years horses have been used for such things as ploughing, to pump water, to pull carts, barges, coaches, guns and to provide the power for machinery; and Jason Hribal argues that animals should be understood as a part of the working class.[4] In industrialising Britain it was horses and donkeys who pulled the heavy barges full of coal and other commodities and thousands of pit ponies, often actually small horses, who did the heavy and dangerous work as the coal was hacked out around them. These animals seldom saw the light of day and might be kept underground for years. This extract from *The Animal World*, dated September 1918, describes their terrible treatment:

> Placed in the hands of ignorant lads who shamefully abused the powers entrusted to them without fear of punishment, worked often in double shifts of sixteen consecutive hours...the horses are...kept below ground for years without seeing daylight, left without any form of inspection worthy of the name, their lives were a standing outcry against cruelty and injustice.[5]

Bertie Coombes, a miner in South Wales writes the following in his book *These Poor Hands* published in 1939:

> I have seen a horse blind in one eye rubbing its nose against sharp stones so it could feel the way to turn and being whipped for not coming round fast enough. Every day horses are worked for sixteen and more hours straight off. What I have seen I know to be true-and I have seen it regularly. Very often they have no water at all during those long hours in the hot places of the mine. Within the last years I have seen horses drop from exhaustion several times during a shift.[6]

They were at daily risk of serious accidents and the terrible employment conditions which prevailed due to the greed of the mine owners, often set up miner against ponies in the cruellest way:

> Often a man must choose between forcing an exhausted horse and being sent home on the dole. He must choose whether the horse shall suffer or his wife and children.[7]

Horses, along with other animals also toiled for long days and nights in the factories, on the tow paths and roads and on the streets of industrialising Britain.[8] Hribal describes some of the work done by horses in the 18th century:

Originally, fibers such as wool or cotton had to be disentangled, pulled into strands, and spun by human hands and feet. These tasks took considerable time and much effort, but, from Lewis Paul and John Wyatt's 1738 machine patent, this was no longer to be the case. Spinning frames and carding devices could now be powered via a trotting horse. So whether in Paul and Wyatt's Birmingham operations, Richard Arkwright's Nottingham mill, or in John Lee's Manchester factory, these equine laborers lived on-site, and spent their days and nights "treading the wheel." Work normally began at 7.00 a.m. during the winter and at 6.00 a.m. in the summer with the average shifts lasting 12 hours. Night shifts were not uncommon. Indeed, in the 18th century factories, horses were the ones who scribed, carded, spun, sheared, and fulled.[9]

James Watt the Scottish engineer chose the name "horse power" as a unit of measurement for the power output of the new machines which were coming into operation and it turned out to be a good sales pitch as the term is still with us today.

On the quayside of the city of Liverpool's waterfront is a monument titled *Waiting*, depicting a large "working horse" in harness standing patiently. The artwork commemorates the many horses who transported goods to and from the docks and warehouses in the busy city and it is estimated that at the height of their exploitation there were twenty thousand horses on those streets.[10]

A Hackney Cab today refers to an iconic black taxi but originally a *hackney* was a horse for general use, the term possibly originating from the early 14th century when horses were raised in the area of Hackney.[11] The name and its derivatives have various meanings:

> Extended sense of "horse for hire" (late 14c.) led naturally to "broken-down nag," and also "prostitute" (1570s) and "a drudge" (1540s), especially a literary one...[12]

A hack is now a common pejorative term for a run of the mill writer especially a journalist while hackneyed means something which is worn out or run down. Unsurprisingly the harsh conditions experienced by horses in the different forms of exploitation exacted a terrible toll on their health. For example, those on the mail coaches were run into the ground and, when no longer able to be as fast as their "owners" wanted, they were sold off for other uses:

> During the 1800s, the average working life of a horse was only about four years on a fast coach and seven on a slow. On the mail-coaches, they could only handle about three years before their bodies gave out. Even more unfortunate, there was no retirement for these employees. They would either be sold to farmers or, worse yet, livery stables. These stables would then lease out their services on a part-time or full-time basis for commercial transport, personal carriages, cab service, or public buses. So once again, these same horses would be sent out to work in the already crowded streets.[13]

Horses and other animals, as well as exploited workers, were, ideologically speaking, just tools to be used for the maximum profit and discarded when they began to falter.

## War and memorials

War is another human activity into which many animals have been forced over the centuries. It is estimated that in the First World War alone eight million horses lost their lives. On the edge of Hyde Park in London stands the Animals in War Monument and the Memorial Fund website explains its purpose as follows:

> This monument is a powerful and moving tribute to all the animals that served, suffered and died alongside the British, Commonwealth and Allied forces in the wars and conflicts of the 20th century.[14]

This memorial has undoubtedly been set up by compassionate people who care about animals but no animals have ever actually "served" in any wars anywhere; they were physically and mentally coerced into doing what we have wanted them to do. It might be comforting to think that they assisted the military actions with the achievement of their objectives but the truth is that the animals on both sides shared a common enemy.

On Remembrance Day it is the custom in the UK and other countries to wear red poppies to commemorate those people who have died in wars, but some groups hold remembrance services and distribute blue or purple poppies to remember the animals who also died.[15]

The Horse Memorial in East London is one of a number in South Africa which commemorate the many thousands of horses who died in the Anglo Boer War and it shows a British soldier kneeling before his horse to give her water. It was unveiled on 11 February 1905 and bears this moving inscription: "The greatness of a nation consists not so much in the number of its people or the extent of its territory, as in the extent and justice of its compassion."[16]

## Different animals?

The British Horse Society claims that today there are 1.3 million regular horse riders in Britain, seventy-four per cent of whom are women, and that equestrian activities are the second best attended sport after football.[17] It makes the following point about how horses are viewed in the UK in relation to other animals:

> Unlike the rest of the European Union, in the UK, the horse is not considered to be an agricultural animal because we do not consider them to be a food animal.[18]

Not an *agricultural animal* and therefore not a *food animal* is an interesting contention, a classification which means the difference between life and death.

Anyway, it seems safe to say that overall in the UK, horses are animals who are admired for their power, speed, faithfulness, bravery, loyalty and so on. There are paintings of British armies going into battle on horseback, knights in armour, sturdy horses pulling the plough; horse racing is said to be the sport of kings and of course there are films such as Blue Velvet. Horses are generally well liked and even revered by many people in the UK.

## Eating horses

For the most part the British have never eaten horses. Horsemeat has been sold in Britain but it has never really been popular and has tended to be looked down upon as food only for the poorest of the poor or for cats and dogs.[19]

Mark Roodhouse describes a major banquet which took place at London's Langham Hotel in 1868 bearing the grand title, the Banquet Hippophagique and it was organised with the explicit purpose of promoting the eating of horsemeat, the plan being to persuade people that the flesh of horses could be used to feed the poor.

Susanna Forrest points out that this and similar banquets thrown with the same intent, had some rather unusual qualities about them:

> Firstly, they are classic, high-Victorian feasts, with more courses and dishes than we 21st-century folk can contemplate without rummaging through the nearest bathroom cabinet for antacids. Secondly, they are typically full of puns. As these hippophagic meals are always for male dinner guests alone, I guess the puns are at least partly a reflection of somewhat schoolboyish amusements in gentlemen's clubs. They mock the modish obsession with French restaurants and also make it clear that they are all sophisticated enough to translate and enjoy the in-jokes. I'd guess also that the puns are meant to defray the anxiety involved in eating horseflesh. There's something of the ogre's feast to it as a result.[20]

In this particular banquet two cart horses and a carriage horse were eaten, one four-year-old, a twenty-year-old and a twenty-two-year-old. Dishes listed by Forrest include:

> Purée de destrier (puréed warhorse soup)....Filet de Pégase rôti aux pommes de terre à la crême (roast Pegasus filet with potatoes in cream)....Kromeskys à la gladiateur (minced horsemeat rolled in bacon and fried. The French racehorse Gladiateur won the English triple crown in 1865)....Langues de cheval à la troyenne (Trojan horse tongues)....Gelée de pieds de cheval au marasquin (horse hoof jelly with cherry liqueur)....Gâteaux vétérinaire à la Decroix (cake made with horse oil instead of butter; named for Decroix himself)....Baron of horse (sirloin and legs. Carried in by four men and accompanied by "Roast Beef of England". It weighed 280 lbs)...and Boiled withers.[21]

Around thirty items were on offer from the menu and naturally all were served with the appropriate booze. But while the event itself apparently went off very well, it failed miserably in its overall aim:

> Feelings of disgust, concerns about cruelty and disease, anger at the patronising attitude of the upper class reformers, patriotism and the growth of cheap meat imports ensured that "knackerine", as Northerners called it, did not become part of the working-class diet.[22]

Another reason suggested for this conspicuous lack of enthusiasm was because eating horses was seen as a disgusting foreign (European) habit. In addition:

> For some, enthusiasm for horseracing and empathy with a fellow beast of burden made

the thought of eating this aristocrat of domesticated animals distasteful. For others, the suggestion made by well-heeled dietary reformers (who would never dream of eating horse themselves) that workers eat a meat usually fed to cats and dogs was an insult. Concern was also expressed about inhumane treatment and unhygienic conditions in slaughterhouses and knackers' yards.[23]

"Empathy with a fellow beast of burden" is a telling phrase, supporting Hribal's assertion about animals being part of the working class and highlighting the intersectional nature of the oppression being practised.

Even at this time there was food fraud with horse flesh being passed off as beef. Later, during the Second World War and for a few years afterwards, there was once again an increased interest in horsemeat in some quarters with yet another round of food fraud to accompany it. The business of selling horse flesh did flourish for a little while though, peaking in 1947 when 19 000 horses were killed and although it tended, at least in theory, to be food for the poor, the trade was brisk. So brisk in fact that things started getting rather out of control:

Hunts complained that they could no longer get horsemeat to feed to their hounds. At auction, horsemeat dealers outbid farmers seeking cart horses, while rustlers targeted ponies on Dartmoor, Exmoor and in the New Forest. In 1948, the Animal Defence and Anti-Vivisection Society caused a national scandal when it exposed the extent of this black market trade.[24]

What are things coming to when you can't get horse flesh to feed to your hunting dogs?

## What's the problem?

But in modern Britain, in the days of the Horsemeat Scandal, the question was being asked, why is it that the British don't want to eat horse flesh? The BBC News magazine tried to help out by trying to find the reasons for the population's lack of enthusiasm by drawing upon the expertise of a number of specialists.

First of all, an animal psychologist says it's is all illogical anyway:

There is no real logic as to why plenty of Britons are perfectly willing to eat cows, pigs, and chickens, but see horses as taboo, according to Dr Roger Mugford, an animal psychologist who runs the Animal Behaviour Centre.

"I'm a farmer and there is an irony. Why are horses different from pigs and lambs?" he says. Part of the reason is people frequently see horses as pets, and humans tend to put "extra qualities and values" on animals they call pets...[25]

He continues:

Horses helped out in warfare. There have been huge sacrifices alongside riders in historic battles. And there are sentimental depictions like War Horse.[26]

It is not clear what extra qualities and values we might put onto pets and hopefully he doesn't eat any of his patients but what is certain is that horses never "helped out" in warfare; nor did they make "huge sacrifices" alongside their riders. They were forced to do what we wanted them to do and were horribly traumatised and killed doing it.

Then we have insights from other experts, this time in the field of Food History:

> Their widespread use as working animals has had a lasting effect, argues food historian Ivan Day. "We have to remember at one point, before railways, horses were the main means of transport. You don't eat your Aston Martin."[27]

And another food historian makes a similar claim:

> Food historian Dr Annie Gray agrees the primary reasons for not eating horses were "their usefulness as beast[sic] of burden, and their association with poor or horrid conditions of living."[28]

The claim in both of these excerpts is that the British do not eat horses because they are useful for other things. But very few people in the UK use horses as a means of transport today or to carry loads and most in fact have never used them for anything at all. And they are certainly not associated with poverty – rather the opposite. So, all this seems just a little bit unlikely.

But whatever the actual reason or reasons, logical or illogical, it is clear that the British generally just do not want to eat horses, so what reactions were there when they were surreptitiously fed equine flesh?

## Horse flesh in the news

The press is perhaps a good place to get a feel for public sentiment, so what did the newspapers say as the UK population faced the great horsemeat threat? To get some idea I looked specifically at how the horsemeat scandal was reported on the websites of two newspapers between 1 January and 31 May 2013, a period which might be called the height of the scandal. I looked at the UK *Sun* newspaper and South African Timeslive websites. The *Sun* was the highest selling newspaper in the UK by far at the time and had almost 13.5m readers for the print and website combined.[29] The Timeslive website is an award-winning South African site and serves both the daily Times and the weekly *Sunday Times* newspapers.[30] Taking two popular newspapers, one in the UK and one outside, I analysed seventy-three articles in total allowing for both a local British perspective and one from a greater distance which had insight from foreign journalists and syndicated copy from various sources.

## Constructing the story

A scandal can be described as "An action or event regarded as morally or legally wrong and causing general public outrage..."[31] and what happened over this period is repeatedly described as some type of scandal with *Horsemeat Scandal* a popular term. The word scandal appears 133 times in 49 of the articles and it was clear from the media and public reaction at the time that people felt that something terribly disreputable had taken place. They felt entitled to be outraged, they wanted answers and accountability and demanded that something be done about this heinous state of affairs. One newspaper article explains:

> The horsemeat scandal has caused outrage across the country. Brits are up in arms over
> the fact horse has been passed off as beef by some well-known food brands.[32]

And this about goatmeat being found in ready meals which were supposed to be lamb:

> The discovery follows the scandal over horsemeat found in beef burgers in January.[33]

And then, ominously, in yet another article we read:

> Horsemeat found in Nestle products as scandal grows.[34]

Linked with the discourse of scandal were those around science and food standards as large amounts of laboratory testing results made their way into the public domain revealing disturbing findings:

> The pre-prepared cottage pie lunches had been delivered to 47 schools kitchens in just
> one county. Lancashire County Council confirmed that horse DNA had been found in
> the meals – but officials refused to disclose which sites had served them.[35]

And

> Twenty-nine beef products out of 2 501 tested in Britain have been found to contain
> more than one percent horsemeat, the Food Standards Agency said on Friday.[36]

Science was a trusted measure of the extent and depth of the scandal as the public came to terms with the numbers, percentages and DNA testing.

There is also an interesting and related discourse concerning the idea of "tainted" or "contaminated" flesh. The word tainted appears 13 times in 12 sources and "contamination" or "contaminated" has 37 references in 22 sources. Even without saying it directly, the suggestion lurks in many of the articles that this exotic flesh is not quite right, there is something corrupt about it and it is sullying the food in some way. The polarisation of purity vs impurity is in play as if the contaminating flesh is in some way unclean. How exactly it is impure or affects quality is never made clear – but it sounds menacing all the same.

Understandably, the substitution of beef with horse or pig flesh was a concern to members of some faith communities and there was also a worry that the secret replacement of one flesh with another showed that all was not well deep in the big food machine.

## Flesh on the move

The story as it unfolded inevitably brought to public attention the wandering of many thousands of tons of flesh on a daily basis. All sorts of animal body parts were making their way from one country to another we learned, being repackaged, sold on, perhaps mixed with other flesh or even re labelled. Individuals who had once lived in one European country were having their remains spread all over the continent as part of a gigantic carnal diaspora. A whole transport network was revealed, a literal flesh trade, a corporeal slicing, grinding, chopping and transporting machine networked over thousands of kilometres going in and out of nation states. This gave rise to suggestions in some articles that the whole problem was one which had its genesis outside of the UK, a sort of dodgy foreigner discourse, and that "buying British" would be the safest option.

But on no occasion was this big carnal mechanism ever described as being in any way unusual or wrong but just the usual, bog standard, regular trade; good old fashioned capitalism powering a mega transportation of the wandering dead.

And in addition to all this, as might be expected, there was also a financial discourse with descriptions of drops in sales, plants closed, discussions about cheap food versus expensive food, loss of product, contracts, workers not working, compensation, legal action and even a boost in sales for some.

## Representing animals

The animals in the texts are mostly portrayed in terms of their flesh and the uses their flesh is put to. There are fifty photographs representing animals. Thirty four of these depict body parts, six live animals, six models of horse's heads, a photograph of a goat with a speech bubble saying "That really gets my goat", a giraffe model, two people in a horse costume and a Nestle company sign depicting a bird feeding babies in a nest. This latter is rather ironic from a company which makes a considerable amount of money from milk obtained by depriving calves from receiving their mother's milk. The models of horse's heads relate to restaurants or butcheries which specialise in selling the flesh of horses.

There is no link between the few photographs of living animals and the many depictions of animal body parts, no narrative of that transition. It is true there are some references to slaughterhouses and the industrial euphemism, "meat processing plant" but no mention of what happens inside these places. This part of the story, the taking of a life, remains a hallowed void, completely untouchable; a gap in reality you could fly a small planet through. But ignorance about this would only present a problem if we actually wanted to know about it – which it is very clear we do not. We are happy with the silence because then it hasn't happened, and it is certainly not going to sell any newspapers.

Compare this to when humans are killed in wars, terrorist attacks or murders. We want to establish the story leading up to violent deaths, we want to know what, why and how. Such events are meticulously documented, scrutinised and investigated and we want to find out who is responsible. Human dead bodies are treated with great reverence; flowers, processions, music, special clothes and special rituals. Photographs of post mortems are not usually published nor photographs of the bodies of murder victims nor those killed in war. Human dead bodies are either hidden from view or sometimes displayed with great reverence.

Not so for animals. For example, one of the texts carries a photograph of a horse's carcass, split down the middle and hanging headless. It carries the description, "Horsing around – meat scandal". No words about violence suffered, no individual recognised, no reverence or sadness, just the opportunity for a joke using this animal's dead body as a prop.

Incredibly, in all of the texts, there is only one direct reference to death and this is about a human death from coronary artery disease, although in another article mention is made of horses being "fatally injured" in racing. The article has nothing to do with the welfare of the horses but is focused on the disposal of their bodies and making sure their flesh "cannot enter the food chain."

## Making jokes

Quite often this whole affair is treated as a big joke, at least with respect to animals. This is especially true of the *Sun* newspaper which has a style of writing where word plays are used ad nauseum, but even the authors of more serious newspapers just could not resist a pun here and there.

*Sun* headlines include, "Binned tin beef half nag", "Nagging Doubts", "Cow about that?" and in reference to a famous "racehorse" who was kidnaped a number of years earlier and never found, "Shergar 'n' fries".

The South African *Sunday Times*, often using syndicated reports, did not display the *Sun*'s sense of humour but tended to take a more factual approach reporting news from the UK as well as France, Denmark, Czechoslovakia and Germany. However, it did carry the headlines, "Slow nags did not go to pot" from the *Daily Telegraph* and Reuters, "French pooh-pooh neigh-sayers over horse meat" from Reuters and "Burger King tells horse-meat supplier 'nay'" from Sapa-AP. Perhaps overall the propensity for puns and attempts at humour reflect a degree of discomfort with the subject and it is interesting that in the extract earlier about horse banquets, Forrest mentions the jokey, pun ridden side of the Victorian hippophagic feasts.

## Amorphous flesh

The widely used term *horsemeat* is anthropocentric in that horses do not have *meat* in a similar way that potatoes do not have chips because chips only make sense when humans cut and cook the potato in a certain way for consumption. Meat only has meaning because of human intentionality; it has nothing to do with the animal in any intrinsic way whatsoever. Meat is a creation of the human mind.

The word "horse" is sometimes used in the texts as in, "No horse was found in this food" or "I am happy to eat horse" and used like this, horse is a mass noun describing amorphous material. This is very different from saying "I eat horses" or even, "I eat the flesh of horses", both of which at least acknowledges that horses are discrete entities – individuals. *Meat, horse* and *horsemeat* are all mass nouns which objectify and remove individuality.

## Looking behind the facade

On the surface the horsemeat scandal appears to be all about crooked dealing, deception, fear of harm, financial losses and gains and the security of the food chain. Yet in so many ways this makes no sense. Of course, people were upset because they did not get what they paid for although some would argue that they may have gained a better deal as the flesh of horses often sells for more than the flesh of cattle and certainly the nutritional value is about the same or even better. There was no threat from drugs lurking in the flesh of horses used in racing and nobody became ill. Interestingly in South Africa some meat products on sale around this time were reported (rightly or wrongly) to contain donkey, kangaroo, water buffalo, giraffe, mountain zebra (a protected species) and even some human DNA but it caused little fuss, and was mostly greeted with a collective shrug of the shoulders.

So why such an outrage in the UK? It all seems so out of proportion. If people had found a few strawberries in their blackcurrant jam, it would have been no big deal. Could we imagine the *Sun* leading with "What's the current state of play?" or "Fruit criminals should be jammed up." Well, yes, quite possibly but it is doubtful that anyone would have been too bothered and there certainly would not have been ministerial meetings, police raids or banner headlines.

No, this is stranger than it seems and what is not said, what the texts are silent about, might be the most important thing of all. But something significant did break through once in these texts, only once in all of those words; when a young woman was reported as saying she feels it is wrong to kill horses. Did she say something that others felt unable to say?

Could it be that the British don't like the idea of killing horses and eating their flesh because they feel a bond with them, admire them, love them? That they perceive them as other beings? This seems quite reasonable from what we know but perhaps it is not a point of view which is able to be articulated in such a situation because it opens the door to possible ridicule as well as problematic questions about other animals such as cows, sheep, pigs and goats which people quite happily do eat. The difficulty lies in holding two conflicting perspectives. The first maintains that it is perfectly acceptable to eat animals, the second that it is wrong to eat horses. If these ideas can be kept apart, as they can most of the time when there is no horse flesh on the table, then the issue stays buried. But if not, then there is a problem.

So perhaps all the outrage is really a bit of a smoke screen and this has more to do with the abhorrence of eating a fellow traveller and friend whom we love and admire and less to do with scandal, economics, fiddling and health. Here we find a truth which cannot be spoken because it is too dangerous and all sorts of problems and difficult questions would need to be faced. Safer to stay with outrage and scandal and hope it never happens again.

Next, we go to the world of the macabre; a story of money, science, dodgy dealings, perverse philosophy and death. Welcome to the world of animal experimentation.

# Writing wrongs

*As nightfall does not come at once, neither does oppression. In both instances, there is a twilight when everything remains seemingly unchanged. And it is in such twilight that we all must be most aware of change in the air – however slight – lest we become unwitting victims of the darkness.*

William O. Douglas[1]

## Labs and language

WORLDWIDE, IT IS estimated that well over 100 million animals are experimented upon every year.[2] The true figure is unknown as is the range of experiments carried out upon them, under what conditions these experiments are done, what species of animals are used and how the animals are housed and transported.[3] Unknown numbers of unknown victims subjected to unknown experiments under unknown conditions.

Animals in laboratories are used for a great variety of things such as testing drugs, seeking basic scientific information, developing weapons including chemical and biological weapons, testing household and industrial items such as cleaning fluids, air freshener or motor oil and for work on addiction to alcohol, cigarettes and drugs. Organisations which use animals include universities, many veterinary and medical schools, research institutes, commercial testing labs, military establishments and agricultural research agencies.

When it comes to language around animal experiments, we have the language in the legislation, the language of the laboratory and its reports and the language of the animal testing business. Each of these areas offers us an opportunity to look at the discourses and the ideologies being employed.

Vivisection literally means live cutting and is something which dates back thousands of years and describes live animals being cut open to try to discover the answer to some question or other. A term which more accurately describes what is done to many animals in research today is *animal experimentation* and although live cutting is still done there is a much greater variety of *procedures*, to use the legislative term, carried out now. A common euphemistic term for the practice is *biomedical research* which Dunayer claims is good for public relations because the name suggests the twin concepts of healing (medical) and life (bio).[4] Plus of course it makes the animals used linguistically disappear altogether.

But let's begin by looking at legislation and see what it is able to tell us about a world where experimenting on animals is legal, encouraged and often compulsory.

## Language in the legislation

In many countries, carrying out experiments on animals needs some kind of permission from an authority and the UK is claimed to have some of the most stringent controls in the world so this is perhaps a good place for us to look, bearing in mind that legislation elsewhere might be quite similar or pretty much non-existent.[5]

Legislation which regulates animal experimentation in the UK is to be found in a document titled *Guidance on the Operation of the Animals (Scientific Procedures) Act 1986* and is essentially a clarification and updating of the 1986 act. It talks in great detail about licencing and who is able to carry out experiments and what the different licence holders are allowed to do to animals. Applications must be made in order for the person planning to carry out the experiments to get permission to do what they wish to do. Some of the legislation, although not a great deal, actually refers to the animals themselves.

The document defines who can legally be experimented upon and tells us that, rather bizarrely, such an individual is described as a *protected animal*. It explains that a protected animal is "any living vertebrate, other than man, and any living cephalopod".[6] This does not mean that "man" is unprotected, just the opposite. Man is not a protected animal because it is assumed that humans can never even be considered to fall within this legislation. Permitting those things which can be done to nonhuman animals under this act, to be done to any humans would be unthinkable as well as illegal. Man is neither a protected animal nor an unprotected animal but transcends these lowly categories. Apparently, we exist in some other moral universe, as the silence of the text and ideological common sense both confirm.

## Legal killing, forms of dying

Killing occupies a substantial part of the legislation which refers directly to animals. This is what it says about their deaths as an experimental outcome:

> 2.3 Death as an end-point
> Death as an end-point must be avoided as far as possible and replaced with an early and humane end-point.[7]

"Death as an endpoint" means using death to provide a data point for an experiment: a dot on a graph or a number in a column. That this signifies the end of a sentient life with all that this life entails both in itself and its relations with others, is considered of no consequence. This fact alone is something worth stopping to consider as it speaks volumes about our frightening ability to abstract ourselves into a meticulously censored reality so that we can continue to act with thoughtless instrumentality to fulfil our desires.

In the explanatory sentence, the term "humane end point" sounds benign but it is euphemistic for killing the animal with supposedly less suffering than the experiment would cause if it continued. Whether or not this will be done is open to question but the gathering of data clearly remains the priority.

The document continues:

> Where death as an end-point is unavoidable for the purpose of achieving the scientific aims of the procedure, measures should be taken to ensure as few deaths as possible and to reduce the duration and intensity of suffering prior to death to the minimum possible.[8]

The text makes clear that *achieving the scientific aims of the procedure* takes priority over any suffering the animals may be forced to endure; that the scientific aims are paramount and the suffering of the animals secondary. This is an example of the big deception which we meet again and again in animal experimentation.

What do we really mean by *scientific aims* which supposedly must be achieved? These aims appear as if they are independently existing entities emanating from the discipline of science and requiring specific actions by the experimenters for their fulfilment. Attaining them is the justification given for imposing suffering and death on the victims. It seems as if those who order and carry out the experiments simply have no choice in the matter and are therefore relieved of all responsibility.

But this is complete rubbish. In reality, the scientific aims are nothing more than the aims of the experimenters themselves and their institutions. They are what these people have decided they wish to achieve and what they believe they will be able to realise by using certain methods. Certainly, they will make use of scientific techniques and theories but science, as such, has no aims or goals but is a method of working and of constructing ideas about the world. There is nobody else driving this train except the experimenters and their organisations.

Importantly, we have here an ideological construction of science to support the oppressive social practice taking place. Invoking the name of science also draws on its social power for support and justification while simultaneously deflecting responsibility from the true originators of the activities being undertaken. The language in this legislation and elsewhere, hides this agency, allowing for an abdication of culpability by those concerned.

## Who kills and how

Later, the legislation discusses the act of killing; who can do it; how they are allowed to kill and where they are allowed to kill. It describes the ways in which different *protected animals* may legally have their lives taken away provided that the person who does it is the holder of a suitable licence – literally a licence to kill. For smaller animals we read:

> Overdose of an anaesthetic...exposure to carbon dioxide gas in a rising concentration, dislocation of the neck...concussion of the brain by striking the cranium...

And for ungulates:

> Destruction of the brain by free bullet using appropriate rifles, guns and ammunition, or ii) captive bolt or electrical stunning followed by destruction of the brain or exsanguination before return of consciousness.[9]

All very matter of fact, very official, very scientific.

And that is about it for the victims because there is surprisingly little about them in this document and no arguments at all for any ethical justification for what is done. The bulk of the document is about administrative matters; applications, types of licence holders and sites where this and that can be done and so on.

In order to gain some perspective on these regulations, it is worthwhile taking a diversion at this point to look at some international guidelines for experimenting on humans.

## Experiments on humans

Any medical research which does take place on humans is incredibly strictly controlled. A document with the imposing title of *International Ethical Guidelines for Biomedical Research Involving Human Subjects Prepared by the Council for International Organizations of Medical Sciences (CIOMS) in collaboration with the World Health Organization (WHO)*[10] lays out the do's and don'ts in some detail and offers us a good insight into the ethical thinking overseeing this research. We will just look briefly at its guiding principles.

In the section titled "General Ethical Principles" it says:

> All research involving human subjects should be conducted in accordance with three basic ethical principles, namely respect for persons, beneficence and justice.[11]

Under the first principle, two other principles are also included which are, firstly that those who can make decisions about their participation must have their decisions respected and secondly:

> ...that those who are dependent or vulnerable be afforded security against harm or abuse.[12]

The second principle, beneficence, is explained as:

> ...the ethical obligation to maximize benefit and to minimize harm...

and the document continues by explaining that this:

> ...further proscribes the deliberate infliction of harm on persons; this aspect of beneficence is sometimes expressed as a separate principle, nonmaleficence (do no harm).[13]

The third principle is justice and refers to:

> the ethical obligation to treat each person in accordance with what is morally right and proper...

and the document once again draws attention to vulnerability:

> ...special provision must be made for the protection of the rights and welfare of vulnerable persons.[14]

It explains that vulnerability refers to a substantial incapacity to protect one's own interests and then offers examples including, "being a junior or subordinate member of a hierarchical group."[15]

It also emphasises that the onus is on the researchers to protect the prospective participants, even if the participants themselves are not aware of their vulnerability or are unable to understand their vulnerability. There is a duty of care to the point where researchers should exclude participants if it is thought that they are unable to give full informed consent even when they wish to consent.

And then tucked away under Appendix 2, in the World Medical Association Declaration of Helsinki, section five, we read about priorities:

> In medical research on human subjects, considerations related to the well-being of the human subject should take precedence over the interests of science and society.[16]

The strict guidelines outlined in the document reflect high ethical principles:

- Respect for choices made by the individual:
- Beneficence; do no harm
- Justice; an individual must receive treatment which is morally right and proper
- Special care and protection must be exercised for the vulnerable such as those seen as lower down a hierarchy
- The wellbeing of subjects takes priority over any considerations of science and society.

Contrast this with how animals are legally treated in animal experimentation:

- Individuals are not allowed any choice
- Individuals are harmed and killed
- Subjects are not treated justly
- All of the individuals are vulnerable but receive no protection
- The considerations of science and society take precedence over the wellbeing of the subjects.

We have complete ethical mirror images; day and night, heaven and the abyss. All the individuals of just one species receive all the protections imaginable while all the individuals of all the other species on earth receive none of those protections. One species alone is supposedly justified in carrying out carnage against all of the others. The duplicity of this ideological facade is shameful but governments and prestigious institutions around the world are happy to subscribe to it.

## Animals in The House

Laws and regulations do not arise from a vacuum but are usually the result of a long processes of enquiry, discussion and eventually promulgation in legislatures. It is here we might expect to find the foundational reasoning behind such acts and regulations. The House of Lords is one of the two houses of the British Parliament and in 2002 produced a report titled *British House of Lords Select Committee on Animals in Scientific Procedures* which looks at animal testing and its regulation.[17]

The document is eighty-two pages long with chapter two, titled *Ethics,* examining the moral and ethical arguments relating to experiments on animals. Unfortunately, the chapter is only one page long and contains a mere five paragraphs.

This very short discussion takes a simple form and describes only two perspectives. It uses the format: some people opposing testing say this, some people in favour of testing say that and concludes with, we unanimously think this.

To its credit it does use the terms "human beings" and "other animals" in the same sentence acknowledging that humans are also animals and the authors say they recognise that the issues raised in their investigations are not only practical but moral and ethical and "centre on the question of how human beings should treat other animals."[18]

This mini chapter devotes less than ninety words to describing the view opposing testing on animals while it employs over two hundred words explaining the position in its favour. Meagre though this offering is, it still has much to reveal when we examine it more closely.

Concerning the view opposing experimentation it refers to Jeremy Bentham and his famous quote about animals and equality in suffering citing seventeen of his words saying:

> There are those who, following a suggestion by Jeremy Bentham in the late 18th century, hold that all creatures capable of suffering are on an equal footing with human beings, regardless of "the number of the legs, the villosity of the skin, or the termination of the os sacrum".[19]

Significantly though, it makes no mention of Bentham also saying in the same note:

> The day may come, when the rest of the animal creation may acquire those rights which never could have been withholden from them but by the hand of tyranny. The French have already discovered that the blackness of skin is no reason why a human being should be abandoned without redress to the caprice of a tormentor.[20]

Why, it seems fair to ask, does it fail to mention this call by Bentham for rights for animals and his assertion that these are withheld by the "hand of tyranny"? And his comparison with slavery?

And Bentham also says this concerning the law

> Other animals, which, on account of their interests having been neglected by the insensibility of the ancient jurists, stand degraded into the class of things.[21]

Here he points to animals being treated as things in law and by extension being property, and makes it clear that he believes they have interests. All of the above are extremely important points whether we agree with Bentham or not and considering that this is a document from the highest court in the land these omissions are either serious oversights or deliberate exclusions.

The report goes on to discuss what it describes as the "animal rights" position saying:

> These people hold that being sentient confers a moral right on animals that they should not be used by human beings for research whose purpose is mainly to benefit humans...[22]

This seems hopelessly confused. The philosopher Tom Regan in his book *The case for animal rights* makes the claim for animals to have rights on the basis that they are experiencing beings and are the "subjects of a life".[23] Nonhuman animals have an inherent value of their own, as do human animals and with this go moral rights such as the right to life, freedom and bodily integrity. Individuals who are the bearers of basic rights possess these protections irrespective of the desires of others. These rights are certainly not dependent on *who* any research is intended to possibly benefit.

Then confusingly, a footnote to the text explains, "This is the view taken by philosophers such as Peter Singer..."[24] Peter Singer, the author of the famous book, *Animal Liberation,* is a utilitarian philosopher who makes the case for animals by arguing for decisions in a particular situation to be based on weighing the interests of all concerned but not by the granting of rights. Utilitarianism is not mentioned anywhere in the document.

After getting itself tangled up in this bit of philosophy, the document incredibly goes on to say about animal rights that, "Some activists are prepared to uphold this view by violence."[25] But it's footnote to this assertion reads:

> None of those who presented evidence to us said that they endorsed violence, though we did not receive written evidence from some of the more extreme animal rights groups.[26]

The veracity or otherwise of these vague, unsubstantiated claims of threats of violence by shadowy groups who might or might not exist, has no bearing whatsoever on evaluating the validity of the ethical arguments opposing animal experimentation. Surely the Select Committee would know this. So, why is it even mentioned at all by the authors? It appears as a rather clumsy attempt to smear the opposition position on animal testing; a position which the report has already failed to even describe coherently.

It is interesting to note at this point that nowhere in the discussion is the pro-testing position ever portrayed as supporting the use of violence. This is because it is ideological common sense, that however violent the animal testing practices actually are, they cannot be defined in this way. It is a prime example of dominant power naming the world. In this ideology, the problem of violence in animal testing simply does not exist, cannot exist, and so there is no case to answer.

When the report turns to views in favour of using nonhuman animals in experiments it says:

> More commonly, there are those who hold that the whole institution of morality, society and law is founded on the belief that human beings are unique amongst animals. Humans are therefore morally entitled to use animals, whether in the laboratory, the farmyard or the house, for their own purposes. And this belief is sometimes combined with a further belief that there is a moral imperative for human beings to develop medical and veterinary science for the relief of suffering, among both humans and other animals.[27]

This is essentially the position which the committee will unanimously support a mere ten lines further down the page.

The first sentence, claiming that morality, society and law are founded on the belief that humans are unique among animals is illogical because all animals are unique. But leaving this aside, the next few words are truly breath-taking. They assert that because of this unique nature of humans, "Humans are therefore morally entitled to use animals.... for their own purposes."

How does "being unique", which from the text we infer to mean advanced in some way, even if that were actually true, confer a moral right to use another's body for our own purposes? There is absolutely no explanation offered for this outrageous claim, not even a hint of how it could possibly be supported. Not only is it illogical but it is a deeply offensive and is the form of argument which has been used to justify abuse as in sexism, racism, slavery and other vile practices.

If humans are advanced (whatever that means), then we surely have an exacting duty of care towards the more vulnerable and are bound to protect them from harm even if it means that we ourselves are harmed in the process. This is a far more reasonable, although perhaps less convenient, argument.

Then, towards the end of this one-page chapter, we come to the not very surprising conclusion:

> 2.5 The unanimous view of the Select Committee is that it is morally acceptable for human beings to use other animals, but that it is morally wrong to cause them unnecessary or avoidable suffering. (bold in the original)

It has taken five trifling paragraphs to get here. A short exercise in muddled philosophy followed by a predictable endorsement of the status quo and a depressing reminder that the ideology of the Great Chain of Being still flourishes in the corridors of the House of Lords.

## Dead right

To complete our brief exploration into legislation let's go on just a little further and see what we might discover by looking at corpses and body parts. A bit odd perhaps but it is surprisingly revealing.

What you can legally do with a corpse depends upon where you live and the species of the corpse we are talking about. Naturally there are public health regulations to be followed concerning what should happen to the dead and these have at their core the protection of the living and so there are laws about burials and cremations and other forms of treatment of corpses, but there is more. There is the idea that human dead bodies must be treated with respect and that there are just some things which we are not allowed to do to them or with them. One of these is pretending that the corpse is alive:

> At common law, it is an offense to treat a corpse indecently by keeping, handling, and exposing it to view in order to create the impression that the deceased is still alive.[28]

So presumably taxidermy and decorating your home or a hotel lobby with bits of human bodies is a non-starter. We can't put Auntie May's head on the wall, however much we claim we loved and respected her, and a stuffed Uncle Alfred in a diorama sitting amongst the rocks and wild flowers is definitely out.

Nor is it allowed to chop up human corpses without the authority to do so:

> The mutilation of a corpse is an offense at common law, and under some statutes, the unauthorized dissection of a corpse is a specific criminal offense. Someone who receives a corpse for the purpose of dissection with the knowledge that it has been unlawfully removed is subject to prosecution.[29]

All this is totally the opposite of what we can do to the dead bodies of animals where we can do pretty much whatever we feel like, including literally getting inside their skins.

## War

Even when people are killing each other in war, actually trying to cause as much damage as possible to each other, there is a responsibility to look after human dead bodies and one of the main requirements is that they must not be damaged or mutilated. Customary International Humanitarian Law (IHL) rule 113, "Treatment of the Dead" says:

> Each party to the conflict must take all possible measures to prevent the dead from being despoiled. Mutilation of dead bodies is prohibited.[30]

Committing mutilation is a war crime both in international and non-international conflicts and the International Committee of the Red Cross explains why:

> The prohibition of mutilating dead bodies in international armed conflicts is covered by the war crime of "committing outrages upon personal dignity" under the Statute of the International Criminal Court, which according to the Elements of Crimes also applies to dead persons...[31]

It continues:

> In several trials after the Second World War, the accused were convicted on charges of mutilation of dead bodies and cannibalism.[32]

Human dignity as a concept in law is now widespread although defining what exactly is meant by it and where it originates from is no easy matter. In the text above there is the concept of a human corpse having dignity and offending that dignity being actually a crime. Rule 90, concerning "Torture and Cruel, Inhuman or Degrading Treatment" clarifies the reasoning:

> The notion of "outrages upon personal dignity" is defined in the Elements of Crimes for the International Criminal Court as acts which humiliate, degrade or otherwise violate the dignity of a person to such a degree "as to be generally recognized as an outrage upon personal dignity". The Elements of Crimes further specifies that degrading treatment can apply to dead persons and that the victim need not be personally aware of the humiliation.[33]

Humans, dead or alive, have dignity which can be offended to such a degree that doing so is a crime warranting punishment through a court of law. Conversely, we construct living, sentient animals as having no dignity and not worth even the protection which is afforded to a human corpse.

Even if we look at the treatment of human tissues, these are also protected and need to be respected. The code of practice of the UK Human Tissue Authority says "Human tissue should be treated with respect, without placing a disproportionate burden on staff or resources."[34] And that "Dignified treatment and separate disposal are the minimum considerations involved in disposing of stored tissue."[35] Even human tissues need to be treated with respect and afforded dignified treatment.

Here again is the ideological creation of mirror ethical universes and in this case even dead humans still come off better than living animals.

## Flipping flesh

While we are in the general area of laboratories and flesh let's have a short detour to complete the chapter and look at research investigating growing animal cells in the laboratory to make "cruelty free" meat. This is promoted as a way to save animals from suffering and possibly help the environment whilst still supplying people with flesh to chew. Naturally, the cells which are grown in the laboratory must have some form of nutrition, such as sugars, amino acids, fats and vitamins and so on which will presumably come from plants and will have to be produced somewhere, processed and brought in. The cells must also be kept warm and cared for in other ways so it will be interesting to see how efficient this process will be in comparison to eating plant food directly, which presumably is the most efficient because plants derive their energy from chemical synthesis powered directly by sunlight. As animals we have to steal food from plants or animals and at each transfer along the food chain there is a loss of energy which is of course why eating plants is far more efficient than eating animals. However, these efforts deserve to be applauded and they offer all sorts of interesting possibilities.

I think this work could potentially, if inadvertently, make major contributions to the growing of tissues and organs to be used for transplantation, medical reconstruction and in laboratory experimentation. As the technology develops, new and improved techniques will surely come into use and there will be a better understanding of what the project of growing animal cells in large numbers entails. It would not be the first time that research in one area has made a significant contribution to another and so rather than feeding the flesh habit it might end up saving human and nonhuman lives directly.

But an interesting question also arises; why grow nonhuman animal cells to eat, why not grow human cells? These would be nutritionally perfect for eating by humans and provided they are infection free what could be better? Real men, the advertisements tell us, eat real meat but now real men could eat real Man or Woman flesh. Woman burgers, Man Burgers and pre sexed nuggets could be available to titillate our chromosome preferences. Using starter cells from diverse nationalities or from a range of so called "races", might produce variations in texture, shear strength, marbling, taste, etc., we just do not know. And I suppose organisations such as the KKK and the racist right could choose their own ethnic group to eat and xenophobes their own national strains. Brave new world indeed.

But would it be legal? The answer appears to be yes. No individual, is being killed so it is not murder and no mutilation of corpses is taking place so that's OK, but eating human flesh seems to fit the definition of cannibalism, which could be a bit of a problem. However, rather surprisingly, in the UK, the USA, South Africa and quite possibly many other countries, there are no specific laws which make eating human flesh or the practice of cannibalism illegal.[36] Eating human placenta has become popular with some high profile personalities and one person has already consumed human flesh twice in public; on one occasion the mouth-watering morsel was donated tonsils and on the other a slice of testicle.[37,38,39]

With that wonderful picture lingering in our minds, let's go right into the laboratory itself with its special language, its players, equipment, techniques, discourses and ideology.

## CHAPTER 11

# Lying by telling the truth

*For the powerful, crimes are those that others commit.*

Noam Chomsky[1]

## Language of the discipline

WE OFTEN THINK of the practice of science as being completely objective, unadulterated by the everyday world and as a great collaborative project for incrementally uncovering Truth. But this is not how it works because science is a human activity and like other human activities it has its own ways of doing things, its own special language, discourses, ideological perspectives and internal power struggles. It is easy to forget that today's ideas and theories are to a great extent transient, just as those of the past were and that the practice of science is culturally, socially and economically influenced.

Michael Halliday is a linguist who developed a theoretical understanding of language called systemic functional linguistics and points to the power of scientific language in separating those who know from those who don't and repeatedly reinforcing the belief that humans occupy a unique, superior position in the world:

> The language of science, though forward-looking in its origins, has become increasingly anti-democratic: its arcane grammatical metaphor sets apart those who understand it and shields them from those who do not. It is elitist also in another sense, in that its grammar constantly proclaims the uniqueness of the human species.[2]

In this chapter we will look at a few examples of scientific writings relating to animal experimentation to see what they might reveal. We begin with standard tests on animals.

## Standardised suffering

There are many standard procedures carried out as routine in laboratories and some of these include experiments on animals. A common example is the *Rodent Forced Swim Test*, also known as the *Behavioural Despair Test* although this name, it has been suggested, should no longer be used because it might have anthropomorphic connotations. The idea behind the test is that a drug, for example an antidepressant, will be given to an animal and the animal's response examined to see if it displays any sign of a change in motivation. What happens is that a mouse or rat is put into a clear sided beaker of water and left to swim until a specific times elapses or he/she finally gives up. Their desperate struggle to try to escape and not to drown is used as a measure of their mental state. One article puts it this way:

> Mice are placed in an inescapable transparent tank that is filled with water and their escape related mobility behaviour is measured. [3]

Notice how a desperate struggle to survive drowning and get free is described as the more benign sounding and abstract *escape related mobility behaviour* – a language practice which is common in scientific reports. This test is clearly unpleasant and very stressful but others are worse; much, much worse and in everyday use around the world.

The Organisation for Economic Co-operation and Development (OECD), has the motto "Better Policies for Better Lives", which sounds really good. It has thirty-five member countries and a budget of 370 million euros and says this about what it does:

> The OECD provides a forum in which governments can work together to share experiences and seek solutions to common problems. We work with governments to understand what drives economic, social and environmental change. We measure productivity and global flows of trade and investment. We analyse and compare data to predict future trends. We set international standards on a wide range of things, from agriculture and tax to the safety of chemicals.[4]

It also provides guidelines on how to carry out experiments on animals. For example, in its document 403 titled *Acute Inhalation Toxicity*, it describes how the $LC_{50}$ test should be done.[5] The $LC_{50}$ is the concentration of a chemical which, when inhaled, will cause the death of half of the individuals tested. The document explains:

> Primary features of this Test Guideline are the ability to provide a concentration-response relationship ranging from nonlethal to lethal outcomes in order to derive a median lethal concentration ($LC_{50}$), non-lethal threshold concentration (e.g. $LC_{01}$), and slope, and to identify possible sex susceptibility.[6]

Here is dense scientific lexicalisation with *concentration-response, median, threshold, slope* and so on, but despite the fact that this is about animals inhaling substances which will cause terrible suffering, this aspect is totally absent from the text. Only the science has any importance and death is just a scientific endpoint. Enough of these endpoints will provide the figure for the median lethal concentration. Perhaps this can best be described as a discourse of psychopathic, technical objectification.

The next excerpt shows once again how the scientific objectives, which are in reality the objectives, the experimenters and various organisations, are given overriding importance:

> However, the targeted concentrations should not induce severe irritation/corrosive effects, yet sufficient to extend the concentration-response curve to levels that reach the regulatory and scientific objective of the test.[7]

The instruction that the animals should not be irritated or burned too severely by the chemicals concerns the best scientific approach rather than any care for their suffering. But in what appears to be at least some acknowledgement of the victim's sufferings we read:

> Moribund animals or animals obviously in pain or showing signs of severe and enduring distress should be humanely killed and are considered in the interpretation of the test result in the same way as animals that died on test.[8]

Killing the animal still allows her/his death to be used as a piece of data in the same way as if that individual had died from the effects of the chemical alone. As we saw in the UK regulations, the paramount consideration is achieving the so called "scientific objectives". Everything else is secondary.

The document goes on to discuss the fine details of exposure methods saying that "nose only" includes "head only" and also that whole body exposure may sometimes be needed if there are "special objectives" for the study.

In the final excerpt, these guidelines paint a grotesque scenario of utter misery and reveal a complete disregard for the sentience of these suffering individuals:

> Animals exposed whole-body to an aerosol should be housed individually during exposure to prevent them from filtering the test aerosol through the fur of their cage mates.[9]

Is this directive because the animals try to sleep close to each other for support or because of their desperate attempts to avoid, as much as possible, the aerosol they are being forced to breathe? I don't know the answer but a moments reflection evokes the misery and torment of this scene. The individual is breathing toxic air which cannot be avoided; she is stifling and choking at what will be the end of her life, but the methodology is all important and dictates that she will not even have the meagre comfort of being with others of her kind, but must suffer and die alone as a sacrifice to data points, objectives and the ruthless idol of scientism.

## Absent agents and disappearing animals

Research reports of experiments on animals are not in short supply. They are described in a huge range of academic journals, in papers presented at conferences, in master's and PhD theses, reports for companies of the testing carried out in commercial laboratories and in work which goes on in secret facilites.

To find a few examples, I did a simple search of an academic database and received numerous returns. We will look very briefly at excerpts from just four of the papers which were some of the first to come up. These papers are not particularly unusual or special in any way.

First is something from the *Journal of Pharmacology & Pharmacotherapeutics* and this article reviews toxicological screening methods. The section we look at outlines a way to look for negative effects which might be caused by the test substance being administered during pregnancy. The testing is carried out on nonhuman animals:

> The compound is administered between the 8th and 14th day of pregnancy, and embryolethal effects are studied. At the end of the study or on the 21st day of the study, a caesarean section is performed and parameters such as fetuses with hemorrhagic bullae, limb malformations, exencephaly, cleft palates, open eyelids, and tail deformities as well as the mortality and the numbers of dead and live pups are noted.[10]

This is densely scientific writing and all about technical matters and as is standard in science it is written in the passive voice meaning there is no agent who carries out the actions described. The compound *is administered*, embryolethal effects *are studied*, a caesarean section *is performed*, and a whole range of things such as limb malformation, other deformities as well as the deaths of foetuses *are noted*.

Severe abnormalities such as "fetuses with hemorrhagic bullae, limb malformations, exencephaly, cleft palates, open eyelids and tail deformities" and the number of dead and living babies are described as *parameters;* they are merely information to be collected. Using the word *parameters* is a lexical choice causing a disconnect from sentience and objectifying the animals.

There is no affective content of any kind in the writing, no emotion at all. Any suffering caused to the animals is completely irrelevant and ignored. Although this paragraph actually speaks of the death of babies in the womb, the brain being formed outside the skull, deformities, blood filled blisters and limb malformations, these are treated in the same that we might record the contents of a box of chocolates. Overall the text is about using tools to generate data.

The paper continues in similar vein and below I have highlighted more agentless phrases:

> During the study period, the animals are observed for signs of toxicity. Parturition, the number of offspring and their sexes are recorded. The number of dead and live pups are noted, and live pups are weighed in the morning and evening each day during the first 4 days. After the termination of the study, the animals and pups are sacrificed and subjected to a histopathological examination...[11]

Note the usual scientific euphemism for killing – *sacrificed*, which in addition to obscuring the act suggests an air of selfless giving in this slaughter without a slaughterer. Dunayer notes that killing might be expressed with a range of euphemisms including "produce lethality", "destroyed", "put down", "put to sleep", "discarded", "dispatched", "disposed of", "terminated", "go into the data" and when "surplus animals" are killed it might be said that their holding areas are "depopulated" or "housecleaning" has taken place.[12]

## Material beings and being immaterial

The next example concerns a report about what happens to heroin when it is taken into the bodies of rats. It is common when writing scientific papers to use standard formats with sub headings such as "Introduction", "Results", "Discussion" and so on and in this paper under the heading "Materials and Methods" we find recorded "six-month-old male Wistar rats."[13] The animals are classed as materials to be consumed in the experiment.

Wistar rats are a special breed of rats i.e. genetically manipulated, who were first bred by the predecessor to the Charles River company (more on them later). The company website tells us this about these animals:

> Ideal For: general multipurpose model, infectious disease research, safety and efficacy testing, aging, surgical model.[14]

Here is the ideology of purpose again and in this case the purpose of these animals is to serve as models for research.

This is what the article says was done to them:

> The animals were divided into two groups:
>
> 1. control group (10 animals) – upon weighing, were treated with physiological solution (about 1 mL) and sacrificed after 15 minutes, and
>
> 2. experimental group (20 animals) – upon weighing received 25 mg/kg b.w. (about 1 mL) of the prepared heroin solution (10 mg/mL), and sacrificed after: 5, 15, 45 and 120 minutes, each time 5 animals.
>
> Heroin was administered intraperitoneally with the aid of an insulin syringe (1 mL), and after treatment the animals were kept in separate cages. The animals were sacrificed by decapitation.[15]

The animals were given saline or heroin by injection into their abdomens using a needle and syringe and then beheaded in groups over a period of two hours. The report is agentless and very technical; the rats non-beings. The story it tells will always be the experimenter's because he has the power and control, he sets the agenda and so his story is the only one in town. The other story, the animals' story, is never told because they have no power and for them this is a tale of extreme violence. It may seem strange to even think about it in this way but that in itself is testimony to ideological power which is all but total.

## Pigs become kidneys

The third paper is about how kidneys from small pigs were removed, stored and then re transplanted into the same pigs. Once again, we find the animals listed in the "Materials and Methods" section but this time the paper also has an ethics declaration:

> 2.2. Animals. We used 12 minipigs with an average weight of 40 kg. All the procedures were approved...and animals were cared for in accordance with applicable legal regulations in Directive 2010/63/EU and RD 53/2013, on the protection of animals used for experimentation and other scientific purposes.[16]

The phrases, "animals were cared for", "legal regulations" and "protection of animals" all suggest that the animals were kept safe and well protected from harm. And they probably were, that is, before they were violated and killed. As is the case in animal experimentation generally, they were legally abused by people who are officially allowed to abuse them and who earn money by doing so. In the dominant ideology, where humans are believed to have a moral right to do this to animals, it is considered a logical, ethical and totally acceptable practice.

The section continues;

> After laparotomy and isolation of the kidney, warm ischemia was accomplished by applying a vascular arterial clamp to the right kidney for 45 min, with subsequent nephrectomy and cold storage of the organs for 24 h in UW solution. The kidneys were then autotransplanted ($n = 6$). A second group of kidneys ($n = 6$) underwent the same protocol...[17]

In everyday English, a large cut was made in the abdomen of each pig and one kidney removed. This was kept in the cold for 24 hours and then put back into the animal. While the pigs began as just materials in the "Materials and Methods" section of the paper, in the last line of this excerpt they no longer exist at all and we read that "a second group of kidneys...underwent the same protocol..." The pigs have disappeared. In fact, they are only named as pigs once in the whole of the article after which we never hear of them again. Not even their deaths are mentioned.

## Dogs and jaws

In the final example, we look at research on dental implants. This paper also lists the animals under "Materials and Methods" and says that the experiments were performed on:

> 24 long snout dogs of both sexes, weighing 30–35 kg, with normal bite, at the age of 20–24 months.[18]

The dogs had dental implants surgically inserted into their mouths by the researchers and were then killed one month, three months or six months later. The excerpt above, which appears at the start of the paper, is the first and last time we ever hear of the dogs named as dogs. However, some time later the authors are able to tell us that, "As a result of the experiment, we prepared and studied 24 units of jaws from experimental animals..."[19] The dogs are *experimental animals* (ideology of purpose) and become transformed into merely "units of jaws".

Only their jaws are valued by the researchers; the animal's lives and all they might have meant have been lost and their jawless bodies thrown away. We have no idea and will never know, what trauma and pain they endured both physical and psychological. Not even the extraction of their teeth is mentioned in the article let alone what happened as the implants were inserted into their jaws and how they managed to eat, if indeed they did. The animal's lives and suffering are erased, they are non-beings, tools which do not require our attention, sympathy, guilt or ethical consideration.

There is another very important point to note here. When experimental work such as this is reported in publications, the narrative gets modified in a particular way. Those parts of reality which are deemed irrelevant are erased and never make it into the report. This is a learned and accepted way of reporting in science, an automatic self-censorship process. There is never any blood or struggles, no gnawing at restraints, self-mutilation, no splinters of bones as holes are drilled into skulls, no howling, no screams, no fear in the eyes, no sadness or confusion and no terror. Not because these didn't happen but because they are understood as being unimportant and because they would interfere with the ideological representation of the practice. This censorship, along with the objectification of the animals and the agentless actions are extremely powerful in sustaining the myth of experiments on animals being nonviolent.

So, are these scientific reports untruthful? Are they simply misleading by omission or are they lying because they are telling the truth but not all of it, a practice known as paltering? However we think about them, we must never mistake modern scientific reports for anything like true and full representations of what actually took place. That would be a mistake.

This extremely brief dip into the huge number of papers produced globally each year shows how animals are portrayed as having purposes to serve; as materials, tools and models for scientific experiments and who are violated by unspecified agents and written out of existence in reports. The carefully selective, anthropocentric, sanitised version of events portrayed in experimentation reports holds the stage and scaffolds the lie that animal experimentation is not violent.

## Dollars and death
But this practice has a commercial side too and experimenting on animals, selling animals for experimenting upon and selling equipment to use on animals is big business. So, our next stop will be the market place, where suffering and abuse keep the accountants busy and the shareholders happy.

CHAPTER·12

# Paying the price

*We know we cannot defend or be kind to animals until we stop exploiting them – exploiting them in the name of science, exploiting animals in the name of sport, exploiting animals in the name of fashion, and yes, exploiting animals in the name of food.*

Cesar Chavez[1]

## Selling suffering

A PROFITABLE, GLOBAL industry has grown up around animal experimentation. It sells animals, equipment, consumables, experiments and expertise. Recently some of the big testing labs have amalgamated producing a brand new company called Envigo which "...has been created through the integration of Huntingdon Life Sciences, Harlan Laboratories, GFA, NDA Analytics and LSR associates."[2] Here is some information about the new company:

> Envigo employs 3,800 people and has sales approaching $500M. The company is a top-three provider of non-clinical research services and research models and services to the pharmaceutical, chemical and crop protection industries, as well as academic institutions and government agencies worldwide.[3]

The business will work like this:

> The RMS business unit provides high-quality research models, lab animal diets and bedding, and support services from 30 sites worldwide. The CRS business unit offers a comprehensive range of drug development and environmental sciences services, including safety assessment, analytical, metabolism, CMC, and regulatory consultancy from nine contract research facilities in Europe, the U.S. and the Middle East.[4]

What is going on here is a mega social practice of making money from experimentation on animals. The overriding discourse we might describe as capitalist–scientific with goods and services both being on sale.

Charles River is an example of another of the big players in the industry and in its annual report it says this:

> For nearly 70 years, we have been in the business of providing the research models required in research and development of new drugs, devices and therapies.[5] In 2015,

we reported revenue of $1.36 billion, a 10.4% increase over the previous year in constant dollars.[6]

The "research models" it refers to are usually genetically damaged and transgenic animals, some of which it is possible to patent in a number of countries.[7] This takes our present "ownership" of animals to a new and chilling level.

Here is a piece about a particular Envigo mouse "model" which is just going on the market:

> Dr. Adrian Hardy, Chief Operating Officer of the Huntingdon and Harlan organization, commented: "We are delighted to make available our innovative SHrN hairless NOD. SCID mouse to the worldwide research community. The new model will help our customers in their important research that leads to bringing innovative therapies to patients."[8]

This mouse has product specifications as well, just like a car or washing machine. Here are some of those specs:

> Phenotypically hairless (sparse, intermittent hair growth possible), Inbred, Deficient in T and B cells, NK cell functional deficit, No circulating complement, Decreased macrophage function, Decreased granulocyte function, Decreased dendritic cells, Severe Immunodeficiency, Coat: Albino[9]

A single animal can be expensive although the monetary price is nothing compared to the cost to the individual animal. The reason given above for producing such "models" is to help customers in order to help patients, but for the company the real reason is to make money. That is, after all, what companies do and the information we saw earlier suggests these companies do it pretty well. Money is generated by exploiting those who are powerless.

We later learn from Envigo that the new mouse has been "developed" to be more effective and more convenient than the "standard" model. But while *developed* suggests improvement these mice have, in reality, been made severely disabled. In this discourse, *development* does not apply to the animals but is anthropocentric and is all about what customers want to do to the bodies of those individuals they are buying. And nobody bats an eyelid at this because it is just ideological common sense.

We are told that "SHrN production will be managed in multiple Harlan facilities in the United States and Europe or put another way, the animals who are being offered as tools of science, will be produced at multiple global sites and sold as commodities."[10] Here is a discourse of production as part of a global capitalist ideology where everything has a price and it's all up for sale.

On its website, Charles River offers a whole range of what they describe as animal "models" and these are divided up depending upon the specific work they might be used for – cardiovascular, renal, oncology, etc. or, alternatively, prospective customers can simply browse and see what takes their fancy. On the page "Find a model", yes that is really what it says, we are offered merchandise such as:

**AKR Mouse** Ideal For: Atherosclerotic model, cancer research, metabolic research, diet-induced obesity Inbred Bred In: US
**Athymic Nude Mouse** Ideal For: Tumor biology and xenograft research Immunodeficient Outbred Bred In: US, Germany, UK
**p110beta PI3K-D931A (129)** Ideal For: Oncology, fertility Genetically Engineered Bred In: US
**p110beta PI3K-D931A(BALBc)** Ideal For: Oncology, fertility Genetically Engineered Bred In: US [11]

The list goes on for twelve pages. On offer are rats, mice, rabbits, guinea pigs, gerbils, hamsters and "Large Models." Exactly which *Large Models* is not clear and attempts to find more information are met with a log-in page and access can only be made once a reader has applied for permission and has supplied suitable personal details and a (presumably acceptable) company name. Applicants are contacted later; the page informs the enquiring reader.

Given this total objectification of living beings it is enlightening to read the Envigo site's explanation regarding their new name. The site explains that the name comes from two roots; *en* – to enhance or enrich and *vigo* being vigorous and also having as its root, life. It explains "...Envigo means a strong, active company whose purpose is to enhance and enrich life." [12] Well, let's be honest here, that rather depends on whose lives we are talking about.

## Behind the websites and the walls
Some further insights into what these types of companies do may be gleaned from what they offer as services and products. However, we should be aware that the information available is carefully controlled and the dense scientific jargon does a great job of making what is really being offered, rather opaque.

Company websites reveal the language in use but we also see photographs of pristine laboratories, equipment, people in gleaming white coats or scrubs, smiling yet somehow serious and these also make their contributions to the discourses.

On its website, Envigo leads prospective customers through a whole host of experiments on animals which the company will do for you at a price. The site mentions things such as affordability and world-renowned quality and talks proudly about its team of "tox specialists" – people who specialise in knowing about and investigating what poisonous substances do to living beings.

Information about experiments on mice, rats or rabbits is easily available but when it comes to other animals, especially primates, the site becomes rather coy. Information about testing on primates requires applying for a log in and password and the enquirer is told that these will be granted if their application is approved. Approved by whom and on what grounds is unclear.

Under the title "Our Capabilities" another company, Convance, uses a drop-down menu to show prospective customers what it has on offer. It proudly lists:

Core Toxicology Services, Infusion Services, Ocular Development Services, Nonhuman Primate Studies, Juvenile Toxicology Studies, Neurotoxicity Study Services... [13]

Then on a link at the bottom of the list, it chirpily says, "Let's Start the Conversation".[14] This is online shopping and the site is just like others we can find selling all manner of everyday products and services. For the broad categories such as "core toxicology", "infusion services", "ocular development", "juvenile toxicology", and "neurotoxicity study services" there is the opportunity to learn more by clicking the relevant button. Let's click on Core Toxicology Services.

In the welcoming way of shopping websites, this displays an outline of what can be purchased under this unit and the page is divided into three columns which are headed "Species", "Duration" and "Administration".[15] Under "Species" it offers:

> Rodent, Rat, Mouse, Rabbit, Hamster, Non-rodent, Canine, NHP (nonhuman primate), Mini-pig, Feline.[16]

It does not say *rats* or *mice* or *dogs* or *cats*; nor does it use scientific species names. *Rat* is offered as is *Canine, Feline* and *Mouse* and used in this way the names are mass nouns where sentient individuals are portrayed as amorphous material, in this case specifically for human use.

In the column headed "Duration" it offers, "Single-dose / special range-finding, sub-chronic, chronic and carcinogenicity".[17] These are indications of how long the animal will have to endure the treatment before being killed.[18] Then in the column "Administration" it offers different ways in which substances can be introduced into the individual's body, offering:

> Dermal, Gavage, Implant, Intracutaneous, Intramuscular, Intranasal, Intraperitoneal, Intrathecal, Intratracheal, Intravenous, Rectal, Subcutaneous, Vaginal.[19]

Some of these words may not be familiar so just to clarify a few;
*Gavage* is introducing substances directly into the stomach – from the French to force down the throat, derived from force feeding poultry for market[20,21]
*Intrathecal* – directly into the cerebrospinal fluid
*Intratracheal* – directly into the trachea (wind pipe)
*Intraperitoneal* – injected into the membrane which lines the wall of the abdominal cavity.

If you are wondering what happened to putting substances into the eyes of animals the answer is that there is a separate page altogether for this which is benignly titled "Ocular Development Services".[22] Included here we find "ocular toxicology" and twenty-seven other options plus the opportunity of watching a presentation by a Convance scientist"...discussing Species Selection for Ocular Studies". And if we still want more we can also listen to some podcasts.[23]

The Charles River company also sets out its stall in a similar way saying:

> Charles River leads the industry in the fields of developmental and reproductive toxicology, ocular research, inhalation toxicology, infusion toxicology, immunotoxicology, phototoxicology, bone research and other specialty toxicological assessments.[24]

It displays a sidebar with six of these fields, ready to be clicked on for further information. At the end of the final paragraph and veering into the utterly obscene, it says in large type, "You might also be interested in..." and offers "inhalation toxicology", "infusion toxicology", "musculoskeletal toxicology" and "neurotoxicology" for the reader's further indulgence.[25] Presumably if you are interested in blinding rabbits you might also be interested in poisoning cats by intravenous infusion.

The company offers under its ocular services a "Model of Retinal Degeneration and Neuroprotection" explaining:

> Charles River offers a blue light exposure model that induces retinal damage and cell death to be used as a screen for investigating potential neuroprotective properties of new chemical or biological entities (NCEs/NBEs) prior to subsequent nonclinical testing.[26]

Perhaps this is a little unclear but a technical sheet is also available which explains it in more detail. Essentially albino rodents are blinded using a blue light source.[27] This may be over a longer or shorter period of time and various examinations are made to see if substances under test have managed to prove protective and healing. Tests are made by, for example, looking at the electrical impulses sent from the retina (electroretinograms) and by examining, microscopically, stained sections (thin slices) of the eyes.[28]

Behind this online shopping experience, behind each of these categories, lies unimaginable misery. Hours, weeks, months or more of agony and fear followed by death. Some religions have their hells but so does science and we know for sure that this one exists; it is happening now and it is advertised on the internet.

## Do it yourself

Some companies concentrate on selling equipment to enable experimenters to carry out their own experiments on animals. Such essential supplies go from cages and food right through to specialised surgical and restraint equipment. For example, a company named World Precision Instruments offers a Micro Drill for Surgical Applications and informs the reader:

> Animal researchers use a micro drill for making holes in bone or teeth during small animal surgery. Our micro drill can also be mounted in a stereotaxic frame.[29]

The stereotaxic frame is a device for holding the animal immobile while procedures are carried out upon them. The company warns that the drill is not "certified for use on humans."

This market place is surprisingly big but the website *LabAnimal* will help you to find what you are seeking and says:

> Welcome to Lab Animal's Buyers' Guide. This is your guide to the lab animal science marketplace, the most comprehensive database of suppliers, products and services in laboratory animal care.[30]

The term "animal care" seems to be stretching things a bit as a description for this sordid trade but the site lists 551 suppliers from various countries and even offers a monthly journal, unsurprisingly called "Lab Animal".

The discourses we have fleetingly looked at in this chapter legitimise the practice of animal experimentation as a business to the point where it is understood as a natural and commendable, moneymaking enterprise. They hang a sign over the door with the lie that no animals are really hurt and this is just business. Trust us, we know what we are doing and it is in everyone's best interests. The discourses of capitalism and science are woven together, co creating an ideology which claims that animals are both tools for science and commodities for sale.

## Looking back

A little later, we will go on to consider the current debate around animal testing and what it tells us, but I think it is helpful to consider how we got where we are and to look at a time when the vivisection debate was a real headline grabber. In the next couple of chapters, we will meet heroic women, protesting workers and the disputes which raged around vivisection at the turn of the 19th century. This story highlights, amongst other things, the nature of animal liberation as an intersectional struggle, the effects of power and the varieties of its victims and rehearses many of the arguments we still hear today.

## CHAPTER 13

# Scientific victims and sexual fantasies

*The animal rights movement is a part of, not opposed to, the human rights movement. Attempts to dismiss it as anti human are mere rhetoric.*

Tom Regan[1]

## History of animal experiments

VIVISECTION HAS BEEN practised since antiquity. It was carried out by Alcmaeon of Croton (6th–5th century BCE), Aristotle, Diocles, Praxagoras (4th century BCE), Erasistratus, and Herophilus (4th–3rd century BCE) although it is perhaps with Galen of Pergamon who lived in the 2nd–3rd century and was a prolific experimenter and recorder of investigations that we mark the real start of animal experimentation.[2] However, Galen's practice fell into disuse relatively shortly after his death, being replaced notably by the Empiric school who believed that vivisection as well as the dissection of human bodies was cruel, wrong and useless.[3]

The vivisectors of those early times interpreted their findings as researchers still do today which is through the lens of how they understand the world to be – through their theories about how the world works. So, this was not science as we understand it today but we would recognise it as vivisection.

In the 16th century the practice re-emerged, notably with the anatomist Vesalius who carried out the illegal dissection of human bodies but also used the vivisection of animals as a teaching method.[4] Experiments on animals continued into the 17th century as the "Age of Enlightenment" gathered pace. Some scientists drew not only on their contemporary understanding of science in order to explain what they observed but also used Descartes' picture of animals as machines in order to justify the ethics of their methods. This justification, while convenient, might have been misrepresenting Descartes to some extent because he did see animals with a degree of compassion and as being able, given the "right organ", to experience pain and that they could show "fear, anger, hope or joy".[5] However the claim that animals do not suffer pain but only display pain-related behaviour is one which still lingers with us today.

Animals were still on the same moral footing as they had been in Ancient Greece and this also applied to some humans as well. Nuno Franco points out:

> While the Enlightenment marked the beginning of the departure from Christian theocentrism, in the new anthropocentric view, animals continued to have no moral

standing on their own. In perspective, it should be noted this was a time in which the slave market thrived and women were seen as inferior.[6]

In France, the physiologist Magendie (1783–1855) became one of the best-known vivisectionists who was admired by some for his work but also had a reputation for imposing terrible suffering upon his experimental subjects. This drew criticism even from supporters of vivisection.

> His public presentations became the most notorious, particularly one he performed in England when he dissected a dog's facial nerves while the animal was nailed down by each paw, and was left overnight for further dissection the following day.[7]

Magendie performed his vivisections without anaesthesia or analgesia even when these were available to him and his victims would be left to suffer for hours or given to medical students to carry out their own investigations once he had finished.[8] It is a sobering thought that a man could practise such pathological cruelty on a routine basis yet still hold high academic office with all that this responsibility entails.

Vivisection around that time was frequently carried out for group teaching and public interest. Descriptions could be vivid and Conner describes how in 1847 Horace Nelson, a lecturer at the Montreal School of Medicine and Surgery in Canada, along with fellow professionals, an artist and a group of medical students, investigated anaesthesia on a dog.[9] After a few minutes, the dog was anaesthetised and:

> Nelson then removed one of the dog's ears, made an incision from a hind leg to its neck, partially flayed it and finally amputated a foreleg.[10]

But he was interrupted in his demonstration and went off to see a patient, returning over half an hour later by which time the anaesthetic had worn off. It is difficult to imagine what type of state the poor animal was in but Nelson continued with his vivisection and removed the remaining ear with the dog crying and howling. This was to show that the dog was no longer "asleep". He then strangled the animal.[11]

A few days later he managed to get another dog and went on to "prove conclusively" the effects of anaesthesia. Nelson's report of this demonstration is tense and dramatic, evoking a feeling of actually being in the room.[12] To start with, the dog was anaesthetised and completely flayed. Then Nelson reports he:

> ...passed over the quivering flesh a poker heated to whiteness. Several deep incisions were made into the muscles of the back. The right leg was entirely separated from the body excepting the vessels and nerves and I once more applied to poker to staunch the bleeding of several small arteries; not a moan was heard, not the least starting of a nerve was perceptible; the flesh smoked and the iron hissed. By means of a crucial incision, I laid open the abdominal cavity, and took out on the table the mass of intestines; my students had then the advantage of a demonstration of the peristatic motion of those organs, and I could observe the rising and falling of the diaphragm assisting most powerfully the respiratory act. The intestines were cut through in different places, the liver and spleen torn and wounded, every step followed by the application of the heated

poker. Finally the thorax was laid open, several of the ribs forcibly fractured, and the intercostal muscles lacerated.[13]

The vivisection lasted around forty-five minutes and then this grotesquely mutilated dog was allowed to regain consciousness. He struggled to lick his many wounds but was so weak with blood loss and his terrible injuries that he fell back on to the table exhausted. The experiment was brought to an end by his being strangled.[14]

This is a picture of absolute horror, something of which the experimenter himself seems very aware when he refers to "these cruel and lengthy experiments".[15] But as Connor notes, in some ways these descriptions are unlike anything we would read today.[16] They offer an intense rendition of what actually took place and we have a feeling of what it is like being there as "the flesh smoked and the iron hissed". Nelson clearly says that it is he who is doing this, using the pronoun, I, repeatedly. As such, the account is so very different from the self censored, agentless and sanitised reports we find in today's literature.

## Claude Bernard

In the middle of the 19th century Claude Bernard (1813–1878) appears on the scene. He is an aspiring playwright who has worked as an assistant to the physiologist Magendie for ten years at the College de France and who will have a momentous influence on the status of vivisection and animal experimentation in the years to come.[17] In his book, *An Introduction to Experimental Medicine* he makes this justification for vivisection:

> Have we the right to make experiments on animals and vivisect?...I think we have this right, wholly and absolutely. It would be strange indeed if we recognized man's right to make use of animals in every walk of life, for domestic service, for food, and then forbade him to make use of them for his own instruction in one of the sciences most useful to humanity. No hesitation is possible; the science of life can be established only through experiment, and we can save living beings from death only after sacrificing others. Experiments must be made either on man or on animals.[18]

In these few words from over one hundred and fifty years ago, he confirms the ideology which is still with us today, of the right to use animals for human purposes, including animal experimentation. But additionally, makes the crucial claim that only through experiment can the "science of life" be understood. This idea, which prioritises laboratory experimentation on animals over other forms of gaining knowledge eventually takes a strangle hold on scientific and popular thinking, which is as suffocating today as it has ever been.

It is claimed that Bernard was a rigorous scientist although his experiments were often gruesome and cruel, such as cutting open animals who were paralysed by curare or "cooking" them alive in ovens.[19] His personal life was a disaster. His wife left him, taking their two daughters with her, who would grow up to hate him and she became an antivivisectionist and opened rescue shelters for dogs.[20]

Although vivisection was popular with some sections of the medical and scientific establishment not everyone was cheerleading it – not by a long way and if the practitioners thought they would be left to continue their experiments without opposition they were seriously mistaken. But to really understand the vivisection debate in the 19th and early 20th century and the clashes it produced, particularly in Britain, we need to look at the social and economic conditions which prevailed at that time.[21] We will also see, as this story unfolds, how the treatment of women, working people and the poor in so many ways echoes our treatment of animals or what we today recognise as the intersectional nature of the struggle for animal liberation.

## Poverty and power

For the poor in Britain, living and working conditions were dreadful. Over years many families had lost access to land owing to the enclosures acts and had been forced to migrate to large centres in a desperate attempt to survive:

> Between 1750 and 1850 alone parliament passed about 4,000 individual enclosures acts, each transferring a single piece of land out of common ownership and into the ownership of farmers and landowners.[22]

Even today, "...6,000 landowners own some 40 m of Britain's 60 m acres of land, and... 70% of the land is owned by 1% of the population." [23] Conditions in the cities were appalling with crowded, damp accommodation, poor sanitation, open sewers, contaminated drinking water and scarce food of variable quality. It is hardly surprising that diseases such as typhoid, cholera, tuberculosis and typhus were rampant as well as disorders associated with poor nutrition. In the industrial towns and cities life expectancy was low, working conditions severely exploitive and protection for workers practically non-existent.

Informal jobs supplied a lifeline for some but they were often unpleasant. There were coal heavers, cress sellers and scavengers; bone grubbers who searched the streets and bins for any rags, bones, bits of metal and other assorted items which might be sold or eaten; pure finders who collected dog faeces and sold them to the tanneries and toshers who worked down the sewers looking for coins or any interesting items which had been washed or flushed underground and might be sold.[24] There was a great deal of prostitution, much of it a desperate survival strategy, allowing for the purchase of food, fuel or other essentials. Edwards suggests that in 1850's Liverpool, there would have been around 10 000 prostitutes and claims that prostitution would have made a significant contribution to the economy of the city.[25] Both women and men acted as prostitutes with the term used to describe them both as "gay".[26] William Thomas Stead, editor and investigative journalist, writing about London, exposed one of the great scourges of the time, child prostitution, which was an industry in itself.[27]

For the poor, margins were very fine and no work meant the real prospect of starvation. If there was work available it often required very long hours and started early in life.

Children worked in factories, mills, coal mines and many other places and they worked long days, often being beaten for falling asleep at their jobs. But they were extremely cheap labour giving the owners greater profits. Scavengers as young as four years old would be expected to gather the cotton waste which collected beneath the machinery in the mills – a particularly dangerous task with flying mechanisms hammering away just centimetres from small limbs, fingers and heads. Accidents were common in the workplace resulting in terrible injuries or death. Some children were even sold to factory or mill owners by parents in the hope that this would ease the burden on the family but also as a way the child might survive the grinding poverty into which they had been born.

Spencer writes that the Inspector of Recruiting had difficulty finding enough suitable men to fight in the Anglo–Boer War (South African War) and the Director General of the Army Medical Service, Sir William Taylor on looking into this, "found men with weak hearts, inadequate sight and hearing, deformities and bad teeth" and informed parliament of this dire situation.[28] In 1883 the government had reduced the minimum height for recruits from 5 ft 6 ins to 5 ft 3 ins but it was reduced even further, this time to 5 feet.[29] Malnutrition was widespread in the country with people living close to starvation and many of these men with stunted growth and deformities, having grown up in such conditions, would have been the victims of that dire situation.

But things had started to improve somewhat during the 19th century and trade unions were legalised in 1824, although not necessarily well tolerated by employers and there was also an increased interest by the authorities in public health. But no women had the right to vote and up to 1884 only thirty percent of men had suffrage – a privilege dependent upon having wealth and property. This meant that only fifteen percent of the total adult population could vote. Later the percentage of men with the vote was increased to 60% although this was still related to the ownership of property. So at the start of the 20th century, all women and forty percent of adult males were still denied voting rights giving a total of seventy percent of the population without suffrage. The government of Britain with its great colonial empire was voted in from a pool of only fifteen percent and then later, thirty percent of the adult population, all of whom were male and all of whom were wealthy. To be poor or female – or worse, both, meant a person had no political influence, no economic influence and negligible social power.

In 1881 the Liverpool Medical Officer for Health, was pleased to announce that the average age of death of a city female had increased to twenty seven point three years, a big improvement from the 1840s when it had been only twenty three.[30] Formal education for the poor was scanty. For some there was the possibility of schooling if the family had any extra pennies to pay for it but for those families with nothing, education would be informal. The Ragged Schools movement worked to enrol the children of families who had no chance of paying – the children whose clothes were rags, and their schools were often taught by volunteer teachers. From around 1870 free primary education began to be available.

Men from well-off families would receive an education while the women would likely have some education, probably with a governess but this might be quite limited and directed more towards literature and home-making skills such as sewing and embroidery.

While illness affected all sectors of society the greatest burden fell upon the poor. Hospitals were able to help to some degree and a number of these were attached to universities and functioned as teaching hospitals. Anaesthetics were coming into more general use but surgery was still extremely hazardous and mortality rates were high.

## Rough treatment

But not all hospitals treated their patients well. Women, especially working-class women, often endured terrible degradation in teaching hospitals. For gynaecological examination they would be strapped to a board with their feet in stirrups often with a group of male medical students standing around watching the examination. It was taken for granted by some doctors that this exposure and the unpleasant comments which would be made would not be a problem for poor women as they were used to a rough life.[31]

> Frances Power Cobbe, who was both a feminist theoretician and the most prominent female antivivisectionist in late nineteenth-century Britain, decried the casual disregard hospital doctors had for the modesty of the "shame-tortured woman" patient, claiming that "decent women, afflicted with some of the most dreadful diseases of humanity, find in these so-called charitable institutions, moral tortures of outraged modesty added to their bodily anguish."[32]

It was also feared by some, especially the poor, that in teaching hospitals poverty-stricken patients might be used for experiments and in some cases, even though an anaesthetic was available, it was not used during operations. The parallel between vivisection and the treatment of the poor was not lost on Dr Anna Kingsford, one of the few female doctors of the time, who writes:

> Paupers are thus classed with animals as fitting subjects for painful experiment. And since no regard is shown for the feelings of either, it is not surprising that the use of anaesthetics for the benefit of the patient is wholly rejected. Even the excruciating operation of cautery with a red-hot iron is performed without the alleviation of an anaesthetic.[33]

Kingsford also describes the treatment of a woman, a pauper, who is dying of consumption and is lying desperately weak and unconscious in her hospital bed. If left alone she will die in a state of unconsciousness, but she is used by the physician as an experimental subject.

> Bending over her, the physician shouts at her to make her open her eyes. She tries in vain to obey him. Taking a pin from his coat, he thrusts it into the under surface of each eye lid. She utters a cry and he withdraws the pin, saying "You feel that do you? Why don't you open your eyes then?" He then pricks her hands and legs, each puncture eliciting a faint cry and effort at resistance.[34]

He eventually gets her up into a sitting position although she is totally unable to do this for herself.

Elizabeth Blackwell, another of the few female doctors of the time, writes:

> ...vivisection tends to make us less scrupulous in our treatment of the sick and helpless poor. It increases that disposition to regard the poor as "clinical material" which has become, alas! not without reason, a widespread reproach to many of the young members of our most honourable and merciful profession.[35]

The young author, W. Somerset Maugham, who was employed as an obstetric clerk in the 1890s seems to have absorbed the stereotyping of poor women as rough living and therefore being in less need of sympathetic care. He also suggests a scientific reason why women might react differently to pain than men and conveniently observes in his *Notebook*, "If women exhibit less emotion at pain, it does not prove that they bear it better but rather that they feel it less."[36]

## Sex and nonsense

Not only were women seen as less intelligent than men, it was almost as if they were unfinished men and there was even a view that the clitoris and hymen were parts of an undeveloped penis.[37] The imagined shortcomings of women also meant that very few had the opportunity to be trained in medicine and even those who did faced barriers. Elizabeth Blackwell found that when she joined St Bartholomew's Hospital in London, she was allowed to work in any area of the hospital except one – the section dealing with women's diseases. This was because, it was claimed, the discipline needed the less excitable temperament of the male for successful treatment.[38]

While it was expected that men would be interested in sex, interest shown by women was to be frowned upon and might be seen as an aberration. Kathryn Hughes explains about women, sex and marriage.

> At the same time, a young girl was not expected to focus too obviously on finding a husband. Being "forward" in the company of men suggested a worrying sexual appetite. Women were assumed to desire marriage because it allowed them to become mothers rather than to pursue sexual or emotional satisfaction. One doctor, William Acton, famously declared that "The majority of women (happily for them) are not very much troubled with sexual feeling of any kind.[39]

As mentioned earlier, prostitution was very common, including child prostitution, and there was a sex trade in young women out of Britain to continental Europe. Figures for rape are difficult to find and, in any case, it is likely that many rapes were not reported. In addition, under a ruling from the 17th century made by Sir Mathew Hale, rape was not possible within marriage and so a woman could not be raped by her husband.

> The husband cannot be guilty of a rape committed by himself upon his lawful wife, for by their mutual matrimonial consent and the contract the wife hath given up herself in this kind unto her husband, which she cannot retract.[40]

This judgement was only overturned in 1991.

And one doctor of the time even maintained that child sexual abuse and the rape of women seldom even took place at all.

> Dr Lawson Tait, a prominent early gynaecologist, claimed in a medical textbook that positive clinical evidence discounted almost all accusations of sexual interference with children; he also used his professional authority to cast doubts on most claims of rape: "When a full-grown healthy woman makes a charge of a completely effected

assault against one man, the charge ought to be presumed to be false, unless the woman was first stupefied by drugs. I am perfectly satisfied that no man can effect a felonious purpose on a woman in possession of her senses without her consent."[41]

## Pornography, gynaecology and stables

During this time, the literacy rate was increasing and reading matter of all kinds was becoming more readily available. This included pornography. Victorian Britain, prudish, on the surface, had a growing pornography trade but unlike earlier portrayals of sexual romps much of it was taking on a darker, more oppressive aspect. According to Coral Lansbury, this newer abusive pornography has intersections with our treatment of animals. In these stories, women are restrained using a range of devices, controlled and whipped. She writes:

> And in Victorian pornography, women are "broken to the bit," to use the expression that John Cleland made popular in Fanny Hill (1750). The language of pornography is the language of the stable: women are made to "show their paces" and "present themselves" at the command of the riding master who flogs and seduces them into submission...[42]

And

> In a great many pornographic novels published between 1870 and 1910, women are repeatedly subdued and tied down so that they can be "mounted" more easily, and they always end up as grateful victims, trained to enjoy the whip and the straps, proud to provide pleasure to their masters.[43]

But something else was also happening in the literature of the time. Ruth Padel surveying the pornography of the era as well as more standard novels featuring women, describes how there was the appearance of women's voices including, significantly, the feminine narrator – a female "I".[44] Then into this flux, in 1877, comes the novel *Black Beauty* which is published just a few months before its author, Anna Sewell, dies at the age of fifty six. It is her only book and it is remarkable in many ways.

Sewell was born into a Quaker family and would no doubt have been aware of a range of social issues of the time. She would also have been encouraged to think for herself and act in a way which she believed she was called to act, whether this was popular or not. So, she wrote about what it was like to be owned by another, the cruelty and neglect that horses endured at the hands of men and such things as the check reign or bearing reign which was used to hold a horse's head up – a fashion of the time causing much pain, discomfort and harm to horses.[45]

The book describes the life of a horse; his carefree upbringing on a farm, getting sold from one owner to another and his treatment by them as well as the treatment meted out to other horses he knows. With the publication of *Black Beauty* there is a quiet but seismic shift. For the first time in an English language novel we have the animal "I" as the narrator, accompanying the reader into his being.[46] The full title of the book reads, *Black*

*Beauty: His grooms and companions. The Autobiography Of A Horse. Translated From The Original Equine, By Anna Sewell.* Yes, a book by a horse; what a courageously foolish and revolutionary idea. Sewell takes us on an expedition across that great anthropocentric chasm between species and into previously disregarded worlds, but in time many others would follow that track, making it into a highway. Exactly one hundred years later, Richard Adams published his story, *The Plague Dogs*, a satire about animal testing where two dogs who are used in experiments go on the run from the Animal Research, Scientific and Experimental facility or ARSE.

*Black Beauty* might not sound much like a book which would take the world by storm but it turned out to be hugely successful. Groups concerned about animal cruelty promoted it and thousands were distributed to horse handlers, drivers and schools. By 1923 the publisher would claim that it was the sixth bestselling English language book in the world.

But there are still other facets to this volume. Padel compares the story of Black Beauty to the standard pornographic style of the time and claims:

> But the shape she gave it, her language, and the variety of suffering her characters undergo reflect the patterns and recurrent themes of classic porn.[47]

Padel notes that the "breaking" of Black Beauty and the forcing of the bit into his mouth parallels a Victorian male fantasy of fellatio as in Cleland's *Fanny Hill*, although in this case the horse is full of revulsion at this invasion and violence.[48] Ginger, a friend of Beauty and a "spirited young mare" who is eventually destroyed by being ridden too hard by young men and ends her life wrecked and dying on the streets of London, also tells her story of being broken in.

The conversation with Black Beauty takes place as the two horses are relaxing in a meadow, but the scene she describes can be compared to a gang rape – her fear, helplessness and violation are palpable. Ginger says this:

> But when it came to breaking in, that was a bad time for me; several men came to catch me and when at last they closed me in at one corner of the field, one caught me by the forelock, another caught me by the nose and held it so tight I could hardly draw my breath; then another took my under jaw in his hard hand and wrenched my mouth open, and so by force they got on the halter and the bar into my mouth; then one dragged me along by the halter, another flogging behind, and this was the first experience I had of men's kindness; it was all force.[49]

The process of breaking Ginger's spirit is underway as she is kept confined in her stall and day after day taken out and made to run and run in circles until exhausted. Early one morning the old master's son, who Ginger says only thinks of her as "horseflesh", makes her run once again but later puts a saddle on her and a new type of bit in her mouth. She fights him and he uses his whip and spurs her on in an attempt to subdue her but she eventually throws him off. She is now exhausted, hurt and bleeding because of the whip and the spurs. The physical and mental domination which will cruelly define her life have been initiated, her world will never be the same again and she will never be free.

Sewell might not have read any of the pornography of her time, but despite being an invalid she was very active in social outreach work and would be well aware of the current values and practices in her society including its treatment of women, the poor and animals. Padel says that, "The animal story began, it almost seems, as anti porn; Black Beauty (1877), its great forerunner, reads almost as one of the great feminist texts".[50]

We do not know what Anna Sewell had in mind when she wrote *Black Beauty* and every great story is a unique entity with multiple influences woven into it and the potential for multiple interpretations. It is undoubtedly a vibrant protest against animal abuse but can also be read as opposition to the exploitation of the poor, to the horror of slavery and to the oppression of women. These do not have to be understood as either/or choices because in many ways the practices are very similar, being forms of domination and exploitation, drawing upon a hierarchical ideology of the world to motivate and justify the abuse inherent in them.

Lansbury notes that two of the recurring characters in the pornography of the time are the doctor who straps his patients down and uses all sorts of contraptions on them and the riding master who similarly controls his victims. The gynaecologist's rooms and the stable were popular settings for such stories. The apparatus used to exploit and abuse animals in vivisection and in other uses had parallels with the instrumentation of both.

In this powerful passage, opening with Jack the riding master violently "breaking in" Victoria, a young woman who he has trapped in a stable, Lansbury describes the abusive nature of some typical Victorian pornography.

> Screaming in protest, Victoria is first flogged and then sodomised by the riding master; she ends politely asking for more. It cannot be emphasized too strongly that this male fantasy was repeated endlessly in later Victorian pornography; what must horrify any sane reader is its lack of eroticism and its emphasis on cruelty. Straps, whips and ropes signify the victim's loss of freedom. All that is left for the young woman is to accept gratefully the domination of a man and learn to like it, just as Back Beauty must accept the bit without complaining for, "it must be so". As Ginger says: "Men are strongest, and if they are cruel and have no feeling, there is nothing that we can do, but just bear it – bear it on and on to the end".[51]

This last sentence is deeply poignant, reflecting the unrelenting misery we cause to the powerless in so many ways and the stoic nature with which our innocent victims bear their suffering...on and on to the end.

With this brief backdrop, we now move on to the great debate which raged around vivisection; to the workers, the mad women and one victim of vivisection who activists made certain would never be forgotten.

## CHAPTER 14

# Mad women and the brown dog

*What I fear most is power with impunity. I fear abuse of power, and the power to abuse.*

Isabel Allende[1]

## The Great Debate

As VIVISECTION GREW so did opposition and it came from a variety of sources including such notables as Voltaire (1694–1778), Jean-Jacques Rousseau (1712–1778), Jeremy Bentham (1748–1832) and Arthur Schopenhauer (1788–1860), as well as various religious groups including Quakers and even from Queen Victoria.[2,3] Claude Bernard records a visit by a Quaker, name unknown, to Magendie sometime in the 1840s to challenge him about vivisection. The Quaker sets out his argument in this way.

> Thou performest experiments on living animals. I come to thee to demand of thee by what right thou actest thus and to tell thee that thou must desist from these experiments, because thou hast not the right to cause animals to die or make them suffer, and because thou settest in this way a bad example and also accustomest thyself to cruelty.[4]

The Quaker asks about rights and by what authority does Magendie take the lives of animals and cause them to suffer. This is still a central question – by what right, on what authority, do we do these things? According to Bernard's account, Magendie sets aside what he is doing and engages in a discussion where he defends vivisection and explains:

> "It is necessary," he replied to the Quaker, "to place yourself at another point of view in order to judge experiments on living animals. It is certain that if they did not have for their aim and their result the service of humanity, they might be taxed with cruelty. But the physiologist who is moved by the tiiought [sic] of making a discovery useful to medicine, and consequently to his fellow man, does not merit such a reproach.[5]

The experiments are not cruelty, according to Magendie, because they are done for a good reason, which is to help humans. It is the aim which justifies the means and the aim is to help humans.

> "War," continued M. Magendie, "would itself be a barbarous cruelty, if one did not consider its aim and its result for humanity. But what one can condemn is perhaps the chase, for then animals are caused to suffer and are killed merely for pleasure."

***[sic] certainly," interrupted the Quaker, "I condemn war and hunting just as much as I condemn experiments on living animals. In all these cases man gives himself rights which he has not got; that is what I wish to prove and I am traveling in order to cause to disappear from the world these three things, war, hunting and experiments on living animals."

Magendie says that hunting for pleasure might be seen as wrong, a position with which the Quaker agrees, but he goes on to say that in undertaking war, hunting and experimentation "man gives himself rights which he has not got." Some Quakers in the late 19th century opposed vivisection because they maintained it conflicted with the Peace Testimony of the Society of Friends and it was also seen as a moral disease as were slavery and war.[6] Barnard sums up the meeting in this way:

> Without doubt the Quaker was not convinced by M. Magendie, and no more was M. Magendie by the Quaker.[7]

These excerpts encapsulate what are still today two of the major opposing positions concerning animal experimentation. The Quaker claims that we have no right to do such things to others while Magendie draws on an hierarchical ideology which places humans above other animals, and claims that because the aim is to benefit humanity, that in itself is sufficient justification.

## A growing force

The antivivisection movement was no blip on the radar of history but a movement of substantial weight with serious activists in its ranks. Britain was something of a hotbed of resistance in the 19th and early 20th centuries with a cast of fascinating characters. This is what a few of the better known ones had to say:

> Charles Dickens, novelist (1812–1870): "The necessity for these experiments I dispute. Man has no right to gratify an idle and purposeless curiosity through the practice of cruelty."

> Robert Browning, poet (1812–1889): "I despise and abhor the pleas on behalf of that infamous practice, vivisection… I would rather submit to the worst of deaths, so far as pain goes, than have a single dog or cat tortured to death on the pretense of sparing me a twinge or two."

> Lewis Carroll, mathematician and author of *Alice in Wonderland* (1832–1898): "Forbid the day when vivisection shall be practiced in every college and school, and when the man of science, looking forth over a world which will then own no other sway than his, shall exult in the thought that he had made of this fair earth, if not a heaven for man, at least a hell for animals."[8]

The resistance was organised, vocal, influential and drew together activists who were also deeply committed to other social change movements. The debate provoked widespread public interest.

The upsurge of animal research in Britain was accompanied by an intensification of the antivivisectionist struggle. In 1875, the first animal protection society with the specific aim of abolishing animal experiments was founded: the Victoria Street Society for the Protection of Animals Liable to Vivisection (later known as the National Anti-Vivisection Society), led by Irish feminist, suffragist, and animal advocate Frances Power Cobbe (1822–1904). Vivisection became a matter of public debate, only matched in Great Britain that century by the controversy around the 1859 publication of Charles Darwin's (1809–1882) On the Origin of Species...[9]

Frances Power Cobbe is a very interesting woman with the "Power" in her name being particularly appropriate. She was educated at home except for two years of expensive schooling which, "she regarded as an interruption to her education and a complete waste of time."[10] She was a feminist, advocated for women's suffrage, was concerned about victims of marital abuse and wrote a pamphlet titled, *Wife Torture in England*; she worked for better care for delinquent girls, wrote articles and pamphlets on diverse subjects, was an antivivisectionist, a powerful speaker and a lesbian.

The Society for the Protection of Animals Liable to Vivisection, which she started, included in its membership such well known personalities as Charles Dickens, Wilkie Collins, Robert Browning, Benjamin Jowett, Mathew Arnold, Charles Kingsley and John Stuart Mill along with vice presidents Thomas Carlyle and Cardinal Manning and the president, the Earl of Shaftsbury.[11] However, it is worth bearing in mind that it was women who made up the bulk of the opposition to vivisection despite the fact that they had few opportunities for personal or professional development in life at this time.

## Border skirmishes

To get an idea of the atmosphere around the vivisection debate we can have a look at a few of the clashes which took place. Charles Richet (1850–1935) the famous French physiologist became embroiled in the defence of vivisection by writing a long essay in which he advanced the argument that animals do not suffer in the same way as humans and that in any case analgesia and anaesthesia were widely used so in fact the animals did not suffer at all. As part of his argument Richet described a hierarchy of beings and claimed that the pursuit of scientific knowledge is a higher purpose for which sacrifices needed to be made – at least by some. However, he got himself into deep trouble when he further elucidated his argument. Michael Finn reports that:

> In this part of his essay as well, he appears almost to equate non-Europeans to the animals that he calls degraded in the series of beings. Searching for an example to parallel and support his argument for ends justifying means, he asks, "What if a few hundred or thousand obscure coolies die digging the Panama canal?" Their loss is simply a sacrifice for a higher purpose."[12]

He was heavily challenged concerning his account of vivisection by a number of people and Anna Kingsford was one who did not agree with his views. She had qualified from the Faculte de Medicine of Paris in 1880, was said to be "wilful but stunningly beautiful" and submitted her thesis on the subject of vegetarianism. Being well aware of the methods of Claude Bernard she took issue with Richet.[13, 14]

> Kingsford responded to Richet's arguments by attacking his claim of scientific supremacy, the claims about anaesthesia and by describing horrific experiments "about breaking animals' limbs and about Bernard's special oven where he conducted burn experiments by roasting large dogs alive."[15]

She not only challenged the factual claims of Richet's but also his ideological claim regarding the supremacy of science.

In his other contemplations, Richet looked forward to the continuing reduction in the numbers of wild animals in Africa and their eventual disappearance as well as the day when barbarism there would be replaced by civilisation and it could become like France. He went on to be awarded the Nobel prize for his work in physiology.

Another very interesting woman of this time is Marie Hout who was a poet, writer and an outstanding activist. In October 1892 she gave a speech to the Société de Géographie calling for women to be allowed to have the choice of whether or not they should become pregnant – a radical suggestion to be sure and one which undeniably confirmed her feminist credentials.

She fiercely opposed animal cruelty and on one occasion reportedly interrupted a lecture by Luis Pasteur at the Sorbonne because he experimented on dogs. She also beat the successor to Claud Bernard over the head with an umbrella because he had vivisected a monkey and the same weapon was used on a workman who, while digging a ditch, had threatened to use his pick axe to hurt a cat. This time Hout ended up at the police station.[16, 17] She is also reported to have helped a Swedish anarchist to attack two matadors during a French bullfight.

Her close friend was the novelist Rachilde (Marguerite Vallette-Eymery) another exceptional character, who had at one time actually worked in a laboratory where vivisection was carried out. Rachilde had been extremely upset by what took place and had smashed up the laboratory and taken the mice who were being used in experiments with her as she left.[18] On another occasion, during a debate, she had pierced a doctor's ear with a hatpin apparently in an effort to make a point about sensitivity.

In the final decades of the 19th century and early years of the 20th, women were asserting themselves and attempting to employ their talents, but it would still not be until 1928 that all women and all men would be given the vote in Britain. Women's growing power was often resented and questioned – not surprisingly by many men. The world of Western Europe and the US was male, elitist, capitalist and human centred; it was viewed through men's eyes and ideologies and with their power they defined much of its reality. These ideologies found expression in the physical world, in colonialism, the exploitation of the poor and the treatment of women, other nationalities and animals. Some of these attitudes are glaringly obvious when it comes to so called "women's disorders" of that time.

## The sick sex?

The control and domination of women by men produced significant mental and physical damage to women. In a section titled "The Hysterical Female" the London Asylum website writes this about those pressures.

> With so little power, control, and independence, depression, anxiety, and stress were common among Victorian women struggling to cope with a static existence under the thumb of strict gender ideals and unyielding patriarchy.[19]

As the medical and scientific establishment was almost completely male, women's bodies and experiences were foreign to it and it seems that women were continually compared, consciously or unconsciously, by many to some ideal male. Maleness was the benchmark and women naturally fell short. This is not to say that women were despised but just that they were other than men and when it came to the really important things, not really as good.

And when their strange disorders arose, and it seems there were many of these, women were examined, diagnosed and fixed by the male medical hierarchy. This meant that women were treated for a whole range of "complaints" which had imaginary causes and objectionable remedies, but this was the science of the day. One popular remedy for a range of disorders was the removal of the ovaries.

> ...the removal of normal ovaries, known as Battey's Operation – began in 1872 and became the fashionable treatment of menstrual madness, neurasthenia, nymphomania, masturbation and all cases of insanity. This practice was supported by distinguished gynecologists and psychiatrists, becoming one of the great medical scandals of the 19th century.[20]

In the latter part of the same century, Isaac Baker Brown, a respected doctor and Fellow of the College of Surgeons, was advancing the idea that clitoridectomy could help cure a range of women's disorders. He maintained that their problems were caused by "Hypertrophy and Irritation of the Clitoris" in other words, masturbation, which seems to have got the blame for many things around that time.[21] The usual cure for such a malady was "...leeches to the labia, cold baths and a gentle diet..."[22] However, Brown in his book *On the Curability of Certain Forms of Insanity, Epilepsy, Catalepsy and Hysteria in Females* claimed that the operation he carried out, which was complete excision of the clitoris, was the answer to these maladies in women.[23] In his book he described the many patients he had treated.

His enthusiasm was not shared by a number of his colleagues and he was eventually expelled from the Obstetrical Society of London and his clinic closed down, although it is claimed that this actually had more to do with the issue of consent for the operation and who should give it – father, husband or the woman herself, rather than any technical arguments or the welfare of women.[24] The operation was also frowned upon in the United States although it was carried out there as late as the 1890s.[25]

Another disorder which could supposedly display a whole diverse compendium of symptoms was known as hysteria and this was believed to arise from the uterus or womb.

> hysteria (n.)... nervous disease, 1801, coined in medical Latin as an abstract noun from Greek hystera "womb," from PIE [Proto-Indo-European] *udtero-, variant of *udero-

"abdomen, womb, stomach" (see uterus). Originally defined as a neurotic condition peculiar to women and thought to be caused by a dysfunction of the uterus.[26]

Here we have what we would normally describe as psychiatric or neurological symptoms, if in many cases we can even call them symptoms at all, being attributed to a problem with the uterus. This was a very popular scientific theory of the day and the reason men did not get hysteria was simple – they did not have a uterus. Observation, interpretation, explanation and treatment would be made through the lens of patriarchal science. Anne Scott describes one such interpretation.

> Henry Maudsley, for example, used Darwinian theory to argue that women were, by nature, close to hysteria, and that their overexpenditure of energy on intellectual or competitive activities could bring about a nervous breakdown.[27]

Thinking and competing were clearly not sensible things for women to do.

It seems the capability of the uterus to cause difficulties could hardly be overestimated and here is an account of the terrible symptoms it might cause as well as the problems of treatment faced by those who sought to cure the afflicted. It is a text which probably tells us a great deal more about ideology than about its subject – uteromania.

> I dread to treat no form of insanity more than utromania, for of all derangements it is the most violent and persistent, and yet it is a very common disorder … Tilt the [womb] a little forward [in the pelvis] – introvert it, and immediately the patient forsakes her home, embraces some strange and ultra ism – Mormonism, Mesmerism, Fourierism, Socialism, oftener Spiritualism. She becomes possessed of the idea that she has some startling mission in the world. She forsakes her home, her children, and her duty, to mount the rostrum and proclaim the peculiar virtues of free-love, elective affinity, or the reincarnation of souls…They entertain bitter and unnatural dislike for everything which has helped to make their lives happy, useful and pure. They trample upon the sacredness of their marriage relations and despise their religious obligations. They regard their husbands as tyrants bent on their enslavement, and they are likely to forsake their homes for positions of public trust for which they are unfitted.[28]

## Mad women

It was this idea of women having peculiar ailments which would be employed as a new weapon for attacking the opposition to vivisection. As things stood, antivivisectionists accused the vivisectors of cruelty and torture but were in turn portrayed by vivisectors and their supporters as being cranks, perverts, impudent ignoramuses, fanatics and mentally disturbed with the vivisectors looking upon themselves as rational men.[29] The new form of attack would add an extra dimension to this conflict.

In the United States, Charles Loomis Dana, the President of the American Neurological Institute and defender of vivisection wrote in a paper in 1909, about the existence of a condition he named zoophil-psychosis.[30] Now, zoophily was a term already known and can be described as meaning love for animals although at this time its use actually had much broader implications, relating to creating a better and fairer world for all.

> The early antivivisectionists used the term "zoophily" to describe the ethical premise upon which the movement was based. Implying more than simply love for animals, zoophily conveyed the reformers' conviction that the spread of mercy was the great cause of civilization. To them, cruelty – the opposite of mercy– had take [sic] hold of medical science.[31]

It is very clear that caring for the interests of animals was part of a wider vision and is what we today might understand as a form of intersectionality. The sentiments of a kinder world for all are also echoed in what came to be the antivivisectionist hymn known as The Bells of Mercy.

But Dana's concept of zoophile-psychosis is something very different and describes a disorder in which there is an "excessive" care for animals as exhibited by antivivisectionists and others. He offered three examples to illuminate his diagnosis.

The first was a man who had developed a great devotion to horses and could not bear to see them mistreated which meant he did not want to go into the city any more. The doctor was able to discuss his "obsession" with him and over the years the patient apparently managed to become a great deal better – whatever that means.

The second example concerns a woman, and Dana apparently finds this case both more difficult as well as somewhat different. The woman was about forty years of age, childless and had developed an affection for cats. She looked after sick cats and would take them into her house and try to help them. It was felt that she neglected her family duties and drove her husband to distraction. Unlike his male patient, Dana refused to treat her but incredibly recommended surgery instead and that she should seek treatment from a gynaecologist. He understood her concern for animals as a form of laziness claiming it is easier to nurse a sick dog or cat than "nurse the sick, provide thoughtfully for the poor, or keep watch over the temper and make a household comfortable."[32]

In his third example of this disorder Dana, rather astonishingly, examines a character from fiction, a young man from Joseph Conrad's novel *The Secret Agent* which was published in 1907.[33] He cites an episode in the story where Stevie, who has mental development problems, jumps down from a moving cab and protests because the driver is lashing the horses. Describing this, Lori Kelly notes how Dana conflates mental disorder with antivivisection sympathies:

> In his paper, Dana is at pains to point out that Stevie's reckless action is not only a manifestation of a mental disease, it is also a trait that is "not uncommon in mentally defective children." Dana thus effectually equates the efforts of those such as the antivivisectionists, whom many in the medical establishment viewed as animal extremists and quacks, with individuals lacking in mental capacity.[34]

The existence of zoophile-psychosis meant that opposing vivisection could be explained as being due to a disorder found mainly in women and mentally challenged children. It was therefore, not a moral, scientific or religious position to be answered but a symptom to be treated. Unsurprisingly, the vivisectionists and their supporters loved this and one editor of the *New York Times* seemed to think it explained and condemned antivivisection activities very satisfactorily. Various learned folk also joined in to support the cause, including Fredric S Lee who testified about the disorder before the New York legislature, and James E Wabasse who in his own text book describing how to carry out vivisection discussed zoophile-psychosis in his concluding chapter. He even introduced a claim by a German scientist that there are two types of women, the mother type and the prostitute type and those who had a great love for animals fell into the latter category.

In France it was a similar story. Finn records how Dr Valentin Magnan claimed that antivivisectionists suffer from a form of hereditary madness and offered a few case studies to support his thesis including one of a woman, a vegetarian, who visits slaughterhouses to try to stop the killing of animals.[35] And Magnan was not alone as Finn explains:

> Other doctors, such as Élie de Cyon, also espoused the madness argument, characterising prominent individuals such as Richard Wagner, who had written an anti-vivisectionist pamphlet, as a lunatic (Cyon, 1883: 13). Cyon notes that Protestant countries produce far more anti-vivisectionist agitation than Catholic France, and he then provides the explanation: "le catholicisme ouvre aux vieilles demoiselles exaltées un refuge dans ses couvents"[Catholicism opens to old ladies exalted a refuge in her convents" Google translation] (1883: 15). By contrast, English spinsters, with no such outlet, become spiritualists or get involved in fantastical charities.[36] (Translation inserted)

The accusation of suffering from a disorder if a person, especially a woman, was opposed to vivisection was so convenient it continued to be used as a form of abuse against antivivisectionists well into the 1920s. Buettinger observes:

> The concept of zoophile-psychosis combined neurological theory with the contempt men in scientific circles felt for the antivivisection movement. Zoophil-psychosis gave clinical credentials to the vivisectionists charge that criticism of medical science was a product of mental disorder...Dana claimed antivivisection sentiment sprang from flaws of the female mind and a mental malfunction in some males. For the vivisectionists of Dana's day his diagnosis was the preferred way to characterise the opposition.[37]

This process of literally doctoring the system, no doubt enabled women to see evermore clearly the power structures dominating themselves and other living beings. Women had connected the dots and powerful men, especially in science, did not want to look at the ugly picture it made. Women were experimental subjects in many circumstances including the quite benign sounding "hypnotisme experimental" which often involved doing more to women than simply hypnotising them:

> In France, the kind of triumphalism that surrounded the notion of experimental science preyed on certain feminists' sensibilities for a very special reason. Here was the irresistible machismo of the male scientist harnessed to a specialty that required subjects. It was not lost on feminists that the powerlessness and suffering inflicted on animals by the experimental vivisectionist had a parallel in the way females were treated by hysteria doctors who employed "hypnotisme expérimental".[38]

This background offers us some insights into the undercurrents swirling around at the time and with these the stage was set for events which in the early years of the 20th century would bring together diverse strands of resistance to oppressive power in a most unusual way. And the focal point of all this would be a small, brown, terrier dog.

## The Brown Dog

In 1902, two Swedish women, Louise Lind-af-Hageby (1878–1963) and Leisa K. Schartau (1876–1962), enrolled to study medicine at the London School of Medicine for Women, an institution which did not carry out vivisection.[39] They were activists who wanted to gain medical training in order to more effectively oppose the practice of vivisection at the Pasteur Institute in Paris "they had seen hundreds of animals dying in agony".[40] Unfortunately, the physiology part of their course was to be taught by University College London which did practise vivisection. So, when the time came, the women duly attended classes but diligently kept diaries and recorded what happened in the vivisection demonstrations.

In February 1903, they were present in the lecture theatre when a small brown terrier dog was brought in strapped onto a board. He was to be used for a vivisection demonstration but they noticed that the dog already had an existing abdominal scar suggesting he had been experimented upon previously and relatively recently. The dog's abdomen was cut open by Henry Starling of the Department of Physiology who was occupied examining him for about forty-five minutes. After this, the dog's wound was clamped shut and he was passed to Richard Bayliss from the same department who made a second incision to expose the salivary glands and continued to carry out other experiments (unsuccessfully) in that region. According to the two women there was lots of noise and laughter in the room from medical students. Tacium gives us more details on these events:

> The brown dog, likely a stray found wandering the streets of London, was first used in a dissection by Starling in December 1902, when he opened the dog's abdominal cavity and ligated the pancreatic duct. For the next two months, the dog lived in a cage and reportedly upset people with his continual howling. He was brought back to the lecture theatre in February 1903, during which he was strapped to the operating board and muzzled, according to standard procedure of the day. The experiment reportedly included a re-opening of the abdominal cavity, inspection of the ligation and exposure of the salivary glands, with an unsuccessful demonstration of the independence of salivary pressure from blood pressure.[41]

After the demonstration, the dog was killed.

The two women's report of these events and descriptions of other vivisections they had witnessed, were to be incorporated into a book they were writing and which would have the ingeniously worded title, *The Shambles of Science*. When they took the draft of their book to Stephen Coleridge, Honorary Secretary of the Antivivisection Society, for possible publication, he noted that a serious infringement of the 1876 Cruelty to Animals Act was described in its pages. The Act declared that an animal could not be used for vivisection and then re-used for a second such experiment.[42] In addition, the dog should have been anaesthetised and also was possibly killed by an unlicensed person.

But getting a prosecution would be very difficult plus there was also a statute of limitation on such offences so instead, Coleridge decided on a plan which would publicise both the cruelty of vivisection and the shortcomings of the current Act. At the annual meeting of the National Antivivisection Society (Jerome K. Jerome, Thomas Hardy and Rudyard Kipling sent their apologies) and in front of some two to three thousand people, he made a passionate speech, repeated the allegations made in the proposed book and accused the scientists of torture.[43] These accusations were duly reported in the press and questions were asked in the House of Commons. Bayliss demanded an apology and when this was not forthcoming, he sued Coleridge for libel, which is what Coleridge had expected would happen anyway. *The Shambles of Science* was published and the case duly went to court.

The court sat in November 1903 and the case attracted a huge amount of interest. The two women would state that they saw the dog before the vivisection and that it was not anaesthetised and that they did not smell any anaesthetic during the demonstration. The anaesthetic which the defence claimed was used was a mixture of ether, chloroform and alcohol which would certainly smell quite strongly. In addition, they had noted movements of the dog during the procedures undertaken. Bayliss and his team claimed the dog was anaesthetised and that any movements which were observed were due to a form of muscle spasm. There was also conflicting evidence from witnesses supporting Bayliss about how the dog was killed and who had killed him – one said by anaesthetic while another claimed to have done it with a knife through the heart.

In the end the court decided in favour of Bayliss and the victory was much to the liking of the establishment press although the liberal and working class newspapers clearly showed their support for the stand Coleridge had taken and felt there had been a miscarriage of justice. Medical students who were supporting vivisection had been very noisy in court during the trial and their actions were described by the Times newspaper as "medical hooliganism" – medical students at the time were generally renowned for their poor behaviour anyway.[44]

In his judgement the Chief Justice, Lord Alverstone, who in his instructions to the jury had described *The Shambles of Science* as hysterical, directed that the section of the book titled "Fun", which detailed the Brown Dog's vivisection, be removed.[45] This was duly done although the authors replaced it with a description of the trial and sales of the book increased. In addition, Coleridge was ordered to pay two thousand pounds plus legal fees, which he did. The *Daily News* opened a fund to help pay the fine and within a month it was oversubscribed.[46] After four months it stood at five thousand seven hundred and thirty-five pounds.[47]

But things were far from over and the antivivisectionists wanted more exposure for their cause. In order to do this, they developed a plan for a very special memorial.

## Fountain of resistance

On the other side of the river Thames from University College London is the borough of Battersea and in time gone by it had been a largely agricultural area, but industry had steadily encroached on the land and it was now full of grimy factories, belching chimneys, foul smells and grinding poverty. It also housed the much-loved antivivisection hospital, a hospital where none of the doctors practised vivisection on animals – or people. It was also (and still is) the site of the Battersea Dogs Home, the largest such institution in England, was founded by Mary Tealb, originally at a site in Holloway when it was known as *The Temporary Home for Lost and Starving Dogs.* In 1885 Queen Victoria became the patron of the Battersea Dogs Home.

Despite all the economic and structural problems of the district, the council was doing what it could to improve living conditions; it had a good record for being democratic and was striving to provide decent housing for its people.

In order to commemorate the death of the Brown Dog and highlight vivisection, funds were raised, particularly by Louisa Woodward, Secretary of the Church Antivivisection League, for a drinking fountain for animals and people which incorporated a statue of the Brown Dog sitting on top of it. Battersea council was offered this egalitarian and practical monument but shied away from receiving such a contentious gift. However, it's district of Latchmere didn't and the drinking fountain was presented to it by Louisa Woodward and Louise Lind-af- Hageby for installation in its Latchmere Recreation Ground.

At a gathering on 15 September 1906, the memoral fountain was unveiled and attending the event were, amongst others, the feminist, political activist and suffragette Charlotte Despard and the playwright George Bernard Shaw. The mayor of Battersea who was also the honorary secretary of the General Labourers Union and secretary of the Battersea Trades and Labour Council, welcomed the fountain with its statue.[48] Reverend Noel led the crowd in the singing of the antivivisectionist hymn, *The Bells of Mercy* or *The Mercy Song,* which has the words, "...speaking for the speechless, lift the load of woe, plain the path of duty we shall find..."[49]

But it was the inscription on the drinking fountain which was going to cause all the trouble. It did not hold back and served both as a sad memorial and as an angry political challenge. It read:

> In Memory of the Brown Terrier Dog Done to Death in the Laboratories of University College in February 1903 after having endured Vivisections extending over more than two months and having been handed over from one Vivisector to another till Death came to his release. Also in memory of the 232 dogs vivisected in the same place during the year 1902.
>
> Men and Women of England
> How long shall these things be?[50]

The antivivisectionists might have lost the court case but they were determined that they would not lose the argument.

And so, the Brown Dog gazed quietly out from above his fountain offering refreshment for humans and nonhumans alike and told his story to passers-by. But in prescience of things to come he had a police guard for company to protect him from any attempts at vandalism. It would be a year before any serious trouble would erupt and this, as well as later assaults, would be chiefly orchestrated by a medical student by the name of William Lister.

It began with an attack by Lister and a group of some thirty students on 20 November 1907.[51] The students who were from University College London and Middlesex Hospital purchased a crowbar and a very large hammer and caught a bus to Battersea. Under the cover of a very foggy day they tried to smash the statue but were prevented from doing so by police officers and local residents.[52] Ten of the students were arrested, fined five pounds each and warned that any such further acts would lead to imprisonment.[53] This did not endear the magistrate, Paul Taylor, to them and he also became a subject of their fury. On one occasion they tried to burn an effigy of him but after failing to get it to ignite they had to resort to throwing it in the Thames.[54] The students were now very angry and began severely disrupting suffragette meetings, causing chaos, and shouting "Down with the Brown Dog".[55] In fact the students became referred to by some people as The Doggers. On 25 November, another attack took place when twenty-five students tried to destroy the Brown Dog but were once again driven back.

Matters swiftly became even more threatening with a mass march and rally planned for 10 December which once again was organised by Lister. He had hoped to get extra support from Oxford and Cambridge students who were in town for a rugby match but that recruitment effort does not seem to have gone very well. Still, it was a large crowd which turned up on the day – perhaps a thousand people assembling in Trafalgar Square. Fighting erupted between pro- and antivivisectionists which was broken up by mounted police and a number of arrests made, but then the students regrouped and began to march on Latchmere.

They made their way through the city and over the Thames, finally reaching Lachmere Park where they were met by more police, trade unionists, suffragettes, local residents and antivivisectionists who collectively drove them out of the immediate area. The students then made the much-loved antivivisection hospital their target but were once again driven back.[56, 57] It is reported that during the fighting one of the students was injured and his friends tried to take him to the antivivisection hospital, but his way was barred by local residents who believed this was just a ploy to get inside the hospital and trash it.[58] For the next few months there were marches, bonfires and violent disruptions of suffragette meetings as well as heated discussions in newspapers, and the conflict continued to smoulder on through 1908 and 1909.

The struggle was also played out on a political front with attempts to draw in high-ranking politicians to help remove The Dog. The police were pressuring Battersea council to pay for the police guard but the council said the police should do more to prevent these attacks and that they were already paying a large amount of money anyway. The Battersea Labour League wanted the students removed from the borough rather than removing the statue from the recreation ground and the Operative Bricklayers Society pledged that its members would defend the Brown Dog.[59]

A public meeting about The Dog took place on 13 January 1908 at the Battersea Town hall and was very well attended. Apart from efforts to have the memorial removed altogether there had also been a suggestion that the inscription on the fountain be taken off but Councillor John Archer proposed a motion resolving that neither the statue nor the inscription be removed.[60] Archer is an interesting character and was amongst other things a politician, photographer and activist. He was born in Liverpool, his mother was Irish and father Barbadian, he was a socialist, and a pan Africanist and would go on to become the mayor of Battersea – the first black mayor of a London borough.[61] The Rev. Dr Wauschauer also contributed to the debate, drawing an interesting parallel saying, "If the drunkard is demoralised by drink, the medical student is demoralised by the practice of vivisection."[62]

Some people present supported vivisection but this clearly did not go down too well with most of those attending:

> Two pro-vivisectionists moved an amendment that the inscription was false and should be removed. This provoked the stormiest scene of a lively evening, and several medical students were in the words of The Daily Graphic "unceremoniously bundled out by the stewards, who numbered over three hundred."[63]

## Political attack

Although political manoeuvring had been going on for some years, the old hospital in the area was to be the first casualty. In 1908 the Battersea General Hospital, also known as the antivivisection hospital, Old Anti or The Antiviv and which was controlled by a board of local residents, had its funding withdrawn. It managed to continue with the help of its supporters including local trades unions, but eventually was sanctioned over its treatment of two patients and finally closed its doors with all patients being transferred to Wandsworth Infirmary.[64] Towards the end of that same year, socialists and moderates lost control of the local council and this would eventually prove to be a turning point. However, support continued for The Dog with more meetings and events and a petition signed by 20 000 people.

Then on 10 February 1910 the new council took a decision that the Brown Dog should no longer have a home in Battersea and gave instructions to remove the statue. This instruction was carried out the very same night under cover of darkness with four council workmen and a one hundred and twenty-strong police guard.[65] When the news got out Battersea went into uproar. Ten days later there was a protest meeting of three thousand people in Trafalgar square and the medical students led violent attacks against the gathering.

Although legal action was instigated to prevent the removal of the statue, the court hearing came too late and the Brown Dog had already been taken away and was later destroyed.[66] And so the residents of Latchmere and the antivivisectionists lost their memorial water fountain and the Brown Dog was silenced. All that remained was an empty space surrounded by railings.

That feelings ran high about this affair is shown by a piece in the *British Medical Journal* of March 1910 which makes its point of view very clear:

> May we suggest that the most appropriate resting place for the rejected work of art is the Home for Lost Dogs at Battersea, where it could be "done to death", as the inscription says, with a hammer in the presence of Miss Woodward, the Rev. Lionel S. Lewis, and

other friends; if their feelings were too much for them, doubtless an anaesthetic could be administered.[67]

This nauseating piece of arrogance is followed by more of the same, this time attacking Sir George Kekewitch who was sympathetic towards the antivivisection movement and had suggested women might abolish vivisection if given the vote:

> We express no opinion about votes for women: but if Miss Woodward, Miss Lind af Hageby and the late Miss Frances Power Cobbe – who loved animals by nature and human beings only by grace – are to be taken as representatives of their sex, and if Sir George Kekewitch is justified in his belief in the way they would use their votes, the welfare of men would have to give way to the comfort of animals if the suffragettes prevail.[68]

These two excerpts taken from the pages of one of the most prestigious medical journals in the world tell us a great deal about the attitudes of many men in the medical establishment of the day. The antivivisection movement is made out to be a big joke and the inevitable machismo surfaces with "if their feelings were too much for them, doubtless an anaesthetic could be administered." The article seeks to depict compassion as weakness and portrays antivivisectionists as feeble and emotional.

The second excerpt names three women antivivisectionists, one of whom is dead. Despite the authors claiming that they "express no opinion about votes for women", they clearly do and make allegations (scare tactics) about what might happen if women get the right to vote and how the *comfort* of animals could/would be prioritised over the *welfare* of men.

The lexical choice of the word *comfort* is particularly telling. *Comfort* communicates ideas of ease or wellbeing, cosiness, freedom from hardship and pain and relaxation, but the antivivisectionists were asking for animals to have freedom from abuse, from having limbs broken, nerves dissected, abdominal surgery, being heated in ovens, being nailed to boards and being killed. To call the prohibition of such acts, *comfort* is an example of power naming the world in order to support its exploitive relations.

If we swop around the identities in this passage, the distorted nature of the word comfort used in this way becomes clear. The writers would never describe their own understanding of comfort as simply not being abused, vivisected and killed. Indeed, it would not be possible for the word to be understood in this way when applied to humans because nobody is legally allowed to treat humans with such violence. So, there is a false choice created: a world with vivisection in it or one where animals live a life of luxury, women have the vote and the welfare of men is degraded. The idea that the interests of women and animals might be seen as deserving of equal consideration to those of men was plainly outrageous to the elitist authors writing in the publication.

## A dog by any other name

Strangely, there is also another dog in this story. The Physiological Society has a web page which describes the Brown Dog affair and also offers this interesting and perhaps rather disturbing parallel about its own dog.

The Physiological Society had a small statue of a dog which was displayed at its meetings until it was stolen from a car boot in 1994 and of which replicas are presented to retiring officers.[69]

The original bronze sculpture of a dog exhibiting the scratch reflex, was presented to The Society by Sir Henry Dale at a Meeting at the Sherrington School of Physiology in October 1942. The inscription it bears describes its own history of being passed from one physiologist to another and reads:

Rudolph Magnus gave me to Charles Sherrington, who gave me to Henry Dale, who gave me to The Physiological Society in October 1942.[70]

The irony of this is that Henry Dale is the same man who was present at the demonstration on that day in February 1903 and who killed the Brown Dog at University College London by stabbing him through the heart.

## The return of The Dog

But the story of the Brown Dog does not end with a circle of old corroded railings forlornly guarding a void in a recreation ground in Battersea. In many ways The Dog continued to speak to people down the years and remained a subject of controversy even if his memorial was no longer able to be seen. Then, seventy-five years after his removal from Latchmere he returned to Battersea, looking a little changed it is true and without his drinking fountain, but telling his story to the world once again.[71]

This later statue of the Brown Dog was erected by the British Union for the Abolition of Vivisection and the National Antivivisection Society on 12 December 1985, the latter society being the same one which was the defendant in the original trial all those years ago. The inscription explains:

On Thursday, December 12 1985, the NAVS erected a statue of a little brown dog in Battersea Park, London, to commemorate the suffering of millions of laboratory animals worldwide, but also, to ensure that the suffering of one dog is never forgotten.[72]

The Brown Dog was still set to do a little wandering and was moved from this location and placed in storage, apparently while renovations were being done – although some people were worried that there might be problems once again. However, all was well and he has finally found a home in a secluded position in the Woodland Walk of Battersea Park close to the Old English Garden. He commemorates the billions of those who, like him, suffered and lost their lives to experimentation and alerts us to the stories of those who are suffering in our laboratories today.

## Bands of Mercy

And just before we leave this fascinating period of history, it is worth pausing to briefly examine two more movements of the time. Whatever else happened around the reign of Victoria there can be no doubt that Victorians did things – all sorts of things. They built roads, bridges, railways, traded, made machines of all kinds and believed in something called progress. And there were some who saw that the world could change and in so doing be kinder to all who lived in it and they believed that this was what progress was really about.

In 1875 in Britain the first Band of Mercy was formed to bring together girls and boys interested in being kind to animals and to offer humane education.[73] It was Catherine Smithies who formed the first Band and four years later it was publishing the Band of Mercy Advocate.[74] Three years later in 1882 the Royal Society For The Prevention Of Cruelty To Animals took over the Band and its publication and in that same year, the organisation began in America through George T. Angell and Rev. Thomas Timmins.[75] By early in the 20th century there were over 27 000 Bands of Mercy in the USA. It was an astounding public commitment to kindness to animals and an exacting revolutionary obligation was placed upon young shoulders.

> Members in Bands of Mercy took the following pledge, which was also recited at meetings and printed on Band of Mercy literature.
>
> "I will try to be kind to all living creatures, and try to protect them from cruel usage."[76]

This is an onerous vow not only to be personally kind but also to actively protect animals from harm.

Also, in Britain another organisation, the Bands of Hope had already taught a Christian gospel calling for compassion for animals and encouraged working class children to become "Christ's Police" as their protectors.[77] This organisation also placed considerable responsibilities on its young members:

> It was not enough for the young Christian to be kind to animals; he had to keep his eyes open for any act of cruelty by an adult and then, like little Joe Green, he must actively help to apprehend the malefactor. Here indeed was the means whereby the child, that individual without rights or authority, could assert itself over the adult world. If children had once tormented animals in order to express a fragile sense of power, they were now presented with the means to assert their moral authority over adults.[78]

The growth of this general and organised concern for animals can also be gauged by just a few of the landmarks between 1824 and 1915:

**1824**: Royal Society for the Prevention of Cruelty to Animals formed (RSPCA)
**1866**: Henry Bergh founds the American Society for the Prevention of Cruelty to Animals (ASPCA)
**1867**: Pennsylvania Society for the Prevention of Cruelty to Animals (PSPCA) is founded
**1868**: George T. Angell founds the Massachusetts Society for the Prevention of Cruelty to Animals (MSPCA)
**1869**: Canadian Society for the Prevention of Cruelty to Animals formed
**1875**: Catherine Smithies forms the first Band of Mercy in Britain
**1875**: Frances Power Cobbe forms the National Anti-Vivisection Society (NAVS) in Britain
**1877**: American Humane Association (AHA) formed

1877: Michigan Society for the Prevention of Cruelty to Animals formed

1882: George T. Angell and Rev. Thomas Timmins start Bands of Mercy in the USA

1883: Caroline Earle White founds the American Anti-Vivisection Society

1886: Humane Education made compulsory in the state of Massachusetts

1888: Rev. S. Massey starts the first Canadian Band of Mercy in St. Henri, Quebec

1889: American Humane Education Society formed

1891: National Canine Defence League founded

1897: Our Dumb Friends' League was founded

1898: Frances Power Cobbe forms the British Union for the Abolition of Vivisection (BUAV)

1905: William O. Stillman and Stella H. Preston form the New York Humane Education Committee

1905: Oklahoma and Pennsylvania legislate mandatory Humane Education in schools

1906: The Animal Defence and Anti-Vivisection Society was established by Louise Lind af Hageby and Nina Duchess of Hamilton

1909: The State of Illinois introduces legislation requiring Humane Education in schools

1910: Detroit Humane Society formed

1912: Our Dumb Friends' League establishes the Blue Cross fund to assist animals injured in war

1915: The first "Be Kind to Animals Week" takes place

1915: Angell Memorial Hospital opens at the MSPCA[79]

It is notable that in some states – Massachusetts, Oklahoma, Pennsylvania and Illinois legislation was passed to make humane education compulsory in schools.

## The central question

The period we have looked at in the last two chapters has offered us insights not only into the arguments for and against vivisection but also the way in which identities were constructed and power differentials came into play at that time. In some ways, not a lot has changed as will become clear now that we turn to examine the debate over animal experimentation today. But we will begin by asking the fundamental question, why does animal experimentation exist at all?

## CHAPTER 15

# War crimes

*Doublethink means the power of holding two contradictory beliefs in one's mind simultaneously, and accepting both of them.*

George Orwell[1]

## Why do we carry out experiments on animals?

WHY DO WE experiment on animals? Given that much of our scientific interest and effort concerns human beings – safety testing, human disorders, human diseases, human biology, better ways to kill people in war and so on, experimenting on animals rather than humans makes little scientific sense.

From a scientific perspective, it is logical that the best research relating to humans is carried out on humans and so human focused research carried out on nonhuman animals is at best second class or worse. Scientists know this but forgo the best scientific method because experimenting on humans is unethical and illegal. Animal experimentation allows the circumvention of this ethical and legal prohibition. The *House of Lords Select Committee On Animals In Scientific Procedures* report we looked at earlier actually makes this point:

> It is true that better quality data on human beings could be obtained were the information gathered by using human subjects. However, animals are used because the majority of people consider that humans are entitled to use animals in ways which would not be acceptable if applied to humans.[2]

It is important to be very clear about this; animal experimentation is not the best science we can do and it is not the gold standard of scientific research as is often claimed.

But there have been times when scientists have chosen to experiment on humans in the same way that we today experiment on animals and I want to look at a few examples. It is a glimpse into the world of experimentation from a very different perspective than the one to which we are usually exposed.

## Experiments on humans

The history we considered earlier suggested that in the 19th and early 20th centuries, some doctors may have used women and poor patients as experimental subjects, but we also know such things continued well into the 20th century and were often carried out on quite a large scale. Some examples are: Japanese researchers infecting prisoners and psychiatric patients with dangerous diseases, US researchers in Guatemala infecting around 1 500 psychiatric patients with sexually transmitted diseases, in Lund, Swedish patients at the Vipeholm Mental Hospital in Lund being given large amounts of sweets in order to investigate tooth decay, mustard gas was tested on volunteer soldiers, healthy prison inmates were given infusions of cancer cells, a mind control investigation organised by the Central Intelligence Agency using drugs, hypnosis, sensory deprivation, verbal and sexual abuse was carried out on Canadian and US subjects, in the Tuskegee syphilis study patients were not told they had the disease and treatment was withheld for decades, and American experiments using radioactive substances were carried out on members of the American public during the cold war.[3,4]

There are some particularly shocking examples which stand out for the severity of what was done and/or the numbers of people affected and we can look at a few of these now.

## Unit 731

Recalling the earlier days of his career, Japanese doctor Ken Yuasa describes how, when he was a medical student in Japan, he had heard reports of vivisection being carried out on humans in occupied China and when he went there in 1942 he was invited to a "practice surgery".[5] He reports that:

> Two Chinese men were brought in, stripped naked and given general anesthetic. Then Dr. Yuasa and the others began practicing various kinds of surgery: first an appendectomy, then an amputation of an arm and finally a tracheotomy. After 90 minutes, they were finished, so they killed the patient with an injection.[6]

This may have been a fairly common practice and eventually he would, from time to time, ask the police for a communist to dissect for training purposes.

A particularly horrific story of extensive experimentation on humans is that of Unit 731 and its subsidiaries. The list of atrocities is long and harrowing:

> From 1933 to 1945, Japanese doctors in China performed thousands of cruel experiments on Chinese, Russians, Mongolians, and Koreans and killed all of them. At Unit 731 alone, at least 3,000 people were tortured and murdered. In addition, similar human experiments and vivisections were done at four branches of Unit 731...[7]

It is likely that Unit 731 near Harbin, China was actually just one of many similar facilities and one estimate is that there were 26 such sites where experimentation and killing took place and that they were located in Japan, China and possibly other countries which had been occupied.[8] The investigations carried out were wide-ranging and often gruesome. For example, one of the interests of Unit 731 was the treatment of frostbite and the unit was based in a place which could get bitterly cold:

> Guards would strip a victim, tie him to a post outdoors and freeze his arm to the elbow by dousing him with water, researchers say. Once the lower limb was frozen solid, doctors

would test their frostbite treatment, then amputate the damaged part of the arm. Then the guards would repeat the process on the victim's upper arm to the shoulder. Another test, another amputation. After the victim's arms were gone, the doctors moved on to the legs.[9]

The experiments were not simply random violence but the whole project was ordered, organised and carefully documented. A medical assistant who worked at Unit 731 describes how he had vivisected a man without using any anaesthetic:

"The fellow knew that it was over for him, and so he didn't struggle when they led him into the room and tied him down," recalled the 72-year-old farmer, then a medical assistant in a Japanese Army unit in China in World War II. "But when I picked up the scalpel, that's when he began screaming."

"I cut him open from the chest to the stomach, and he screamed terribly, and his face was all twisted in agony. He made this unimaginable sound, he was screaming so horribly. But then finally he stopped. This was all in a day's work for the surgeons, but it really left an impression on me because it was my first time."[10]

The victim was part of a plague experiment and echoing the voices of earlier vivisectionists he explains why he believes an anaesthetic could not be used:

Vivisection should be done under normal circumstances. If we'd used anesthesia, that might have affected the body organs and blood vessels that we were examining. So we couldn't have used anesthetic.[11]

In regard to the use of children in experiments he says, "Of course there were experiments on children. But probably their fathers were spies."[12]

As the Russian forces approached the facility at the end of the Second World War an attempt was made by the Japanese to destroy the large complex, but this failed and in addition, many Japanese personnel were captured. What happened next to these prisoners depended on which country dealt with them. Some of the staff were given immunity by the Americans as part of a deal:

Partly because the Americans helped cover up the biological warfare program in exchange for its data, Gen. Shiro Ishii, the head of Unit 731, was allowed to live peacefully until his death from throat cancer in 1959. Those around him in Unit 731 saw their careers flourish in the postwar period, rising to positions that included Governor of Tokyo, president of the Japan Medical Association and head of the Japan Olympic Committee.[13]

Other staff ended up with the Russian authorities and were put on trial for what they had done. They were given prison sentences which they served for a few years and were eventually quietly returned to Japan and freed, hinting at another deal having been struck, similar to the American one.

In the Russian trial the justification given by the accused was that they were simply following orders and a translator from the trial remembers how much this annoyed the Russian prosecutors.

Soviet inquisitors were angered by the testimony of the Japanese. Permyakov still remembers some of the questions and answers from the courtroom interrogation:

> Question: Why did you help to cut out his eyes?
> Answer: I received an order.
> Question: Are you a puppet? Don't you understand that was sadistic?
> Answer: It was an order.[14]

Another exchange is also revealing:

> Question: Are you a Shinto believer?
> Answer: Yes.
> Question: Your belief is gentle and kind; how can you use people in experiments, instead of rabbits?
> Answer: The interests of our mission required this. [15]

That the goal of the mission overrides ethics and compassion and is sufficient to justify the actions being carried out reprises the animal experimentation legislation we have already reviewed. The "scientific goals" are the priority and everything else is secondary. It is also interesting that the Soviet questioner seems to believe that experimenting on rabbits would somehow not breach the Shinto commitment to being gentle and kind.

Takashi Tsuchiya, Associate Professor in the Department of Philosophy, Osaka City University, identifies a number of factors which might have contributed towards these terrible events. Obviously, a wartime situation is one of them but he also lists coercion, an opportunity to use well-resourced facilities, an extremely hierarchical system in medicine with actions sanctioned from above and having suitable ideologies to draw on. Concerning this latter point he says:

> In addition, eugenic and racist ideologies were prevalent in Japan, as well as in western countries. Consequently, most Japanese then had prejudice against people in other Asian and European countries and discriminated against them. They thought Chinese, Korean, Mongolian, Russian, American, English, etc. were beings that need not be treated humanely, especially in wartime.[16]

Here is a hierarchical view of the world utilised to justify abusing those perceived as lower down that hierarchy. The parallel with animal experimentation could hardly be more striking.

## Nazis and the Ravensbrück rabbits

In the Second World War, Nazi doctors conducted a wide variety of experiments on people including hypothermia tests, bone grafting, sterilisation, irradiation, subjecting them to phosgene and mustard gas, and testing the effects of low air pressure. Both adults and children were used and the victims suffered terribly.[17]

In Ravensbrück concentration camp experiments were carried out on a group of Polish Catholic women who were members of the resistance who came to be known as the Ravensbrück Rabbits or Lapins.[18,19]

The group's name came from their treatment as medical lab rabbits – and also, because the cruel experiments often left them with injuries and deformities that meant hopping was the only way they could get around.[20]

The experiments concerned the treatment of infections and are said to have been initiated because of the loss to infection of one of Hitler's close friends.

Ravensbrück's sulfonamide experiments, as they were known, were performed to test the efficacy of sulfa drugs. They studied nerve and tissue regeneration, including bone transplantation from one person to another. Otherwise healthy prisoners had parts of bone, muscle and tissue removed without anesthesia; healthy limbs were amputated.[21]

Some of the women died and others were executed, some even having to be carried to their own executions. One of the things that happened before execution is that the other women would try to make the victim's hair as good-looking as was possible and her cheeks were pinched to make them flush and give her face some colour; all this so that she would look as beautiful as possible on her final journey.[22]

Josef Mengele was one of the most notorious Nazi experimenters and carried out horrific experiments on many prisoners at Auschwitz, a complex of concentration camps in Poland. He established a kindergarten for children whom he planned to experiment on and he could be very kind to them. They had a better diet than other parts of the camp and he would sometimes give them sweets but later he would carry out the most dreadful experiments on them.[23] The United States Holocaust Memorial Museum says this about Mengele:

He had a wide variety of other research interests, including a fascination with heterochromia, a condition in which an individual's two irises differ in coloration. Throughout his stay in Auschwitz, Mengele collected the eyes of his murdered victims, in part to furnish "research material" to colleague Karin Magnussen, a KWI researcher of eye pigmentation. He himself also conducted several experiments in an attempt to unlock the secret of artificially changing eye color.[24]

He tried to change the eye colour of some prisoners by injecting substances into their eyes.

After the end of the Second World War, plans were being made for the prosecution of perpetrators who had carried out experiments on prisoners, but there were problems because suitable legislation did not really exist or at least there was uncertainty about it.[25] Eventually, in a trial which came to be known as the *The Doctors Trial*, twenty doctors were charged with a range of offences, but they argued that they were only doing their jobs and seeking information which could not be obtained in any other way and which was needed in order to help people. This is a familiar defence when it comes to experiments carried out on nonhuman animals. The doctors were found guilty.

The above are only a few examples of human experimentation and we naturally find them appalling. All manner of experiments have been performed on humans and while in a few instances they may have been essentially gratuitous violence, most have been planned, carried out by professionals, scientifically structured and the work methodically recorded. In the examples we considered there were ideological justifications. The perpetrators may have believed, or claimed to believe, in their right to experiment on the victims because those people were considered lower on some scale of hierarchy. In addition, the ultimate benefit to the perpetrator's group and the achievement of the aims of the scientific enquiry were invoked as validations.

It comes as no surprise that all of this sounds so familiar. Experimenting on humans and on nonhuman animals in this way is essentially the same exploitive social practice and employs identical forms of ideological justification. One practice is illegal, the other is championed. And we are undoubtedly at war with animals.

Now we turn to the public discourse on animals and experiments; who says what about who and how various identities are constructed.

## CHAPTER 16

# Animal experiments in the public domain

*To tell the truth is revolutionary.*

Antonio Gramsci[1]

## Waving shrouds and public health

WHERE DOES THE debate about experiments on animals stand today? To get some idea, I looked at the *Daily Mail*, a popular, right wing newspaper, the *Guardian* newspaper which is liberal, *The Royal Society*, a prestigious scientific institution, The UK government's regulations on animal testing and *Understanding Animal Research*, an organisation formed from the Research Defence Society and the Coalition for Medical Progress which promotes animal experimentation.

I analysed twenty-five articles from the *Daily Mail* website which has over 99 million monthly readers and twenty-five from the *Guardian* newspaper site with monthly readership at just over 63 million.[2,3] The Royal Society had one guide and two statements on animal experimentation and I used the UK government document, *Guidance on the Operation of the Animals (Scientific Procedures) Act 1986*. Only ten articles were used from the Understanding Animal Research website as it has a clearly stated position as a pro-testing organisation. Overall there were sixty-four texts giving a total of around 130 000 words. Not a comprehensive survey but it can offer some insights

I found nine major themes, five of these are quite closely related and can be grouped together broadly as technical in nature, they are *Descriptions of Experiments*, often shocking and highlighting neglect, discussions of *Regulation and Control* of testing, a theme of *Reduction in Numbers*, one of *Alternative Methods* to be used and one of *Care for Animals*. While these are very important and interesting in their own right, I particularly want to examine in some detail the four remaining ones.

These are: *Animal Rights and Activists* which concerns the construction of identities of those involved in this debate, and then *Ethics, The Only Way* and *Shroud Waving* all of which deal with the central question of the motivation for and justification of, animal testing.

Let's start with *Ethics*

## Ethical arguments

We now finally turn to the theme which is really at the core of this debate – as the Quaker says to Magendie – by what right do you do this? So what are the ethical and moral arguments we find in these texts? Well there are actually precious few which attempt to deal with this subject. There are differences of opinions about what is acceptable and what is not and here are a couple of examples of these from the newspapers:

> Professor Stephen Harris, from Bristol University, says: "Monkeys are thinking, feeling, conscious creatures. They're not that different to us in many ways. "I've heard it described as a primate slave trade and it's difficult to argue with that description. I struggle to find any legitimate reason why we should treat our fellow primates in such a cruel manner."[4]

And this one is from an interview with a professor who uses monkeys in his research:

> Are any kinds of vivisection unacceptable? "Give me an example." Isn't using animals for testing cosmetics wrong? "That's a very strange argument. People talk about cosmetics being the ultimate evil. But beautifying oneself has been going on since we were cavemen. If it's proven to reduce suffering through animal tests, it's not wrong to use them. To say cosmetics is an absolute evil is absurd."[5]

Perhaps it is unfair to expect popular newspaper articles to look at this in detail, but surely it is not too much to ask from Explaining Animal Research, the UK government or the Royal Society. The UK government's document on animal experiments does not deal with ethics at all and neither could I find anything substantial in the texts I examined from Explaining Animal Research, but The Royal Society does at least make an attempt of sorts.

The Society is possibly the oldest scientific society in the world and at times acts as advisor to the British government and the United Nations. It is very active in promoting science and making it understandable to a wide audience. Of its three texts about animal experimentation two are quite short but the most extensive one is titled, *The use of non-human animals in research: a guide for scientists* and parts of this document do deal with ethics.[6] Let's have a look.

In its opening paragraph it presents a familiar claim, portraying it as fact:

> Humans have benefited immensely from scientific research involving animals, with virtually every medical achievement in the past century reliant on the use of animals in some way...

We will leave aside the dubious nature of this claim and going on we read:

> The majority of the scientific community consider that the benefits that have been provided by the use of animals in research justify this use...

and

> The public also increasingly accepts the use of animals in research...[7]

Even if this happens to be true about some opinion polls which may have been conducted, it does not serve as a justification for animal experimentation because a popular vote is certainly not an ethical argument.

Then, astonishingly, and we are still in the first paragraph on the first page, the reader is instructed on the appropriate moral point of view which should be taken regarding animal experimentation:

> The appropriate moral stance for all use of animals in research is to minimise animal suffering and maximise the benefits to medicine and health, agriculture and fundamental understanding.[8]

As we progress further, we will find that scattered all over the document are text boxes describing what experiments have been done on animals in the past and how useful these have been. They are not there for decoration and presumably are to continually hammer into the mind of the reader the claim that animal experiments are essential to medical progress.

But we do find a section titled "Ethical approaches to the use of animals" which goes into a little more detail about the ethical justifications for experimentation although this discussion and conclusion take up a mere 310 words. The rest of the section deals with degrees of suffering, balancing suffering and benefit, and the care of animals.[9]

It takes an approach very similar in style to the House of Lords report discussed earlier and suggests three possible views concerning animal experimentation. The first is that animals should have the right to life, the second that only humans can have rights because rights are "firmly embedded in a social context" but that we have a responsibility to look after animals, and thirdly that animal experimentation is justifiable because of its potential medical benefit.

It then brings in difficulties relating to "absolutes":

> Both the rights and the responsibilities arguments are sometimes taken as absolutes, over-riding all other moral claims. However, this could also be the case for the moral argument for supporting animal experiments because of their potential medical benefit.[10]

It continues,

> The alternative to such absolutism is to respect the range of views by attempting to both minimise the suffering inflicted on animals used in research while maximising the scientific and medical gain which is consistent with the Royal Society's position on this issue.[11]

At first glance this might seem very reasonable – a compromise helping everyone to move forward. But that would be a grave error because it is nothing of the sort.

The document portrays three original positions so let's look at what was theoretically on offer in each case. We have: 1. animals have a right to life; 2. animals should not have rights but should be protected; and 3. animals should be used for experiments. After the so-called compromise we find that: animals have no rights, they are not protected and can be experimented upon but should only suffer as much as is needed for us to get what we want. The ideas of a right to life and protecting animals just disappear as if they were never really there at all, which perhaps they weren't. This isn't a compromise, it's a stitch-up pretending to be one.

The whole document is heavily loaded in favour of experimenting on animals and offers scientists who might have doubts about this kind of work no discussion of counter views, or suitable ethical debate in any meaningful way.

What we should note is that in the ideology being drawn upon, it is understood that humans have a right to use animals and that it is acceptable that animals should suffer in order to contribute to possible human good. We are left in no doubt that humans are more valuable than animals and we find ourselves firmly back with a hierarchical world view which claims a right to use those who are lower down this hierarchy to fulfil our own desires.

This is a dogmatic account which presents the appearance of being otherwise. The Society's motto "Nullius in verba" meaning "take nobody's word for it" is something well worth bearing in mind.

## My way or you're dead

The next two themes are quite similar and often intertwine in texts. We can describe them as discourses because they construct aspects of the world in a particular way and I have named them *The Only Way* and *Shroud Waving*.

*The Only Way* constructs the idea that there is only one way to do medical research. Here are three excerpts:

> Emeritus Professor David Morton, a vet and bioethicist from Birmingham University, says: "Sometimes you cannot use anything other than primates if you want to get good scientific data. For example, you wouldn't have the polio vaccine if primates had not been used in research".[12]

> Meanwhile, Porton Down itself stresses that tests on animals are conducted only when there is no alternative.[13]

> Scientists insist that new treatments for serious illnesses cannot be developed unless their safety and efficacy is tested on animals. Similarly, they argue that progress in understanding basic biology, which underpins the creation of new medicines, cannot be achieved without animal research.[14]

The general claim of this discourse is this: there exists no way, known or unknown, by which essential knowledge and techniques which we have today could have been gained and no other way, known or unknown, by which such requisite knowledge and techniques may be gained in future. Obviously, this is a hypothetical claim as we do not know what possible methods and techniques might have been developed in the past if animal experiments were not carried out nor can we possibly know what techniques will become available in future. No logical proof is offered to support the claim and it is difficult to imagine how there could be such proof. An historic survey of selected milestones in science, as in the Royal Society document, while interesting in itself certainly does not qualify as anything like a proof of such a hypothesis.

Despite these fundamental deficiencies, the power which science and the scientific community wields means that, more often than not, this claim is seldom seriously challenged.

But the claim also seems very unscientific. As scientists we are always trying to find better, newer, more effective, more efficient, more accurate, more economical, more portable, more environmental ways of doing things. It is one reason why, for example, today we have an assortment of incredibly accurate and informative medical imaging devices which did not even exist thirty years ago, and a whole range of surgery which can be done using keyhole techniques.

Consider this. On 17 December 1903 the first powered flight (although this might be contested) took place south of Kitty Hawk, North Carolina and covered a distance of 37 metres. Less than 30 years later the jet engine was being developed, which would be used to power huge aeroplanes, and on 20 July 1969 humans set foot on the moon. In 2004 the Rosetta space probe was launched to position a space vehicle right next to a minute object floating in the vastness of space, a journey of over six billion kilometres.

> After a journey of more than 10 years featuring three Earth gravity-assists, a Mars assist and two asteroid fly-bys, Rosetta arrives at comet 67P.[15] It travelled 3.8 billion miles and rendezvoused with a tiny object about two and a half miles across which is travelling at 24 600 mph.[16]

A long way from the 37 metre flight made just over a hundred and ten years earlier. Yet when it comes to animal testing, we are continually referred back to this two-thousand-year-old method of animal testing as the bench mark of excellence.

But on the subject of hypothetical claims, perhaps we should consider other ones. Let me suggest one. If we had decided one hundred years ago that animal experimentation was completely unacceptable, then scientific investigation would not have stopped dead but we would have steered our scientific practice into other directions. No doubt one of the things we would have decided to do is put some real effort into cell culture, although in those days it would have been far from easy. We would have been confronted by all sorts of problems as there are in any emerging field, but we would have got better and better as we drove the technologies such as microscopy, micro techniques, dyes for living tissue, making tissue skeletons and so on and our understanding of general biochemistry, cellular growth systems, membrane formation and the functions of nucleic acids would have improved. Our new techniques, as well as our understanding of many different cellular processes would have provided benefits in fields such as bacteriology, virology, general medicine, plant pathology and parasitology antibiotic production as well as an improved understanding of human and animal health.

Despite having put relatively little effort and funding into human cell culture over the years, today we can grow cells and some tissues in laboratories and are possibly on the way to producing organs. Work with stem cells harvested from a patient's own blood is offering all sorts of innovative and less traumatic therapies for severe disorders. For years much of our research efforts relating to cancer treatment, cell regeneration, transplantation, gene control, and lots of other areas have been focused deep into the fine workings of cells – their functioning at the sub-cellular level.

Imagine if we had taken this path long ago, we would be so much further down the road and would already have been working for many years with human cells, tissues and organs. Even if we were only sixty or seventy years in advance of where we are today, that is a huge stretch of time in scientific research. Who knows what we could do and what we would have learnt? But again, this is just hypothetical as is the claim of *The Only Way*.

## Shroud Waving

The second and closely related discourse is *Shroud Waving* which maintains that people will die and scientific progress will slow or grind to a halt if animals cannot be used for experiments. It is dramatic, blaming and misleading. I borrowed the name from a quote by Ian Kennedy in the 1980 BBC Reith lectures: Unmasking Medicine: The New Magicians.[17] In the broadcast he says:

> Not so long ago, a senior civil servant remarked that consultants opposed to shifts of resources from the well-endowed areas of medicine to the Cinderella areas of geriatrics and mental illness have not been averse to using "shroud-waving tactics".[18]

It seems an appropriate description for the scare strategies so often employed in this debate. Here are some examples.

> I have always believed animal experimentation is not only right but a moral necessity. Put simply, without the use of animals in the lab we would not have modern medicine. We would have no cancer drugs, no effective antibiotics, no proper analgesics. Many surgical procedures would be impossible.[19]

Note that the edifice of modern medicine, according to this depiction, rests on animal experimentation. No experiments on animals – no modern medicine it claims. And

> Stephen Whitehead, chief executive of the Association of the British Pharmaceutical Industry, said: "Where medical research is involved, we have a straightforward option – continue with medical research and continue to save and improve lives; or stop medical research and stop our quest to cure Alzheimer's, HIV, cancer and every single disease that is untreatable. For me the decision is obvious – we have to prioritise human life at the same time as continuing to strive to reduce the number of animals used in research."[20]

This depicts medical research and animal experiments as if they are the same thing. The conflation of the two leads to the specious argument that no animal experiments means no modern medicine and no medical progress, resulting in widespread death and suffering.

The next excerpt draws on the same idea but, rather honestly, makes it all a matter of self-interest and power.

> Medical research: while one feels sorry, obviously, for the poor animals, we're not prepared to forgo a cure for Parkinson's for our mother. That seems a pretty unanswerable conclusion.[21]

And the final extract is not even about human lives being saved but rather human lives being created.

> Lord Robert Winston, as the only peer to hold a project licence for animal research, particularly considered the contribution of animal research in IVF, his own field of medicine. "It is interesting to consider that more than one million babies could not have existed without the research that has been carried out on rodents."[22]

With threats of medical progress grinding to a halt and the resultant deaths of millions emanating from the powerful authority of science through its emissaries, it would be a brave person indeed who would stand up to support the ending of animal experiments. That is, if you actually believed all this to be true.

These two discourses, *Only Way* and *Shroud Waving*, construct a world where safeguarding health and gaining scientific knowledge about health are equated with laboratory experiments on animals. We are back with Claude Bernard in the 19th century claiming the only way to study the science of life and care for people is by experimenting on animals.

But is this really the case or is it a picture of the world with a very large chunk missing, rather like claiming that what we see through a keyhole is actually the whole mountain landscape?

## Health care overlooked

Many advances in medicine have not come out of an animal testing laboratory but are the product of such things as careful clinical observation, non-animal laboratory work, sharing of information, good scientific enquiry, imaging, computer modelling, epidemiology and plain good doctoring. But I want to take a little time looking at one, often-overlooked, discipline.

We can divide medicine very broadly into preventive medicine or public health, and curative medicine. Roughly speaking, the first is about trying to make sure people don't get sick and the second with trying to cure them if they do. For the most part when we think about health we think in terms of hospitals, medical staff, intensive care facilitates, new drugs and curing the sick. But while these are essential and make for successful TV shows, the less acknowledged elder sibling quietly goes about doing the job of preventing people from becoming ill in the first place. Public health measures are in place worldwide protecting the health of billions of people twenty-four hours of every single day, every day of the year, but there is little drama and communities are continually protected by the many procedures, systems and protocols in place. Billions of people do not get cured of diseases or disorders because they don't get sick in the first place.

Public health practices have been around for centuries often on a relatively small scale and perhaps linked to cultural practices. It certainly seems that large concentrations of people, such as those in ancient cities, found ways to keep their water safe and dispose of human waste.[23] However, in Europe with the industrial revolution, trade increased, cities grew rapidly and many landless people migrated to urban centres to survive. The result was that large populations lived in the most awful, crowded, unsanitary conditions and life expectancy was very low. According to the historian E.P. Thompson, the average age of death of a labourer in 1840 was as follows:

> ...Truro 28 years, Derby 21 years, Manchester 17 years, Bethnal Green (London) 16 years and Liverpool 15 years.[24]

Appalling as these figures are – and they really are terrible – an interesting process was underway countrywide at that time and it had been going on for some years. Generally, the crude death rate in the country had actually been falling and with an increasing interest in public health it would continue to do so right into contemporary times. This was happening without the use of antibiotics (penicillin only started to become widely available around 1948), surgery was still very risky, and there were few effective drugs for most illnesses.

Public health scholars attribute these ongoing improvements to a number of things, but five stand out: the increased provision of safe drinking water, better housing, better nutrition, proper sanitation and increasing education including specific education such as the training of midwives. It is also interesting to note that after some time, the birth rate also started to decrease despite there being no modern contraception available.

Robert Sharpe in his book, *The Cruel Deception*, examines numerous examples from this period showing diseases declining before specific medication was available to treat them.[25] Infant mortality, deaths from tuberculosis, bronchitis, scarlet fever, whooping cough, measles, diphtheria and typhoid fever all show declining rates well into the 20th century and those rates were often little affected by new treatments or vaccinations when these were finally introduced.[26] Sharpe notes that:

> Over the next 100 years [1850–1950] Britain's death rate fell rapidly, due almost exclusively to the decline of the infections – mainly TB, bronchitis, pneumonia, influenza, whooping cough, measles, scarlet fever, diphtheria, smallpox, cholera, typhoid, diarrhoea and dysentery.[27]

He continues

> ...mortality was already declining before, and in most cases long before, specific therapies became available.[28]

McKinlay and McKinlay survey historical health data from the USA from 1900 to the early 1970s and draw this conclusion:

> In general, medical measures (both chemotherapeutic and prophylactic) appear to have contributed little to the overall decline in mortality in the United States since about 1900 – having in many cases been introduced several decades after a marked decline had already set in and having no detectable influence in most instances.[29]

Public health is critically important and even more so now on our increasingly crowded planet but sometimes for reasons of poverty, mismanagement, or war, public health safeguards are not in place for many communities and the United Nations Children's Fund describes the terrible threats still affecting many children today:

About 29,000 children under the age of five – 21 each minute – die every day, mainly from preventable causes. More than 70 per cent of almost 11 million child deaths every year are attributable to six causes: diarrhoea, malaria, neonatal infection, pneumonia, preterm delivery, or lack of oxygen at birth.[30]

The World Health Organization says the following about diarrhoeal diseases in children:

Diarrhoeal disease is the second leading cause of death in children under five years old. It is both preventable and treatable. Each year diarrhoea kills around 525 000 children under five.

It continues

Key measures to prevent diarrhoea include: access to safe drinking-water; use of improved sanitation; hand washing with soap; exclusive breastfeeding for the first six months of life; good personal and food hygiene; health education about how infections spread; and rotavirus vaccination.[31]

Simple, cheap, but effective measures can literally make all the difference between life and death.

In rich countries and those becoming rich, other problems arise which will cause many people to suffer disablement or early death from preventable disease. This time though, the threat is not from infectious agents but is related to lifestyles. Once again let's hear from the WHO:

It has been projected that, by 2020, chronic diseases will account for almost three-quarters of all deaths worldwide, and that 71% of deaths due to ischaemic heart disease (IHD), 75% of deaths due to stroke, and 70% of deaths due to diabetes will occur in developing countries (4). The number of people in the developing world with diabetes will increase by more than 2.5-fold, from 84 million in 1995 to 228 million in 2025 (5).[32]

It then makes clear that this does not have to happen.

Chronic diseases are largely preventable diseases. Although more basic research may be needed on some aspects of the mechanisms that link diet to health, the currently available scientific evidence provides a sufficiently strong and plausible basis to justify taking action now.[33]

A fact sheet released by the WHO in 2017 about obesity, notes among other things, that:

Worldwide obesity has nearly tripled since 1975. In 2016, more than 1.9 billion adults, 18 years and older, were overweight. Of these over 650 million were obese. 39% of adults aged 18 years and over were overweight in 2016, and 13% were obese. Most of the world's population live in countries where overweight and obesity kills more people than underweight.[34]

There are other examples as well and we have not even touched on the life threatening pollution which we cause, but essentially the preventable diseases of poverty and the preventable disorders of affluence need the application of political will, not experiments on animals. We already know how to prevent millions of people becoming disabled or dying early.

But we should also be aware that curative health has become an industry. The health insurers, private hospitals and private clinics, the equipment companies and of course the pharmaceutical industry pull in some very big money and at the time of writing, even the National Health Service in the UK is being pushed by the government into ever increasing privatisation.

If we have $x$ funds to spend, how do we spend it to save the most lives and prevent as much disability as possible? It seems reasonable that spending it on prevention would be much more cost effective and efficient than trying to find cures for diseases and disorders we already know how to prevent.

Of course, we need a balance between preventive and curative medicine and I want to make it very clear that what I have said is in no way criticising those dedicated professionals who work in curative medicine and carry out this essential work – absolutely not. But I am sure that they would prefer not to have to care for patients who should not have become ill in the first place, but instead give their time and expertise to those who have slipped through the defences or who have disorders which cannot be prevented as yet and need their specialist skills.

Imagine a physician working in a disadvantaged location treating a critically ill child who is sick with severe diarrhoeal disease. She uses all the tools of modern medicine to help her patient to recover intravenous fluids, specialist nursing care, laboratory tests, a range of pharmaceuticals, etc. However, the doctor knows that she will be sending this little girl back into the very same environment which made her sick in the first place and will very likely make her sick again or perhaps even take her life the next time around.

The point here is not about different types of health practices, but to highlight that the discourses of *The Only Way* and *Shroud Waving* portray a world where only curative medicine exists and the only way to gain medical progress in that world is by experimenting on animals. They construct an ideological god of scientific/medical elitism and those who challenge its spurious conflation of medical progress and animal experimentation are deemed both ignorant and dangerous.

Finally, we turn to examine how the identities of those involved in this debate are constructed in these and other texts.

## CHAPTER 17

# Constructing identities

*We know of course there's really no such thing as the 'voiceless'. There are only the deliberately silenced, or the preferably unheard.*

Arundhati Roy[1]

## Who is who?

THE CONSTRUCTION OF public identities is important because rightly or wrongly this influences public opinion. We have three major identities in these texts there are the people who support and carry out animal experiments, the people who oppose them and the victims of the practice. To begin with we can look at the first two identities and there is a clear divide in the ways in which anti-testing activists and those who support testing are constructed with two themes paramount, one is violence and the other knowledge.

## Contestations of violence

The single most prominent construction of animal rights supporters or the shadowy "animal rights extremists" of these texts, is that they are dangerous people, potentially or actually violent. This might be said directly or implied. On the other hand, the institutions and employees carrying out experiments are portrayed actively or by default as nonviolent and possible victims of violence themselves. Here is an excerpt from an article which portrays researchers "reeling" as animal rights extremists attack "science":

> While I was busy raging at scientists for being silenced by animal rights extremists, researchers were reeling from a now infamous series of violent attacks on science...
>
> The combined effects sent a chill wind through the scientific community, which retreated further into its various ivory towers than ever.[2]

This is a barricades and bodies in the streets scenario and claims not only that the scientific community is under attack, but science itself. The words *reeling, infamous, violent, attacks, chill wind, retreated further* paint a bleak picture of science under siege in a dystopian world.

The article references three other articles to support its claim of an *infamous series of violent attacks*. One describes an attack on the managing director of Huntington Life Sciences by unknown assailants resulting in outpatient care. A person from The

Animal Liberation Front is quoted in it as saying they did not condone such attacks and Stop Huntingdon Animal Cruelty campaign said: "We unreservedly condemn any act of violence be it against animals or humans."[3] The second article is about Cambridge University announcing they would not go ahead and build their proposed neuroscience laboratory which would have experimented on primates. There were protests against the laboratory being built and a public enquiry recommended that the building should not go ahead. The third article refers to a dead body being exhumed as a protest against guinea pig farming to supply laboratories for carrying out testing. Four people admitted conspiracy to blackmail.

What is noticeable and very common, is the article's silence about the violent nature of experiments. It is impossible that the writer is unaware of what happens in animal experiments and so must have chosen either to ignore it or believes that experiments on animals are not classifiable as violence. While this may appear simply a linguistic difference of opinion, it is not. Deliberately burning, blinding, breaking limbs, poisoning, injuring and killing individuals are violent acts; they surely cannot be understood in any other way and they are certainly described as violence when they are carried out on humans.

There is a great deal resting on this classification. If such acts are defined as violence then those individuals carrying them out and authorising them, are guilty of abuse. Indeed, outside the walls of a prescribed laboratory such acts against animals are actually recognised as violence and deemed criminal acts for which the offenders can be prosecuted. Once inside a designated facility however, these acts undergo a legal revolution and no longer constitute violent abuse and the perpetrators are no longer counted as abusers.

The same does not apply to human victims, however, because such acts, wherever they are committed, are understood as violence and therefore criminal offences. Overall, it is not, as we might reasonably expect, the *actions* themselves which determine the characterisation and the legal implications but *who* the victim is and *where* such acts take place.

So, in order to avoid dealing with the real nature of animal experiments, ethical principles are bifurcated, truth is discounted as collateral damage and the band cheerfully plays on.

Yet the portrayal of animal activists as violent or who carry the threat of menace seems to be a default position, almost a mantra. Here is another piece portraying vague threats against scientists and progress,

> Until now the unwillingness of the silent majority publicly to oppose the disgraceful tactics used by anti-vivisectionists has enabled a tiny minority to slow the pace of legitimate medical research and at times even to threaten its existence.[4]

It is those who oppose testing who are guilty of carrying out *disgraceful tactics* not those who treat animals violently. And that this *tiny minority* is so powerful that their actions might threaten the very existence of medical research which once again is conflated with animal experiments as if they are one and the same thing.

## Debbie Vincent

The portrayal of animal activists as violent, when in reality the vast majority are completely the opposite, was highlighted in the trial of Debbie Vincent. The *Daily Mail* reports that "The case against Vincent was that she was aware of the militant actions [of some activists] but did not allege that she took part in them." Vincent, an animal activist, had been subjected to repeated police raids over a number of years, none of which had resulted in any prosecutions. She was, in this case, charged with conspiracy to blackmail and the judge had some unkind words:

> Sentencing the 52-year-old, who acted as the public spokeswoman for Shac, Judge Keith Cutler said: "It is difficult for a judge to calculate the repugnance felt by society to such appalling acts. Nothing at all could justify such attacks."[5]

With the words *repugnance, appalling acts* and *such attacks* from the judge, Vincent is construed as not only being antisocial but extremely dangerous to society. Yet the prosecution never claimed she carried out any direct acts against Huntington Life Sciences or its partners or anyone else and she herself has always maintained her innocence. But strangely, the judge also said that she had good character references the *Guardian* newspaper says this:

> But the depictions of Vincent in the court and in the media do not tally with the woman who emerges in dozens of letters from people who have provided references to her legal team. Farmers, vets, bosses of animal shelters and leaders of community projects spoke of a gentle, peaceful woman who was kind to both animals and humans. One read: "I have never known her act without honest or integrity and believe her motive for all she does are in the interest of justice and the greater good."[sic][6]

She was sentenced to six years in prison with extremely harsh conditions imposed on her after her release.

## Facts to the rescue

The website *AnimlRightsInfo.extremism* describes itself as "A global information service about animal rights extremism" and tells us that "AREinformation is produced and managed by Understanding Animal Research (UAR), a not-for-profit company based in London, UK, with guidance from the AREinformation Editorial Board."[7] No points for guessing that the site is pro-animal experimentation but they have at least injected some factual information into this debate which is to be welcomed.

On a world map the site has a pull down menu which lists twenty-seven incidents worldwide of arrests or prosecutions of "animal rights activists" between 2012 and 2016.[8] There are ten prosecutions listed and these are for such things as demonstrating, damaging property, liberating animals, posting posters, conspiracy to blackmail and harassment.[9] Much of this involves one or two individuals. From the information recorded it would appear that over these four years, no "animal rights extremists" caused any injury to any person. Ten prosecutions over four years is two-and-a-half per year globally on a planet with a human population of seven-and-a-half billion. This works out to one case per year for every three thousand million people. Not a huge problem it would seem. So much for this tsunami of violent extremism which inhabits much of pro-testing mythology although apparently not the real world.

Dan Lyons, an academic and activist against animal testing, makes clear in an excerpt from one of the texts examined how skewed he believes the discussion has become:

> "We are an entirely legal and peaceful organisation," said Dan Lyons, of Uncaged. "We have direct evidence that the regulations have been often breached, but nothing is done to punish the researchers. The debate is all about the extremists."[10]

Lyons is well aware of what animal experimentation entails and was the Director of Uncaged when the company Imutran (parent company Novartis) carried out notoriously abusive experiments on a range of animals including primates, while the UK government's celebrated top class regulatory system was completely missing or at best comatose. The publication of the leaked evidence was blocked for two-and-a-half years due to a court case by the companies but finally published in the report titled, *Diaries of Despair*.

The infamous, but continually financially bailed out, Huntington Life Sciences testing laboratory was also involved and the report makes accusations of government collusion in preventing any meaningful enquiry or punitive action:

> The disturbing story of Government malpractice that is revealed by the Diaries of Despair scandal teaches us a sobering political lesson. Behind a wall of confidentiality, the Government has succumbed to the improper advances of big business and the scientific "old guard": together they ride roughshod over democracy, the public interest, the rule of law, and the welfare and rights of animals. However, the Diaries of Despair affair is the most extreme and well-documented example of a deeper pattern of Government misconduct.[11]

Animal rights and animal liberation philosophy in their grounding theories make respect for animals, nonhuman and human, fundamental.

## White coats and occult knowledge

The second area of portrayed difference between pro- and anti-testing identities is knowledge. A common construction is broadly, that those who understand about animal testing support it but those who are ignorant are opposed to it. This may be stated overtly or be an implicit assumption in the text. Here is a sentence from an article about Professor Tipu Aziz, a prominent researcher, that leaves little doubt:

> What is new, though, is that these men have started to fight back against what Aziz describes as the "misinformed and sometimes illiterate anti-vivisectionists who adopt terrorist tactics."[12]

Again, the violent extremists are conjured up although as we saw earlier, they are actually in rather short supply. In this particular extract we have "extremists" constructed as misinformed and sometimes illiterate.

In the next excerpt a line is clearly drawn dividing scientists from activists:

> The animal research story started to change. Instead of pictures of activists in blood-spattered lab coats wielding "animal abuser" placards, the media filmed thousands of scientists taking to the streets in support of building a lab in Oxford, and reported on a new petition in support of animal research.[13]

Those who march for animal testing are characterised as scientists while those marching against it are described as activists. This is a commonly depicted partition and there is an assumption in many texts that those who oppose testing cannot possibly be scientists and therefore cannot understand the issues involved.

The House of Lords report we looked at earlier struggles with this problem when trying to compare perspectives on a range of issues and it sets up a scientists vs non-scientists scenario. We read, "Scientists who use animals...", "Scientists and industry have countered..." "Research scientists argue..." and "The scientific position was summarised..." Those who are opposing experimentation are referred to as, "Other witnesses to the Committee...", "Many of those opposed to the use of animal experiments..." or neutral terms meaning those who have opposing views to "the scientists".

I don't think this is a deliberate ploy to mislead in any way but it has just become the usual frame for the debate and we even saw this when we looked at the 19th and early 20th century vivisection debate. Of course, the dichotomy is not valid and many scientists, including medical doctors, are opposed to animal experimentation.

There is another very important point about this emphasis on the binary portrayal of the debate. The depiction of science vs nonscience makes the debate all about scientific knowledge and completely avoids interrogation of the foundational claim of any justification for animal experimentation – a matter which lies firmly in the domain of ethics. Burying the primary ethical debate is expedient for the support of animal experimentation because it is much easier to play "mine is better than yours" around the scientific playing field.

## Journal wrath

But it is not only in the popular media that we find these two discourses about violence and knowledge. In the prestigious journal *Nature* of 24 February 2011 the editorial is titled, "Animal rights and wrongs" and discusses a self response survey carried out by *Nature* of biomedical scientists and their reports of the "effects of animal-rights activists".[14] There were 980 responses, the journal reports, with over seventy percent of them from people who conduct research on animals.[15] The editorial discussing the issue abounds with phrases related to violence supposedly carried out by people supporting animal rights. We read for example, *physical attacks, campaigns of harassment, fire bombings, violent activist behaviour, violent attacks, destruction of personal property, vandalism, lingering fear, intimidation, corrosive animal rights extremism, tide of violent activity, bully and blackmail* and *terrorize researchers*. Quite a tirade in an editorial of only 765 words. It does not give any specific details of this litany of horrors; no descriptions, dates, times, numbers, individuals, court cases or anything of that nature.

Interestingly, a victim in the survey is defined as anyone who has been "negatively affected" by animal rights activism or "seen somebody else negatively affected" which is, to say the least, a pretty vague, take your pick, make it up for yourself type of definition. Predictably though, in no part of the discussion are animals ever mentioned as *victims of animal experimentation* even though this evidence is fully documented in peer reviewed publications and the number of victims runs into billions. This silence indicates the presumed shared understanding between author and reader, that the animal's lives and their suffering have no place in such a calculus; this recognition is just ideological common sense.

Another page of the same issue gives further details of the survey and has the header "A Nature poll exposes the Battle Scars."[16] Once again, in case we didn't get it the first time, the picture is painted of scientists under attack from violent, destructive, dangerous, animal rights activists. Interestingly though in the graphics section displaying the results there is a rather important bit of information tucked away. It says that, "...33% of respondents had 'ethical concerns' about the role of animals in their current work."[17] Now that seems to be a finding that would have been well worth a piece from the editors.

In another *Nature* editorial, this time in *Nature Immunology* of April 2004, titled "Standing up to bullies" a very similar representation is made of violent activists and scientists under attack, mention of "terrorism in the guise of animal rights" and even a claim that a performance of the English National Ballet had been interrupted by activists.[18] To be fair, this was at a time when "animal rights" activism was probably more high profile than it is today.

However in attempting to make its case against the "bullies", the editorial at one point bizarrely attacks the organisation People for the Ethical Treatment of Animals by claiming that "The Center for Consumer Freedom" [now the Center for Organizational Research and Education] has "... called for revoking the tax exempt status of PETA (People for the Ethical Treatment of Animals) because of suspected financial ties to criminal activities."[19] It gives no further details but the mud has been thrown and this is a direct attack on those with opposing views rather than on their ethical position.

Instead of *Nature Immunology* smearing PETA by simply repeating this claim, it might have been prudent to investigate the credentials of the organisation it cites. The Center for Consumer Freedom has long been mired in controversy of all kinds and Source Watch gives us a feel for some of this:

> It [The Center for Consumer Freedom] runs media campaigns that oppose the efforts of scientists, doctors, health advocates, animal advocates, environmentalists and groups like Mothers Against Drunk Driving, calling them "the Nanny Culture" – the growing fraternity of food cops, health care enforcers, anti-meat activists, and meddling bureaucrats who "know what's best for you".
>
> Based in Washington, D.C., Berman & Co. represents the tobacco industry as well as hotels, beer distributors, taverns, and restaurant chains. Hotels, motels, restaurants, bars and taverns together comprise the "hospitality industry," which has long been cultivated by the tobacco industry as a third party to help slow or stop the progression

of smoke free laws. CCF actively opposes smoking bans and lowering the legal blood-alcohol level, while targeting studies on the dangers of meat & dairy, processed food, fatty foods, soda pop, pharmaceuticals, animal testing, overfishing and pesticides.[20]

So far as I am able to ascertain, PETA has never been prosecuted for having financial ties to any criminal activities and I have no idea if *Nature Immunology* ever offered an apology to the organisation for this implied criminality. But the fact that editorial content of this dubious quality can appear in such a prominent and respected scientific journal speaks volumes as to how deeply and rigidly this ideology of the legitimacy of legalised animal abuse is embedded.

## Silenced voices

We have looked at the construction of the identities of those in favour of animal testing, and those who oppose it, but there is another group to consider, the ones with everything to lose and nothing to gain; the animals.

While the animals used in laboratories are labelled as lab animals, models, materials and all sorts of euphemistic terms, they are real living beings, individuals who have their own identities whether we recognise them or not and are, to use Regan's description, *subjects of a life*. Being other than human does not make them less than human but they are absent to us and the unrecognised and unacknowledged become the unconsidered to whom we are unaccountable. It is time to own our long standing failure in this regard and genuinely reflect on them and their lives.

What principles should we draw upon to assist us in deciding how to act in relation to them? This is an immensely important question and cannot be brushed aside as some administrative detail. We are dealing with a practice which has real world consequences, we are adjudicating on the suffering and death of billions.

In the guidance for human experimentation we examined earlier, there is a non-negotiable obligation to consider first and foremost those who will be experimented upon. The subjects are always the prime focus, their wellbeing paramount, their wishes and choices respected. The welfare of the subject always takes precedence no matter their age, abilities, mental capabilities, verbal ability, nationality, state of health or any other such criteria. There is no question of scientific or social goals overriding this guiding principle. But this is a principle absent from animal experimentation.

Why should we treat nonhuman animal subjects any differently from human ones? It is true that animals who are used in experiments do not use human languages, but nobody can doubt that they communicate in many ways including, like humans, non-verbally. A chimpanzee struggling to escape restraints communicates, at the very least, her or his wish to break away from that imprisonment. This is not anthropomorphic because restraints are made to do just what the name says and struggling against them clearly demonstrates a wish not to be restrained. The very act is one which is semiotic; we are able to understand that there is a desire to be free – not to be part of what is happening. And when it comes to inhaling toxic vapours, irritants in the eyes and even the very fact of simply being kept in a cage, then similar interpretations are not only reasonable, it would surely be perverse to claim otherwise.

It often seems as if we wish to deny any rich forms of communication between animals, yet there is no doubt that living beings both transmit and receive meaning in many ways. The singing of birds, the displays of peacocks, the dance of bees and the calls made by elephants are just a few examples. The academic field of zoosemiotics (part of biosemiotics) focuses on this very capability and is described as "… the study of semiosis within and across animal species."[21]

Accusations of anthropomorphism have long been used as a big stick to threaten researchers studying animals and thereby retarding our deeper understanding of animal lives. Frans de Waal, primatologist and professor of psychology at Emory University, highlights this in an article in the *New York Times*:

> The ape also shows the same ambivalence as a child. He pushes your tickling fingers away and tries to escape, but as soon as you stop he comes back for more, putting his belly right in front of you. At this point, you need only to point to a tickling spot, not even touching it, and he will throw another fit of laughter.
>
> Laughter? Now wait a minute! A real scientist should avoid any and all anthropomorphism, which is why hard-nosed colleagues often ask us to change our terminology. Why not call the ape's reaction something neutral, like, say, vocalized panting? That way we avoid confusion between the human and the animal.[22]

He later points to our elitism and demeaning of other animals especially in regard to thinking:

> Given how partial our species is to intellectual distinctions, we apply such linguistic castrations even more vigorously in the cognitive domain. By explaining the smartness of animals either as a product of instinct or simple learning, we have kept human cognition on its pedestal under the guise of being scientific. Everything boiled down to genes and reinforcement. To think otherwise opened you up to ridicule, which is what happened to Wolfgang Köhler, the German psychologist who, a century ago, was the first to demonstrate flashes of insight in chimpanzees.[23]

Today we are thankfully seeing significant changes in the way many researchers describe how animals behave and they are doing it in ways which not so long ago would have brought them severe censure and could have risked their careers.

We cannot deny that animals make choices, that they have cognitive abilities and that many appear to experience similar things to ourselves including sadness, happiness, affection, fear, depression and even in some cases laughter. They are unique individuals who lead their own lives and I think we can safely say that not one of them has ever given us permission to use them for experiments. Yet we perversely set aside our clearly defined and much prized ethical principles when we want to experiment on nonhuman individuals and supply self serving, anthropocentric justifications for doing so.

## Selective justice isn't justice

Perhaps the concept of justice can assist us with this problem. Fairness is a principle cherished in societies everywhere and when it comes to making a decision where parties have conflicting desires or interests then any decision-making process must be as fair as possible. Natural justice is about being fair to all concerned and requires that in a dispute or perhaps a decision-making process, all parties are given the opportunity to be heard and that any adjudication is made by an unbiased, independent entity. This principle underpins everything from labour disputes to murder trials.

In addition, natural justice demands that the power exercised by the parties, be it economic, social, physical or whatever must play no part in influencing the final decision because the parties must be on an equal footing. It is only the veracity of the arguments, the weight of the evidence and the ethical considerations which are weighed and adjudicated. In other words, it must be a fair process for all concerned irrespective of who they are, what they are and what power they may or may not wield.

This means that when it comes to decisions regarding animal experimentation, if we were to follow a just process, all parties would have their interests and their preferences represented and any decision would be made by an impartial adjudicator. Nothing less would be acceptable.

One objection might be that because animals cannot speak, they would be unable to represent their interests and preferences in such a forum. This is true, but it is also the case for some humans such as babies, young children or adults with neurological problems, but we do not exclude them from such processes. On the contrary, we go to great lengths to make certain that they are fully protected and represented and we do so by appointing advocates on their behalf. So, in the case of animals, and given the demands of natural justice, we would be required to appoint an advocate who would act on the animal's or group's behalf and in their interests.

The advocate would draw upon historic data, for example, any information such as records of previous, similar experiments and how the animals were affected by them. Insights from animal behaviourists and other specialists would assist in understanding such things as the impacts upon the animals and the animal preferences in those situations. In addition, they would consider information from specialists about aversions, fears, pain, socialisation, restrictions, and so on that may have been identified by researchers through observations of aspects like behaviour, gait, posture, sounds, calls, etc. in free-living and captive animals. Other information might also be relevant but in this way, the advocate would then be able to draw up and present an argument going some way towards representing the interests of those animals.

This general scheme could be used for a particular experiment or more likely, be used to generate an institutional decision on whether to experiment on animals or not. In this case the advocate would notionally represent all animals who might be experimented upon in the future by the institution.

There is nothing at all exceptional about this as a process although it might seem strange simply because we normally exclude nonhuman animals' interests from our decision-making. What is really bizarre however, is the system currently used to make decisions about animal experiments. Here is how our current arrangement works.

- The first party is the animals and they have no representation whatsoever.
- The second party is researchers, institutes, government, industry, etc. who wish to

carry out violent and lethal actions against the first party. The second party is able to represent its case in full.

- The second party, or a sub group of it, or a similarly interested party, acts as the adjudicator and makes the final decision.

This is the type of set-up that is used for decision-making in formulating government policy right through to judgements by ethics committees in universities, research institutes and commercial laboratories. It is an embarrassingly corrupt system, a sham with not the merest semblance of a just process. The outcome is inevitably rigged by the influence of human elitism, money, prestige and self interest.

But a just arrangement is possible and could look something like this:

- The first party (animals) and their representatives argue for the interests and preferences of the animals.
- The second party (researchers, institutes, government, industry, etc.) represent their wishes to carry out tests on the animals.
- The adjudicator or adjudicators make the final decision.

Of course, a major problem here is that the adjudicators are members of the human species, but I am sure we could find some who are able to act in an impartial way.

The comprehensive refusal by relevant authorities and organisations to use a process based on the principles of natural justice for deciding whether or not animal experimentation should be practised demonstrates that there is actually no interest at all in having a just process.

But perhaps I am wrong and my comments are unfair and so I want to make a proposal. I challenge any decision-making authorities in colleges, universities, research institutes, governments and the like anywhere in the world to set up a fair and just forum or tribunal as I have outlined above. It must be open to public attendance; all parties must be fully and competently represented and the principles of natural justice must be applied in full to discern a fair and just outcome to the question of whether or not experiments on animals should be carried out. It will be interesting to see if any institutions take up the challenge and if so, what decision is reached. Who is going to be first?

## CHAPTER 18

# Killing mechanisms

*Look, you can see for yourself. They are not like you and me. They do not
behave like human beings. They are here to die.*

Rudolf Hoess[1]

## Structures for violence

So FAR, WE have touched on just a few of the animal texts which are all around us,
speaking of our past and present violence and justifying our exploitive social practices.
These are important to understand but we are still faced with fully explaining the
enormous amount of suffering and death we impose on animals and that we do so
without giving it a second thought. In order to do this, I propose we need to look at two
things; the necessary mechanisms which must be in place to facilitate mass violence
and the ways in which some influences, particularly, ideologies and discourses, affect
our minds.

In this chapter we will look at the first of these and consider what the world must be
like for this large-scale, institutionalised abuse to be practised as a normal part of life.
What must the landscape of the damned look like, what structures and mechanisms have
to be in place?

But where do we look for guidance, because there is nothing else like this, it is unique
in the world, the social practices of a particular species of hominid? Perhaps the closest
we can come to it is by looking at human–human violence.

## Humans killing humans

The social psychologist Philip Zimbardo says this about our puzzlement concerning the
mass violence we perpetrate on other human beings:

> We continue to ask, why? Why and how is it possible for such deeds to occur? How can
> the unimaginable become so readily imagined? These are the same questions that have
> been asked by generations before ours.[2]

Sadly "such deeds" still occur despite or perhaps because of, our organised societies and
apparent sophistication. Zygmunt Bauman writing about the Holocaust expresses the
belief that its examination is able to offer us important insights into otherwise unnoticed
or obscured features of our societies.

I propose that the experience of the Holocaust, now thoroughly researched by the historians should be looked upon as, so to speak, a sociological "laboratory". The holocaust has exposed and examined such attributes of our society as are not revealed, and hence not empirically accessible, in "non-laboratory" conditions. **In other words, I propose to treat the Holocaust as a rare, yet significant and reliable, test of the hidden possibilities of modern society.** (emphasis in the original)[3]

This may also be the case for other such events. It is as if the underlying strata of society becomes exposed during such cataclysmic upheavals, offering a glimpse of what lies beneath the surface. Charles Patterson in his book *Eternal Treblinka* makes extensive and disturbing comparisons between what humans do to nonhuman animals and what happened to people under Nazi rule.[4]

## Genocide

The United Nations Genocide Convention of 1948 describes genocide as an intent to destroy, in whole or in part, a national, ethnic, racial or religious group by: killing the members of the group; causing serious bodily harm; deliberately inflicting conditions which are calculated to lead to physical destruction in whole or part; imposing measures to prevent births and forcibly taking children away to other groups.[5]

This is not the same as our treatment of animals in the food industry, in experimentation and elsewhere although there are important similarities. The first difference is that human genocide is carried out *within* the species, but what is done to animals is done *by* members of the human species against members of specific *other* species. The second is that in genocide the paramount goal is to destroy a particular group by killing them directly or producing conditions which will lead to their deaths, and possibly also by taking away their young and by preventing further births. In the mass exploitation of nonhuman animals, the methods and goals are more varied, but generally we can say that they are formulated in such a way as to use and kill every member of a group, but continually produce young to replace them and then use their bodies in the same ways. It is not a single genocidal act but an ongoing, infinite process of intergenerational slavery genocide.

A third difference is the scale of the killing. The number of nonhuman animals killed by humans is orders of magnitude greater than anything ever recorded in human – human violence. In the 100 years of the 20th century an estimated 60 million men, women and children were killed in different places throughout the world "because the state thought this desirable."[6] This figure may be even higher, but worldwide in farming alone we kill around sixty thousand million nonhumans every year which is over a 150 million a day or 1 736 individual's lives violently snuffed out every second. To put this into context it is the equivalent, in numbers, of wiping out the whole human population of the earth every six-and-a-half weeks or killing every human being in Central and Southern Africa every twenty-four hours; or in European terms, killing all the people in the United Kingdom, Ireland, Denmark, Norway and France every day.[7]

One way to categorize genocide is by using the description of the motives which are given to explain it, and using this system, it can be divided into four categories: retributive, institutional, utilitarian and ideological.[8] Utilitarian genocide most closely resembles the situation with nonhuman animals and it is marked by domination and exploitation in order to obtain what we want. Describing this, Smith writes:

> They are being killed, were killed, because of a combination of ethnocentrism and simple greed. The basic proposition contained in utilitarian genocide is that some must die so that others can live well.[9]

If the term ethnocentrism is replaced by anthropocentrism, this description corresponds very well with what humans do to nonhuman animals. We own their bodies, we use them and we kill them to get what we want.

So, what does history tell us is needed for genocide, what are the essential mechanisms needed for this and other forms of mass violence?

## Bureaucracy and organisation

Genocide may appear to be a spontaneous outbreak of mass violence, but it is both planned and organised. In the Rwandan genocide, the highest authorities in the country took part in its organisation. Information was broadcast on the radio stations in order to incite killings, meetings were held for the same purpose, the government decided who should be killed and local government officials controlled the start and end of the killing:

> Prefects transmitted orders and supervised results, but it was the burgomasters and their subordinates who really mobilized the people. Using their authority to summon citizens for communal projects, as they were used to doing for Umuganda, burgomasters delivered assailants to the massacre sites, where military personnel or former soldiers then usually took charge of the operation.[10]

The killing of millions of Jewish people in the Holocaust could not have happened without a high degree of organisation. The murder of six million people and the subsequent disposal of their bodies was a huge logistical and technical challenge to the Nazis which, in the end, was solved by the power of bureaucracy and the everyday activities of the modern industrial state. Glass notes how established companies used their expertise to provide facilities and supplies just as they would have done for any commercial project:

> The construction of Auschwitz required the help of Topf and Sons of Erfurt, who built the crematory ovens; W. Reidel and Son of Bielitz and Joseph Kluge of Geiwitz, which supplied the reinforced concrete; the construction firm of Robert Kohler; and the Dessau Sugar and Chemical Factories and the German Pest Control Company in Frieberg, which supplied Zyklon B gas.[11]

Weiss points out how people carried out the routine duties they were expected to perform and that the genocide depended on the participation of many thousands of employees in diverse occupations doing their jobs:

> The murder of millions in five years needed the voluntary complicity of tens of thousands. Public and private institutions participated directly or indirectly in the

oppression and killings: army, police, civil service, Foreign Office, railroads, postal services, utilities, bureaucrats, corporations, bankers, lawyers, judges, physicians and scientists.[12]

Nothing extraordinary or new was required for the crime of the Holocaust, it was already in place but simply needed to be redirected for the commission of this atrocity. Feingold writes:

> [Auschwitz] was also a mundane extension of the modern factory system. Rather than producing goods, the raw material was human beings and the end-product was death, so many units per day marked carefully on the manager's production charts. The chimneys, the very symbol of the modern factory system, poured forth acrid smoke produced by burning human flesh. The brilliantly organized railroad grid of modern Europe carried a new kind of raw material to the factories. It did so in the same manner as other cargo.[13]

One of the spin offs from the genocidal process was the availability of slave labour for companies such as AEG, Daimler-Benz, Telefunken, and Siemens where people worked under harsh conditions and it is claimed that some victims were even purchased for use in medical experiments.[14]

Max Weber the sociologist and philosopher identifies at least six major characteristics of an ideal bureaucracy hierarchy of authority, impersonality, written rules of conduct, promotion based on achievement, specialised division of labour and efficiency. It is easy to see how this powerful, instrumental mixture of characteristics can allow a focus on the efficient achievement of short-term goals while at the same time mentally distancing those involved from their participation in the overall horror. Most people who took part in the Holocaust did not directly injure anybody, far less commit murder. They simply did their jobs.

Most individuals involved in animal exploitation do such things as drive vehicles, type letters, build structures, collate information, process accounts, purchase consignments, make chemicals, advertise products and so on. They don't directly harm animals but without them and most importantly, without the millions and millions who support such industries, for example by purchasing their products, this simply could not continue.

## Science and technology

Genocide cannot happen without technology. This may take the form of crude weapons such as machetes, radio broadcasts to orchestrate the killing, trucks to ferry perpetrators around and so on but to confine, transport and murder on a vast scale and over a significant period of time, requires appropriate science and sophisticated technological input. It became clear to the Nazi High Command that killing large numbers of people was a major technical problem and would require time, money and other resources. It would also take a psychological toll on the perpetrators. The "humane" murder of victims was an issue for some of the Nazis including Himmler. Patterson observes:

Those who kill "humanely" often contend that their victims suffer minimally or not at all. This contention helps to ease the guilt and makes the continuation of killing more acceptable. Robert Juhrs of the SS, whose job at Belzec was to shoot the arrivals who were no longer able to walk, said that because of the poor condition of the Jews after their long journey in overcrowded freight cars, he looked on shooting them "as a kindness and a release. I shot the Jews with a machine gun from the edge of the ditch. In each case I aimed for the head, so that each one died instantly."[15]

But shooting large numbers of people and burying their bodies in mass graves would not work. The introduction of technology into mass killings increased the efficiency of the process while at the same time reducing the stress on perpetrators. Technology allowed physical and psychological distance to be inserted between perpetrator and victim and then the problems to be overcome were no longer personal or moral but simply technical:

The Third Reich's use of technology allowed the perpetrator to kill without acknowledging the victim as a person. Killing in gas chambers and crematoria created a vast gulf between killer and victim. In technologizing death, the perpetrator shifts to another level of connection with the victim, one of organization, techniques, the victim important only insofar as he or she presents a problem in organizing death.[16]

Stillman and Pfaff make the point that the mechanized killing in the German death camps arises out of our society; it comes from our "civilization" and inevitably from our ideology:

There is more than a wholly fortuitous connection between the applied technology of the mass production line, with its vision of universal material abundance, and the applied technology of the concentration camp, with its vision of a profusion of death. We may wish to deny the connection, but Buchenwald was of our West as much as Detroit's River Rouge – we cannot deny Buchenwald as a casual aberration of a Western world essentially sane.[17]

This "vision of a profusion of death" sums up concisely our relationship with the billions of nonhuman animals we use.

Patterson describes the similarities between today's slaughterhouse system and what took place in the death camps. Even the final path leading to the point where the actual murders took place, the "chute", "kill alley" or " funnel" is similar. Drawing on work by Donat and others he describes how:

At Treblinka the "tube", which was eighty to ninety yards long and five yards wide, led from the "disrobing rooms" in the lower camp to the gas chambers in the upper camp. After going about thirty yards toward the east side of the camp, the tube made a sharp, almost ninety-degree turn and went straight up to the central opening to the gas chamber building in the upper camp...Guards used fists, whips and rifle butts to force their naked victims to run four and five abreast with their arms raised through the tube.[18]

Bauman claims that the inherent power of science must also be taken into consideration as a factor. Science is instrumental in nature in that it is a tool for enquiry and innovation but it does not evaluate, from an ethical perspective, the solutions which it provides. Science has no moral compass because it isn't supposed to have one; ethics are outside its ambit. This is not to say that scientists are unethical or that scientific choices can't be evaluated ethically, but simply that science itself is not about the process of ethical evaluation. He says:

> What is not pointed out, however, is that more than any other authority science is allowed by public opinion to practice the otherwise ethically odious principle of the end justifying the means. Science serves as the fullest epitome of the dissociation between the ends and the means which serves as the ideal of rational organization of human conduct: it is the ends which are subject to moral evaluation, not the means.[19]

And those ends are not generated by science but are the products of our own desires, the outcomes we alone seek.

Science and technology are omnipresent in the nonhuman animal exploitation industries infiltrating every aspect of their functioning; inventing, adjusting, controlling, monitoring, solving problems, driving ever greater efficiency and profits.

## Coercion
Victims of genocide are coerced physically and verbally living in a constant state of fear and having family members threatened, assaulted or killed. They might be collected together in large groups for ease of control or to satisfy some other desire of the perpetrators.

Animals used by humans are coerced as a matter of routine, often they are beaten and "broken"; restraints and harnesses of all kinds are used as are weapons such as whips and electric prods. They are often confined in large numbers, some living their whole lives indoors.

## The Law
Genocide, like slavery has not always been a crime:

> ...the slaughter of whole groups has occurred throughout history, it is only in the past few centuries that this has produced even a sense of moral horror, much less been thought of as "criminal". Indeed from ancient times until well into the sixteenth century, genocide was not something that men were ashamed of, felt guilt for or tried to hide; it was open and acknowledged.[20]

Within the prevailing ideology of a group, some acts are acceptable while others are unthinkable. For the Nazis, sex with a Jewish woman was unthinkable because it might lead to a dilution or contamination of the genes of the master race if the rape resulted in the birth of a child. The murder of Jews however was acceptable.[21] When the Nazi leadership wanted a legal answer to the "Jewish Question", decrees were issued excluding Jews from business, schools, universities, sports facilities and so on.[22] After attacks on Jews during the night of 9 November 1938, some Sturmabteilung (SA) members were punished for theft, a violation of the code of honour, and some for rape, a transgression of the ban on interracial intercourse, but twenty-four SA members who had killed Jewish people were only reprimanded, with the court requesting Hitler to take no further action.[23]

The Reichstag Fire Decree took away many civil liberties from the population and the Enabling Act known as the "Law to Remedy the Distress of People and Reich" gave Hitler plenary powers and together these pieces of legislation installed a legal dictatorship.[24] The Nazi hierarchy could then make up the law.

Perpetrators of genocide may believe themselves to be acting legally, whether or not this is true, it is an important aspect of genocide that it is collective in nature; there is state authority and legal sanction and so the perpetrators are relieved of feelings of guilt.[25] The mass gassing, in the camps were supposed to be legal, systematic and controlled with Himmler claiming the "right to annihilate this people".[26] SS guards in the camps were told they were valuable soldiers and not murderers and Himmler informed them that "any guilt they felt was because their conscience had been distorted by centuries of Judeo-Christian ethics."[27]

Concerning the genocide in Rwanda, Cook, referring to Mironko's research, writes:

> By recounting their actions using words that imply authorization by some higher power, Rwandans who have confessed to genocide thus appear to take no personal responsibility for murdering innocent men, women and children.[28]

We kill billions of animals every year but not a single life taken is a crime because we, the perpetrators, decide it is legal; we enslave animals as well which we also declare as lawful and in addition deem them our property.

## Authority and power

Power is implicit in authority and authority sanctions the use of power. Authority directs and empowers agents while at the same time absolving the individual agent of the consequences of their actions taken under direction. This is a common story and in their examination of the My Lai massacre in the Vietnam War, Kelman and Hamilton write of other "sanctioned massacres" noting how My Lai had its precursors:[29]

> Elsewhere in the world one recalls the Nazi's "final solution" for European Jews, the massacres and deportation of Armenians by Turks, the liquidation of the kulaks and the great purges in the Soviet Union and more recently massacres in Indonesia and Bangladesh, in Biafra and Burundi, in South Africa and Mozambique, in Cambodia and Afghanistan, in Syria and Lebanon.[30]

This is far from an exhaustive list. Cook points out that in the Rwandan genocide:

> To the extent that these ordinary people saw themselves as participating in ibitero organized and sanctioned from above, it becomes much harder to establish genocidal intent on the part of ordinary perpetrators.[31]

It is a recurring theme in so many acts of mass violence that people claim they were only doing what was asked of them, what was required of them; doing their job, carrying out their duty.

## Secrecy

The removal of victims from view and therefore essentially from the consciousness of the population is important. The Nazi gas chambers and crematoria were far away from densely populated areas and access was strictly controlled. Some members of the population would have seen cattle trucks filled with people but this is not the same as seeing them beaten, stripped naked and gassed. Secrecy was essential so that the truth could be hidden, or at least it would be less obvious. Certainly, the enormous extent of the abuse would likely have been incomprehensible to most people and Schnurer notes the importance of this in obscuring culpability:

> For both Nazis and the animal oppression industries, it was essential that the general public never comprehend the vast system used to divert responsibilities away from consumers and participants in the process of destruction.[32]

Of course, we don't always need great physical distance for this and while slaughterhouses are often on the edges of towns, experimentation labs are usually in smart, expensive modern structures or in prestigious historic buildings right in the middle of our cities, but what happens behind those facades still remains concealed.

And then there is the everyday abuse which is so common, so ordinary, so normalised we just fail to notice; it is all but invisible.

## Discourses and ideology

Glass notes that, while there were those in the Nazi command who bear an enormous responsibility for what happened, "[i]t is naïve to suggest that only a few thousand individuals were responsible for the deaths of millions" and claims that many people enthusiastically endorsed what was happening.[33,34] Haidu points out that the concept of ideology allows contradictions such as the murder of thousands to sit alongside claims of decency on the part of perpetrators and "...informs the discourses and actions of agents and representatives of various kinds including administrators and soldiers."[35]

Ophir draws our attention to the physical potentials of power and discourses and writes of:

> ...the technology of power and the modes of "excluding" discourse which made the Holocaust possible: the discourse which made it possible to exclude a group of people from within the borders of the human race and the technology which made it possible to massively deport them to their deaths.[36]

In the Holocaust there was an already existing discourse of anti-Semitism which was combined with a relatively new discourse from the "science" of eugenics. The lack of moral concern, Glass maintains, was in part because of the climate created by German science, portraying killing Jewish people as simply part of a health policy:[37]

> Science had established its dominance over the belief structure of Nazi Germany. Race lay at the centre of this scientific edifice; and racial hatred elaborated itself as a set of scientific principles obsessed with blood cleanliness, genetic purity, and a phobic

reactivity to the potential of race contamination. These beliefs exercised an enormous influence over scientific, professional, political, and administrative practices.[38]

Proctor puts it this way:

> ...science set the stage for the Final Solution long before the arrival of National Socialism. When the Nazis took over, the preexisting scientific discourse allowed the doctors to become the priests of the cult of the German blood as well as its medical keepers and the exterminators of its potential polluters.[39]

In some cases, victims of the Holocaust were changed from living beings into objects by tattooing numbers onto their bodies, making them just a cipher and obliterating their names and individuality and thereby removing them from the ambit of moral concern. When they died, the authorities in charge of record-keeping would often not use the word corpse but refer to figures or pieces.[40]

Haidu points out that removal of identity and being was an important step in the whole process:

> The desubjectification of the victim was a programmed precondition enabling the perpetrator's enactment of the narrative program of extermination.[41]

In Unit 731 the human subjects of experiments were referred to as *marutas*, or logs – ideologically changing them into objects. Smith notes that in genocide and other forms of large-scale violence the victims will often be dehumanised by referring to them as, for example, "rats", "lice" or "gavours".[42] In the Second World War, Japanese soldiers were described as "monkeys", "baboons", "gorillas", "dogs", "mice", "rats", "vipers", "rattlesnakes", "cockroaches" and "vermin".[43] In the war between Japan and China in the 1930s, the Japanese referred to the Chinese as "pigs". In the Vietnam War, the US army's General Westmorland described the Vietnamese as "termites" and in the Iraq War Iraqi civilians running for cover were described by American pilots as "cockroaches".[44]

In excerpts from statements given by perpetrators in the Rwandan genocide, victims were described as *inyenzi* (cockroach).[45] They were also portrayed as creatures to be hunted and Mironko claims that "[i]n order to understand the genocidal process in Rwanda it is important to understand the use of hunting terms in relation to the narratives of the killers".[46] The genocidal acts are often referred to by perpetrators with hunting terms such as "kwihisha" (to stalk), "kwichira ku gasi" (to kill in full view), "gushorera" (to herd wild animals together), "guhiga" (to hunt or chase), "kuvumbura" (to flush out of hiding) and "gutera" (to attack).[47]

Pol Pot and his cadres imposed the most violent and oppressive rule on the people of Cambodia from 1975 to1979, obliterating the society and causing the deaths of up to two million people. This is how Neou Heang, a nun in the province of Kampong Chhnang, describes life in Cambodia under the Khmer Rouge:

> We had no rights; only they had rights. They killed and got rid of us as if we were animals. Before, the people could eat their own rice and work their own fields and not have enough on their own. During the Pol Pot regime they herded us like cows. If they wanted to kill us they could kill us.[48]

164

How poignant that she draws the comparison with animals and sees herself and other Cambodian's lives under the Khmer Rouge from that perspective. Isaac Bashevis Singer famously writes in his book, *Enemies: A Love Story*:

> As often as Herman had witnessed the slaughter of animals and fish, he always had the same thought: in their behaviour towards creatures, all men were Nazis. The smugness with which man could do with other species as he pleased exemplified the most extreme racist theories, the principle that might is right.[49]

In relation to animals we are their genocidal persecutors though written larger by many orders of magnitude greater than any genocide in human history.

Ideology and the discourses which flow from it are essential in supporting our violent abuse because we need justifications, however spurious, for our reprehensible acts. We like to think of ourselves as good people, people who do the right things.

Smith, writing of human genocide, sums all of this up so well:

> Genocide must be legitimated by tradition, culture or ideology; sanctions for mass murder must be given by those in authority; the forces of destruction have to be mobilized and directed; and the whole process has to be rationalized so that it makes sense to the perpetrators and their accomplices.[50]

## Capitalism and consumer demand

Consumer demand in its many forms is the major engine of animal exploitation. In our hyper capitalist world, we create endless desires and drive an economic system predicated on ever increasing consumption with ever increasing production. Capitalism treats nonhumans as objects to be used, resources to be exploited, products to be consumed and every day, by our participation, we fuel that mechanism.

## Essential mechanisms

From the above we can see that the essential mechanisms for our ongoing animal genocide are already in place and we utilise them efficiently and are applauded and rewarded for our efforts. It is important to understand that they do not function as separate isolated entities but are closely integrated to form a whole. For example, discourses and ideology will be a component part of each of the other mechanisms.

But even allowing for all of the above, we might think that we would feel some deep responsibility for what we do to animals, but for the most part, this is simply not the case and we are deeply anaesthetised against their pain. What is going on here? In order to understand we must return to where we started – to the human mind, where violence is fashioned and absolution for atrocities granted.

## CHAPTER 19

# Shocking revelations

*We used to wonder where war lived, what it was that made it so vile. And now we realize that we know where it lives...inside ourselves.*

Albert Camus[1]

## Experimental social psychology

PHILIP ZIMBARDO DESCRIBES two approaches to examining the "antisocial behaviour of individuals and violence sanctioned by nations."[2] The "dispositional" approach focuses on the individual in order to identify errant behavioural traits or psychological risk factors while the "situationalist" approach looks at the situations which people find themselves in and the influences these have on them.[3] Zimbardo explains the dispositional approach in this way:

> Locating evil within selected individuals or groups carries with it the "social virtue" of taking society "off the hook" as blameworthy; societal structures and political decision making are exonerated from bearing any burden of the more fundamental circumstances that create racism, sexism, elitism, poverty, and marginal existence for some citizens. Furthermore this dispositional orientation to understanding evil implies a simplistic, binary world of good people, like us, and bad people, like them. That clear-cut dichotomy is divided by a manufactured line that separates good and evil.[4]

Lee et al. interviewed and psychologically tested, nineteen murderers in prisons in California.[5] They found that, while ten of the prisoners had long histories of violence, were generally extroverted, had a strong masculine identity and showed poor impulse control, the remaining nine had never committed any criminal offences, had excessive impulse control, were mostly shy and had a gender identity which was feminine or androgynous.[6] Zimbardo notes that:

> These "shy sudden murderers" killed just as violently as did the habitual criminals, and their victims died just as surely, but it would have been impossible to predict this outcome from any prior knowledge of their personalities, which were so different from the more obvious habitual criminals.[7]

It appears that violence can be a product of our societies and the situations people find themselves in and this much has already been hinted at by our brief survey of mass human–human violence. The work of three major researchers in the field, Stanley Milgram, Philip Zimbardo and Albert Bandura along with their colleagues, tell us a great deal more about how this can happen and although their research concerns mostly human – human violence, it is particularly relevant to our enquiry.

## Milgram and authority

From 1960 to 1963, Stanley Milgram was a member of the Department of Psychology at Yale University and carried out experiments looking at the obedience level of experimental subjects in carrying out commands – some of which they believed would cause harm to a test subject or even put his life in danger.[8] This work was destined to make Milgram famous although not necessarily popular.

For a start, he needed to find research subjects and advertised for New Haven men to take part in a scientific study and offered them each $4 plus 50c car fare for about an hour's work. The story he used as a cover was that this experiment was about learning and memory and would involve a teacher (the volunteer), a learner and an experimenter who supervises the process. Here is how Milgram describes the scene:

> The experimenter explains that the study is concerned with the effects of punishment on learning. The learner is conducted into a room, seated in a chair, his arms strapped to prevent excessive movement and an electrode attached to his wrist. He is told that he is to learn a list of word pairs; whenever he makes an error, he will receive electric shocks of increasing intensity.[9]

What the volunteer does not know is that the experimenter is being played by a 31-year-old biology teacher and the learner by a 47-year-old accountant. The room where the "teacher" will sit has an impressive shock generator, apparently attached to the learner and going from 15 volts to 450 volts with labels progressing from "SLIGHT SHOCK" through to "DANGER – SEVERE SHOCK".[10] This impressive machine had 30 lever switches and when one was depressed a red light would glow, there would be an electrical buzzing, a blue light labelled "voltage energizer" would come on, the needle on the meter swung to the right and various clicks were heard.[11] All this and more created a real theatrical atmosphere and perhaps Milgram was even drawing upon his schoolboy interest in stagecraft.[12]

But it wasn't all about show. Milgram actually gave each volunteer teacher a taste of what they believed they would be administering and subjected them to a real 45 volt shock from the generator. No doubt it helped to dispel any lingering doubts they might have about the authenticity of what they were going to be doing.

## How it all worked

There were many variations to the experiment but the general protocol consisted of the learner having to remember which words were linked together in a list of words he had been given. Each time he gave an incorrect answer the teacher gave him an electric shock, announcing the voltage before actually administering the shock. With each succeeding wrong answer, the voltage increased by 15 volts. If the teacher faltered in his duties he would be prompted to continue by the experimenter (wearing a lab coat) who would say such things as, "please go on", right through to "you have no other choice, you *must* go on".[13]

Early on in the project it had become clear that vocal feedback from the "learner" would be very important. Pilot studies had shown, rather worryingly, that having no vocal feedback simply meant that the teacher continued right to the end without a problem and would give the highest shock possible. Mild protests also proved inadequate and, in the end, vehement protests were inserted into the protocol, but even these did not stop many teachers from giving the full range of shocks. This was a disturbing finding and Milgram observes:

> The situation did more than highlight the technical difficulties of finding a workable experimental procedure: it indicated that subjects would obey authority to a greater extent than we had supposed.[14]

In the actual experiments, as the shocks increased the learner protested more and more using a set menu – painful groans at 135 volts; at 150 volts he asks to be released; at 180 volts he cries "I can't stand the pain", at 270 volts there are screams, at 300 volts he insists he will not continue to take part. After this, his non-responses are considered to be wrong answers and shocks are given at steadily increasing levels. The shrieks continue until they fall silent at 330 volts and neither shrieks are heard nor answers appear in the electric answer box above the generator.[15] But the experiment continues until the final voltage of 450 volts is reached. One can only imagine that this must have been quite a gruelling emotional roller coaster for everyone concerned.

It is interesting that Milgram also ascertained what certain groups of people thought would happen in this experiment. He asked three groups psychiatrists, college students and middle-class adults, to estimate how high people would go in giving the shocks to the learner. All three groups grossly underestimated how many people would comply right to the end, believing that only a few might go so far. As it turned out, they were very wrong indeed.

## Proximity

The proximity of the learner played an important part in determining at which point the teacher would defy the experimenter and not carry on giving shocks. In one set of experiments the learner was in another room and could not be heard except for banging on the wall, in another the learner could be heard, in a third there is physical proximity of learner and teacher and in a fourth there was "Touch-Proximity":

> Thirty-five percent of the subjects defied the experimenter in the Remote condition, 37.5 in the Voice-Feedback, 60 percent in Proximity and 70 percent in Touch-proximity.[16]

Clearly, being close to the individual to whom we are causing pain affects us dramatically but surprisingly, out of the 40 teachers in each set of experiments, many still administered 300 volts or over. In the Remote test 65% administered the maximum 450 volt shock (375 volts was labelled "danger: severe shock"), in the Voice Feedback, 62.5%, the Proximity,

40% and even with the Touch-Proximity it was 30% who went to the maximum level. It is obvious that the teachers did not enjoy inflicting pain on the learner and needed to be persuaded to carry on, but importantly, they did carry on.

What was happening here? Milgram uses the term "agentic state" to denote when a person comes under the influence of an authority and a person's autonomy changes so that they become an agent for carrying out the authority's wishes. Not every individual reacts in exactly the same way of course and he discusses some of the different factors which might influence those variations. However, the numbers speak for themselves and Milgram makes these critical observations:

> The perception of a legitimate source of social control within a defined social occasion is a necessary pre-requisite to a shift to the agentic state...
>
> Within this situation, the idea of science and its acceptance as a legitimate social enterprise provides the overarching ideological justification for the experiment.[17]

And later, he offers this clarification:

> The fourteenth century Spanish Jesuit might have eschewed science, but he embraced the ideology of his church, and in its name, and for its preservation, tightened the screw on the rack without any problem of conscience.[18]

The agent renounces his own personal autonomy and cedes it to the accepted authority in order to fulfil that authority's goals.

Milgram observes that for people to behave in this way, they need some ideological validation, where violence can be legitimately sanctioned by authority for allegedly "good" reasons. In these experiments, the man in the white coat represents the authority of science but perhaps he could also, in another situation, be a particular construction of a political ideal, a tradition, a culture, a religion and so on, depending upon how heavily invested the "teacher" is in that particular authority. Our violence against animals is often justified by appeals to science, tradition, religion, culture, health, masculinity and other authorities.

Milgram also notes something extremely important about the shift in responsibility for actions taken and says, "The most far reaching consequence of the agentic shift is that a man feels responsible *to* the authority directing him but feels no responsibility *for* the content of the actions that the authority prescribes."[19] The agent no longer feels responsible for his actions.

Milgram's experiments were surprising and deeply disturbing in that they suggested that ordinary young Americans were willing to follow commands from an authority even if it meant causing severe pain and possibly even killing a person. He writes:

> Many subjects will obey the experimenter no matter how vehement the pleading of the person being shocked, no matter how painful the shocks seem to be, and no matter how much the victim pleads to be let out...It is the extreme willingness of adults to go to almost any lengths on the command of an authority that constitutes the chief finding of the study and the fact most urgently demanding explanation.[20]

Over fifty years later these experiments are still a source of fascination and some controversy, but the central findings remain and are as enlightening and as troubling as ever. Milgram went on to carry out laboratory simulations on over a thousand subjects in various situations and below are some of the "influence principles" to emerge from his research. They are factors which can help to influence people to commit acts which go against what would normally be expected of them.

- An acceptable justification for the actions to be carried out;
- Some form of contractual obligation;
- Having the participant take up a meaningful role which carries learned positive values;
- Providing rules to be followed, even if at some point those rules no longer make sense;
- Changing the semantics of what is being done such as from "hurting" a learner to "helping" a learner;
- Reducing the likelihood that the actor will be personally held responsible for any possible negative outcomes of any of the acts;
- Using small increments in the violent acts and increasing them gradually;
- A gradual change in the authority from, say, just reasonable and rational to unjust, unreasonable and irrational;
- Making the "exit costs" from the activity high.[21]

## Zimbardo and deindividuation

Philip Zimbardo examined, amongst other things, a process known as deindividuation, where the perpetrators, victims or both, have their individuality removed. This changes an agent's willingness to inflict pain or discomfort on another.[22] In one investigation young women, who we will call experimenters, delivered painful electric shocks to other young women over a number of trials. They could see the women through a one-way mirror and they could also hear them. Half of the experimenters were deindividuated at the start of the experiment. They were given numbers as their only identification; they wore hoods and they were treated as a group. The other half had name tags, no hoods and were treated individually. Both groups were told the same story about the experiment and what it was supposed to be about or as Zimbardo describes it, "the big lie they never questioned". What happened was that the deindividuated women delivered twice as much shock as the individuated experimenters. Being anonymous was a condition which allowed significantly more violent behaviour. Extensions of this work and replications, some using military personnel, confirm these general findings and Zimbardo concludes:

> Anything that makes a person feel anonymous, as if no one knows who he or she is, creates the potential for that person to act in evil ways – if the situation gives permission for violence.[23]

## Guards and prisoners

In the famous Stanford Prison Experiment, Zimbardo looked at how ordinary young men reacted to being placed in a simulated prison environment either as guards or as prisoners.[24] In order to do the experiment, Zimbardo and his team converted part of the

Stanford University Psychology Department into "prison cells". The men who took part in the experiment were all volunteers and were screened to make sure they had no history of drug use, crime or violence and no experience of playing the roles of prisoners or guards.[25] The group were given batteries of tests and interviewed and twenty-four of those deemed as the healthiest and most normal, were randomly assigned the roles of prisoners or guards.[26] The "prisoners" were "arrested" by the Palo Alto Police Department, booked in the police station and then taken to the "prison". As far as possible, the participants were made to feel like real prisoners or real guards.

The prisoners had their individuality removed. They had to wear a smock with their ID number on it and a head cover made from a women's stocking in order to hide any distinguishing hairstyles. The guards also lost their individuality and wore military style uniforms and mirrored sunglasses.[27,28] Even at this distance in time, looking at the web site with the old photographs and text boxes it is possible to appreciate how real and intimidating this became.[29]

Although the experiment was scheduled to run for two weeks, it was obvious that problems were developing and it had to be terminated after only six days because:

> Pacific young men were behaving sadistically in their role as guards, inflicting humiliation and pain and suffering on other young men who had the inferior status of prisoner. Some "guards" even reported enjoying doing so. Many of the intelligent, healthy college students who were occupying the roles of prisoner showed signs of "emotional breakdown" (i.e., stress disorders) so extreme that five of them had to be removed from the experiment within that first week.[30]

Zimbardo decided to terminate the experiment not only because of the increasing degradation and violence taking place but also because he was becoming affected himself and was taking on the role of a rigid authority figure of a Prison Superintendent looking after "his" prison.[31,32]

Important aspects of this experiment are the anonymity of the participants, both guards and prisoners, as well as a social structure which allowed for certain attitudes and actions. Zimbardo points out that the situational forces triumphed over the positive dispositions of the people.[33] He also highlights an important difference between the research paradigm in Milgram's experiments and that in this one. In Milgram's work, there is a formal authority prompting the subject to obey but in this research there is none.

> Rather, the situation is created in such a way that subjects act in accordance to paths made available to them, without thinking through the meaning or consequences of those actions.[34]

The situation allowed the guards, or at least some of them, the licence to act on their ideological understanding of what they believed is the right way for a guard to behave towards prisoners and it is worth remembering that these young men were understood to be psychologically the healthiest and most normal of the original group.

Zimbardo describes the essential conditions which were in play in the experiment:

> Central to this mind set were the oppositional issues of power and powerlessness, dominance and submission, freedom and servitude, control and rebellion, identity and anonymity, coercive rules and restrictive roles.[35]

These thirty words from Philip Zimbardo sum up perfectly our relationship with the billions of nonhuman animals whom we exploit. Even though he did not write it about animals he could not have been more accurate.

Zimbardo's thesis about deindividuation and societal channels is supported by other research in very different contexts including eleven year olds playing sport in Germany, violent crime in Northern Ireland and combatants from different cultures.[36,37,38]

## Bandura and moral disengagement

Along with the work of Milgram and Zimbardo we find that of Albert Bandura, which both complements theirs and, in many ways, draws it together. But because of our focus on animals, one experiment carried out by Bandura is particularly interesting and concerns labelling and dehumanisation. Bandura *et al.* set up a situation where college students were able to "overhear" a research assistant speaking to an experimenter about students from another college, some of whom were said to be "nice" others said to be "animals" and the remainder not described at all.[39] Then the original college students took part in an experiment where they were asked to give electric shocks to the students from the other college. The results showed the effects of labelling and "dehumanisation" and Bandura explains:

> The subjects gave the highest level of shock to those labeled in the dehumanizing way as "animals," and their shock level increased linearly over the 10 trials. Those labeled "nice" were given the least shock, whereas the unlabeled group fell in the middle of these two extremes. Thus, a single word – animals – was sufficient to incite intelligent college students to treat those so labeled as if they deserved to be harmed.[40]

Bandura developed a theory of moral disengagement, which describes how a person's moral controls may become disengaged from the consequences of their actions.[41,42] This means that given certain conditions, people are able to carry out or contribute towards, actions which they would normally describe as wrong, yet feel no moral responsibility for supporting them or carrying them out. The conditions he identified are: moral justification; euphemistic labelling; displacement of personal responsibility; diffusion of personal responsibility; disregard for, or distortion of, the consequences of the actions taken; dehumanisation of victims; attribution of blame to the victims; advantageous comparison (it's better than the alternative); and progressive moral disengagement.[43] Without explaining these just at the moment it might already be obvious how many of them can contribute towards the mass violence perpetrated against animals.

Bandura notes that there is no requirement to be a monster in order to carry out monstrous acts:

> The findings from research on moral disengagement are in accord with the historical chronicle of human atrocities. It requires conducive social conditions rather than

monstrous people to produce atrocious deeds. Given appropriate social conditions, decent, ordinary people can do extraordinarily cruel things.[44]

The facilitation of moral disengagement in relation to our treatment of animals functions so smoothly and is so deeply embedded in our world, that fundamental moral questions asked about our violence against animals are often received with confusion, bewilderment or even derision.

## Conditions facilitating moral disengagement

Taking this body of work as a whole we, not surprisingly, find some of the conditions identified by researchers are quite similar, so I have amalgamated a number of them and drawn up a list of what I believe are core conditions facilitating moral disengagement, particularly in relation to ideology and discourses.[45,46,47] In the list below I include a very brief explanation for each one, how it applies to animals and I have added, at the end of each section, a shorthand way of thinking about it.

**Moral justification for the acts carried out.** It is common for people to claim a right to use animals. Animals are often constructed in texts as beings who are part of a hierarchy and that their lower status in this hierarchy justifies them being used by humans. The claim might be based on various forms of the Great Chain of Being, certain understandings of tradition, religion, incorrect science or some other source although it is often simply understood as common sense – ideological common sense. We say they are *only* animals and should be *treated like animals* because animals deserve to be treated in a particular way. They are ours to use. *We have the moral right to use animals as we wish.*

**Meaningful positive roles of the players involved in abuse.** The butcher, animal farmer, animal testing scientist, racehorse owner, etc. are all understood as being upstanding people doing good work. Never are they portrayed as people involved in systems of abuse. We construct such identities again and again in this positive way while those who support animal liberation are constructed as extremists, ignorant, weirdos, terrorists and emotional wimps. *These are good people with proper jobs who would never contribute to violent abuse.*

**Basic rules to be followed or existing societal channels.** Doing what is allowed by the law or encouraged by our understanding of society, religion, tradition, culture or science is one way in which abusive actions can be constructed as acceptable. We might even claim that some of these actions are necessary and required of us. This conveniently absolves the perpetrator of any responsibility. *It is legal, supported by the state, normal, everyone does it and we have always done it.*

**Change of semantics or euphemistic labelling.** Power lexicalises the world. Particular words are chosen to obscure the reality described. We *cull, send to market, process* animals, we sell *mince, sweetbreads* and *braun*. In laboratories, animals are *enucleated, sacrificed* and *donate blood* while those on farms *give milk* and *produce bacon*. Horses *serve* in war and animals don't whimper in pain but make *vocalisations*. *Change the words, change the reality and the moral questions disappear.*

**Deindividuation (anonymity) of the perpetrator.** The loss or submersion of our identity into a group can mean that we no longer exercise the controls which we normally would. We become part of the crowd. But also, being individually anonymous may have a similar effect – our actions do not lead back to us. *Being anonymous lowers the barriers for abuse.*

**Diffusion of responsibility**. What is done to animals often involves many people and so an individual does not feel the burden of personal accountability. The group diffuses this responsibility. In buying products from animal exploitation industries because millions also buy them, there might be little personal ownership of the acts carried out on our behalf. *It was not done for me personally so it's not my fault.*

**Displacement of responsibility**. The decision to carry out abuse was not made by me. I simply do what I am told and I can't accept responsibility for the outcomes of decisions made by others. *I am just doing what I am required to do.*

**Deindividuation of victims**. We make sure that the billions of animal victims used by humans have no names and no individuality. Sometimes they are given numbers. This corrodes any recognition of them as real beings. Often, they are not even referred to as she or he but as it, just as we refer to objects. They might also be described by using mass nouns signifying no individuality or sentience but only amorphous material – hunting *elephant* or eating *horse*. There is no personal connection nor any understanding of them as individual beings or as "subjects of a life" with all that this entails. *No individuals and no sentience mean no problem.*

**Authority.** Authority comes in many forms. There is the authority of governments, organisations, tradition, academia, science, culture, identity, religion and so on. Some interpretations of these construct ideologies which condone abuse. Ideologies shape laws and regulations which give authority to act and sanction the actions carried out. *X gives us the authority to do what we do.*

**Exit costs are high (leaving the system has personal costs)**. It is difficult to step outside of the dominant ideology, discourses and practices of animal abuse and to refuse to be part of the power structure we have been born into. We risk being thought of as strange, abnormal, deluded, weak and becoming an outsider. Refusing to be part of the systems of animal exploitation can come at a devastating personal cost. *Challenging the system can be very bad for you.*

**Advantageous comparison – making harmful conduct look good**. This constructs a reality where what we do to animals is better than the alternative. For example, the claim is often made that animals would need to be fending for themselves and be in danger if they were not cared for on farms and in intensive units where they get medical attention, are kept away from cold and rain as well as being safe from dangerous predators (except of course, ourselves). This is essentially the alibi for Happy Meat and its various spinoffs. Animals in laboratories, we are always told, receive the best possible care. *What we do to animals is much better than the alternative.*

**Disregard or distortion of consequences**. Discourses construct a world where what happens to animals is not really as bad as it seems, or it is just not important enough to consider. In scientific papers animals are not recorded as screaming, bleeding, struggling or whatever and often they just disappear rather than being killed. Farmed animals are not really incarcerated, they don't miss their families, mothers soon forget about their children being taken away and they are killed humanely. *It's not really as bad as it seems and it's not worth being concerned about.*

**Reification.** In so many discourses animals are constructed as things for our use; machines, models, raw materials, objects of research, parts of a production system, as resources and so on. This has now become so normalised that our relationship towards them has become purely instrumental. They are parts of systems, means to an end, but not sentient beings. *Animals are things to be used.*

**Attribution of blame to the victims.** In numerous ways animal's lives are portrayed as having purposes which relate to serving human wishes and we construct identities such as *beef cattle, dairy cows, dual purpose chickens, laboratory rats, game, pack animals, cage birds, race horses* and so on. We tell ourselves, this is their reason for their existence and so there is nothing wrong with using them for that purpose. We conveniently blame the victims for being what we construct them to be. We ask what they are for, not who they are. *This is why they exist.*

**Transformational power of moral disengagement**. The more we employ conditions which facilitate moral disengagement the easier it gets and the more normal and acceptable it becomes, to support or use violence against animals. Eventually the various abusive practices just become ideological common sense and we stop even asking if what we do is right. There is a story which the great South African writer André Brink would tell to his students. Once, when he was visiting Paternoster and Veldrift, which are small towns on the west coast of South Africa, he came across a worker who was boiling crayfish. The man would break off their tails and then throw them into a pot of boiling water. Brink asked the man if it didn't hurt the crayfish when their tails were snapped because they made crying noises, but the man assured him that "They get used to it."[48] *The more we do it, the easier it gets for us.*

## How the system works

After our short journey through this landscape, we can now fashion a better understanding of how we are able to carry out mass violence against nonhuman animals on an unthinkable scale, yet lack of any feelings of responsibility for what we do.

As we have seen from examining human – human violence, the essential mechanisms for carrying out large-scale abuse and carnage already exist in our societies, they just need to be adapted to the particular task in hand, to the practice we want to carry out. We have in place bureaucracy and organisation, science and technology, the ability to coerce, the support of the law, authority and power, secrecy, capitalism and consumer demand, and supporting discourses and ideologies. It is this combination of mechanisms which allows us to seamlessly carry out large-scale, complex exploitive practices against nonhuman animals. And sadly, we know all too well that it works very effectively.

But I suggest that it is the discourses and the ideologies which they draw upon, which are absolutely crucial. They form part of each of the other mechanisms for violence and they supply their specific justifications and rationalisations as needed. The conditions for moral disengagement outlined above are all facilitated to a greater or lesser extent through texts because texts are pathways into our minds. The landscape into which we are born, is awash with texts of all kinds which construct animals and our uses of animals in such a way as to explain, support, authorise, justify and reinforce our exploitive practices. They administer the anaesthetic of moral disengagement and make sure we feel no responsibility for these terrible acts. Without moral disengagement it is hard to imagine how such practices could ever continue and it is the animal abuse system's greatest asset. Without the prop of moral disengagement, the great edifice which is animal exploitation would surely creak and eventually collapse.

Here is a general overview of how the system works:

- Those with power use what is already in place to carry out the exploitive social practice.
- This can only happen through human agency and it requires justifications
- Discourses, drawing on an overarching ideology, supply explanations which at the same time facilitate moral disengagement.
- No moral concerns are raised and the exploitive practice goes ahead.

## System failure

The machinery of moral disengagement does not always run as smoothly as it might and from time to time it falters, allowing dissident views to break out, challenging the status quo and producing real world consequences. We can learn a great deal from these malfunctions, for one thing we can learn how to deliberately make them happen, again and again. Such dissident action is a contestation about power, about the nature of the world we live in and its nonhuman and human inhabitants; we are in a struggle about nothing less than the construction of reality itself.

In the final chapter let's look at a few examples of alternative discourses, the effects they can have, and at possible ways to help us change the world for animals and ourselves. First, we travel into history to look at a few stories about old saints and then, turning to more modern times, we consider the lives of two nonhuman individuals, Pheonix and Jerom.

## CHAPTER 20

# Other voices, other worlds

*What we look for is no longer the* Pax Romana, *the peace of imperial Rome, nor is it simply the* Pax Humana, *the peace among humans, but the* Pax Gaia, *the peace of Earth and every being on the Earth. This is the original and final peace, the peace granted by whatever power it is that brings our world into being.*

Thomas Berry[1]

## Making changes

WE ARE so immersed in the dominant ideologies of our world that at times it is difficult to imagine that the world could be anything other than it is. Indeed, we are often told that this is just the way the world is, the way things are, thereby crushing any hope that things could be otherwise. But there is nothing inevitable about the way our human world is structured, it is not the product of inexorable physical processes, not a facet of the physical universe but an artefact of some human minds and a creation of dominant ideological power. So, change begins by believing that other worlds and other ways of being and interacting are possible.

There is a long history of individuals and communities who have understood the world differently from our present exploitive, anthropocentric and elitist perception and who have seen animals as beings in their own right. Many of these people were devoutly spiritual and while they are represented in all of the major faiths and none, I want to look at a few examples from some old Christian traditions.

## Old saints and animals

Preece offers numerous examples of spiritual groups through the ages who have been either vegetarian or vegan[2] There are good reasons to believe that vegetarianism was practised by many early Christians and in the 5th century St Augustine believed that Christians practising vegetarianism were "without number" (there were an awful lot of them!) and that they were vegetarians because they considered it unethical to kill animals for food. [3] Around two thousand years ago a community of early Christians had grown up in the desert of Egypt to live an ascetic, contemplative life. These people are often referred to as the Desert Fathers and Desert Mothers and it appears many were vegan or vegetarian.

Thus St Athanasius wrote of the desert-dwelling St Anthony that his, "food was bread and salt, his drink only water. Of meat and wine it is needless to speak, for nothing of the sort was to be found among the other monks either."[4]

The same saint was recorded to be at peace with the wild beasts, to have let his camel free when there was a drought and to have said that, "My book is nature and whenever I will I can read the words of God."[5] St Macarius, also known as The Lamp of the Desert, was accused of being gentler to a blind hyena kitten than to his fellow humans.[6]

St Jerome describes how Theron, a monk, would go into the desert at night and being joined by various animals, he would draw water from his well and offer them cups of it for being so kind for accompanying him.[7] The truth of this story obviously cannot be confirmed although there is equally no reason to doubt it, but as Preece points out what is revealing is the spirit behind it. He says that given the significance of wells in the desert and their importance to the family group, "[t]o share one's well with the animals was a mark of great respect and an intimation of closely felt kinship."[8]

Other tales and legends show a similar spirit. In the Celtic Christian tradition, possibly because of the fusion of Christianity with earlier Celtic beliefs, there was emphasis on the imminence of God in the world.[9] According to Bradley, early publications of the lives of the Celtic saints "give a picture of men and women who were deeply attached to animals and birds."[10] Columbanus it is said, would summon the animals and birds who would come to him and play. On one occasion wolves stand peacefully around him as he recites a psalm and on another, he is able to persuade a bear to leave its cave so that he can use it as a hermitage. Otters warmed the feet of St Cuthbert as he came out of the North Sea, and dried him with their fur, and St Serf had a lamb that followed him about and a pet robin and he is said to have raised a pig from the dead.[11] A boar, although savage to begin with, became the first disciple of Saint Ciaran of Ossory and other animals also came and joined him: a fox, a badger, a wolf and a stag.[12] St Mochuas lived a simple life as a hermit but was kept company by a fly, a mouse and a cock.[13] The cock would keep the hour of Matins for him, the mouse would not let him sleep more than five hours a day but if he tried, the mouse would lick his ear and wake him up. The fly would walk along each line of the psalter as he read it and would keep his place until he returned to it for the saying of more psalms.[14]

Then there is the famous story of St Kevin and the blackbird:

> According to his custom he put his hand (in raising it to heaven) out through the window, when, behold, a blackbird happened to settle on it, and using it as a nest, laid its eggs there. The saint was moved with such pity and was so patient with it that he neither closed nor withdrew his hand: but held it out in a suitable position without tiring until the young were quite hatched. In perpetual remembrance of this wonderful happening, all the representations of St Kevin throughout Ireland have a blackbird in the outstretched hand.[15]

And in another tale, we meet an abbot in Lismore who comes across a bird weeping by the path. He is puzzled by this and then an angel comes to explain:

"Hail, cleric!" says the angel "let the trouble of this vex thee no longer. Molua, Ocha's son, is dead. And for this cause the creatures lament him, for that he never killed any creature, little or big. And not more do men bewail him than the creatures, and among them the tiny bird though seest".[16]

Finally, we have the story of Columba. As Columba, who is nearly 80 years old and is living the last day of his life, sits down to rest, a white horse who carried the milk for the monastery, approaches him and senses his soul is about to depart.[17,18]

It went to the saint and strange to tell put its head in his bosom, inspired as I believe, by God, before whom every living creature has understanding, with such perception of things as the creator has decreed; and knowing that its master would presently depart from it, and that it should see him no more, it began to mourn and like a human being to let tears fall freely on the lap of the saint, and, foaming much, to weep aloud.[19]

With all of these tales, it is the compassionate and embracing spirit behind them which is so arresting and they are windows into a very different world. The depth and breadth of this compassion is highlighted in the words of St Isaac the Syrian (c.345–438) who is answering the question, "What is a charitable heart?":

It is a heart which is burning with love for the whole creation, for men, for the birds, for the beasts, for the demons – for all creatures. He who has such a heart cannot see or call to mind a creature without his eyes being filled with tears by reason of the immense compassion which seizes his heart; a heart which is softened and can no longer bear to see or learn from others of any suffering, even the smallest pain, being inflicted upon a creature.[20]

The people we have read about in these examples did not live in some abstracted world of luxury but lived austere, physically and mentally demanding lives, yet they practised deep compassion, love and respect for their fellow beings.

## Phoenix the calf

Next, to something more contemporary, and this concerns a series of events where compassionate discourses relating to animals broke through in a very public way, revealing our often paradoxical beliefs.

As described at the start of this book, the United Kingdom had an outbreak of foot-and-mouth disease in 2001 and the British government attempted to arrest it by carrying out a mass killing of both infected animals and those healthy ones in the areas around affected farms. This caused much anger, mistrust, protest and genuine heartbreak from people in all walks of life. Mounds of bodies and burning pyres were common sights in the media and at least six million animals were slaughtered.[21]

On Good Friday, 13 April, a white calf was born at Clarence Farm near Axminister in Devon. Five days later slaughtermen on their routine foot-and-mouth assignment came to the farm and killed a total of fifteen cows including the calf's mother, about thirty sheep and two calves, both less than a week old, and left their bodies in the barn.[22]

The farmers, Philip and Michaela Broad, could not watch but stayed in the farmhouse with their son. The bodies lay there for five days until more officials from the Ministry came to disinfect them. They opened the barn to reveal a scene of carnage and then, to their surprise, a small white calf who had been lying next to her dead mother got up and walked towards them.[23]

Philip and Michaela were very angry at what had happened and phoned the Ministry giving them an hour to deal with the problem, but when there was no reaction, they contacted a couple of newspapers and informed them of what had happened. But they also did something else which changed everything. They named the little calf and she became Phoenix. She was no longer an amorphous statistic in the cull, or raw material in the food industry she was an individual, a sentient being, an orphan with a name. She was photographed and her picture and story appeared in a local newspaper and then her tale was taken up by the national newspapers.[24]

The Ministry of Agriculture insisted she must be killed even though she had been cleared by a Ministry veterinarian of having any disease. A slaughterer went to the farm in the company of a policeman to carry out this directive, but the owners steadfastly refused and informed the official he would have to go and get an injunction from the court. The police officer also then informed the slaughterer he must leave the farm.

But the story was now well and truly in the public domain and all manner of people became involved in responding to the calf's plight. Browne records the groundswell of outrage:

> But pleas to spare Phoenix flooded in. The Mirror launched a campaign to "Save Phoenix from the Ashes". Animal rights groups and actress Carla Lane threw in their support. Anthony Gibson, regional director of the National Farmer's Union, said the calf's slaughter would "make King Herod look like a humanitarian". Tony Banks, Labour MP and former Government Minister, spat: "I was extremely angry. The idea of slaughtering this animal was totally unacceptable. The officials from Maff [Ministry of Agriculture Fisheries and Food] are Daleks". [25]

Such was the countrywide sympathy for this survivor that newspapers and backbench MPs warned that her slaughter could even mean a loss in the general election for the ruling Labour Party. *The Sun* newspaper had a picture of Prime Minister Tony Blair and the cross hairs of a gun sight focused on Phoenix with the caption, "Vote Labour or the calf gets it!"[26] Then, suddenly, government policy about foot-and-mouth was changed. The government insisted that the timing was simply a coincidence and nothing to do with this case, but it meant Phoenix was no longer a target and would be allowed to live out her life, and as it turned out she did so as both a pet and an international celebrity.[27]

Just as with the Watchtree Nature Reserve and its plaque of commemoration for the animals who were killed, the story of Pheonix is paradoxical. We have two opposing beliefs in conflict, an ideology which understands animals as commodities, objects of commerce, essentially all alike, and another view which recognises them as sentient beings with lives and families and as individuals having their own inherent worth. Provided these beliefs remain compartmentalised in our heads and in our lives, we can do the trick of subscribing to each, but with Phoenix both came into play at the same time and a choice had to be made.

Was it that she became an individual because she had a name, or was it perhaps because her mother was killed and she was an orphan, or that she looked so innocent and alone, or that her story was told on her behalf, or that people felt a direct personal call to intervene to save her? We do not know, but the new way of seeing her disabled the usual mechanisms facilitating moral disengagement and she became a defenceless child in need of our assistance and we responded accordingly. Alternative discourses saved her life.

## Jerom

Our final example is another story vividly highlighting competing beliefs, although in a very different context, and sadly this does not end as happily. I came across this account many years ago and have periodically looked at it, unsure of how it might best be retold but always convinced that this is a story which deserves to be heard.

The author's own words offer us a unique window into a world which is seldom described in such intimate detail, and into her own struggle as she came to terms with the conflicts she faced. She does not speak of ideology or sociological theory or anything like that but with her honesty and the immediacy of her writing we are immersed in a bleak dystopian world; one which due owing to secrecy and the hegemonic power of science and the scientific–economic establishment, lies safely buried behind smart facades and big reputations.

This is the story of Jerom, a chimpanzee in a research establishment, and it is narrated by the young woman who got to know him and who cared for him until his death. It brings together the domination of animals by humans, the power of science over ethics and compassion and the power of men over women. It also echoes many of the themes of the antivivisection protests around the turn of the 19th century. This remarkable account has never been published but was placed on the internet in 1997 and revised in 2001.[28] In its re-telling here I have used many of the author's own words so that the reader can get a sense, a feel, for the way it is written because I think this is also a very important facet of the whole story.

In 1993 Rachel Weiss was a junior at Indiana University in the USA and took a job as a weekend caretaker in the Medical Sciences animal section and later would also work in the Psychology Department's animal facility. She looked after the animals, fed them, gave them water and cleaned out their cages. Some animals had tumours, song birds had their vocal cords cut and rats and rabbits had electrodes cemented into their skulls.

When she graduated, she obtained a job as a Primate Care Technician at the Yerkes Regional Primate Research Center (now the Yerkes National Primate Research Center) based at Emory University in Atlanta. She was keen to be a part of scientific research and proud to be working at Yerkes. After a time and with relatively little training, she was able to work with chimpanzees in the Chimpanzee Infectious Disease (CID) section. She describes it in this way:

The atmosphere in the building was bleak and timeless. Unwashed stains from countless feces wars covered the ceiling; almost every one of the water devices in each cell either didn't run, or ran incessantly. The walls were gray concrete. Cells were formed by interwoven, steel bars creating 3-inch squares forming the front and ceiling of each cage. The side and back walls were concrete; each eight-inch-thick side wall had a slide-door in it, connecting adjacent cells. Incandescent light fixtures hanging from the building's drop-ceiling were the only source of light.[29]

To prepare for their duties, workers needed to put on protective clothing in an anteroom and...

"dressing out" in CID included a full-face shield, a Tyvek jump-suit, several layers of rubber gloves, a thick face mask, and a bouffant hair-cover...[30]

It was in this facility she would meet Jonah, Buster, Manuel, and Jerom as well as other chimpanzees and go on to write about them and their lives, but particularly she would write about Jerom and in 1995 began to keep a diary about him. Although she had chosen to be part of the scientific enterprise and often uses scientific terms, the animals are not portrayed as research objects but as individuals with emotions and meaningful lives. For some reason, her induction into bioscience and her earlier work with animals did not produce a disengagement from these chimpanzees.

She writes both as a scientific observer and as somebody who knows the animals personally. This duality may appear as a mere detail, but it is far from such. It signifies a conflict of ideas about the world, one which would intensify as the months went by and would eventually place an intolerable burden on this young woman. Her writing is a truly remarkable and courageous account of what she witnessed, what she did, and her thoughts and feelings. And at the centre is Jerom, a powerless fellow being with whom she shared her days and who was entirely at the mercy of those in this bare detention facility, who would use his body and take away his life.

When she first meets Jerom he is already sick and being used for AIDS research:

It was difficult for me to get a handle on Jerom at first. He was sick when I met him, and he seemed to spend most of his time sitting on his bed-board (a Lucite and steel shelf jutting out from the wall 6 feet from the floor). I'd been told that he was a jerk, and liked starting trouble especially with Manuel and being generally unfriendly with caretakers. Jerom was dark in fur and face, and of lanky build; he and Buster were half-brothers.[31]

She writes of Jerom as a real individual who is, "dark in fur and face, and of lanky build", and talks about his reputation and his half-brother, and we cannot help but understand that for her, he is a fellow traveller in life. The ideological tension is evident. Yerkes and its staff regard Jerom as a model, a tool to be used for science, but still degrade him, describing him as a jerk; but Weiss, while supporting scientific research, cannot help but see a vulnerable person behind the bars. We find out more information about Jerom as she writes:

> Jerom was born on 23 February, 1982, so he was 13 years old when I met him. When I began to work in CID in the middle of August, 1995, he had been enduring a bout of diarrhea for the previous six months.[32]

She describes how she learns the ropes and gets to identify the individual animals for whom she is caring:

> I had little experience up close and personal with chimps and it took a little while for me to recognize the obvious individual characteristics of each chimpanzee face. But I knew that Jerom was getting sick; the first time I vividly remember identifying him in his social group he was sitting on his bed board, quite emaciated, with wild, sunken, staring eyes. Like the humans I've seen affected by wasting, I could see Jerom's skull under his skin.[33]

The words *meet* and *endure*, and the name *Jerom* can only relate to another individual and for eyes to be *wild* and *staring* means there has to be an experiencing somebody behind them. The enormity of this ongoing recognition cannot be over stated, nor the inevitable ethical drain it places on Weiss.

The first attempt to infect Jerom was when he was only two-and-a-half years old, but he did not become infected that time so other attempts followed until he was eventually super-infected. Along with the other chimpanzees, he was used in various research projects over the years but also spent time simply being held in captivity.

Eventually, the thirteen chimpanzees in the facility are transferred to new accommodation, but sadly this means Jerom is separated from Buster, his long-time cage companion. Over time, Jerom becomes more and more sick until staff believe he is going to die and begin giving him antibiotics and fluids. He is clearly very ill indeed:

> He was so severely weakened by the wasting that he had a difficult time holding his head up. He would sit with his knees drawn up and held his chin in his hand: he had to manually turn his head in the direction he wished to face. At times he would hang his head and sob quietly; other times he would climb down from his bed board and curl up in a fetal position on the floor in front of me.[34]

Here Weiss flouts the discipline of scientific reporting; she describes in plain language the suffering of Jerom, including him sobbing quietly and alone.

Jerom is darted or "knocked down" so that some of his blood can be taken and given to another chimpanzee called Nathan to infect him. Darting is a very stressful procedure for the chimpanzees and it would cause panic when it was about to happen. Some of the chimpanzees were "trained to present" – to offer their arms so that blood could be drawn. They were trained to become compliant agents in their own abuse but it was better than the alternative.

Despite his poor condition, slowly, over weeks, Jerom regains some of his health and Weiss interacts with him as best she can, given the bars and her protective suit and facemask. His health continues to improve and then Buster, his old cage friend, is able to visit. It is a joyous reunion even within those drab walls:

> We stood and watched Buster and Jerom jump and scream, pound barrels, throw balls, each in their own cell, for many minutes. Eventually they calmed down, without more than a few slaps at one another; soon they held hands through the doorway, and even kissed and were soon rolling on the floor happily gnawing on one another.[35]

But after two weeks together, Jerom's health begins to deteriorate once more, and in November 1995 they are separated again. Jerom now has pneumonia, and still continues, after six months, to suffer from diarrhoea. He no longer gets visits from his long-time companion but lives a solitary life. Buster is in an adjacent cage and they are separated by an opaque sliding door. Each spends time looking for the other through the key hole. Jerom understands that a key will open the door to his friend:

> Jerom began to understand that a key opened the padlock that let the door open to let Buster in. Now he would get very excited if he saw me with a key, or he would tug at the padlock (he could reach it with his fingers) and turn it over and then attempt to slide the door open. It was very disheartening to watch him try to get to his friend:[36]

Weiss tries to persuade the person in charge to allow some contact between Jerom and Buster but she is told that the "in charge" feels auditory and visual contact with other chimpanzees is sufficient. In addition, he tells her to stop caring so much about the animals and to remember why they are at Yerkes. He tells her Jerom will be euthanised when he has an undisputed opportunistic infection.

Weis appreciates that Jerom and the other chimpanzees have emotional needs, including contact with others, and that they are able to suffer not only physical but also emotional pain. The person in charge sees Jerom as a research device to be kept alive and in good enough shape to continue to be used until he has fulfilled his purpose or, more correctly, the purposes of the experimenters. The person in charge represents the power of the Centre and the power of science, which together co-construct the social reality of what is right and what is acceptable. Weiss, meanwhile, is obviously starting to colour outside the lines.

The "in charge" is trying to impose his authority in order to draw her back into the "right" ideology, where she is no longer be engaged with and empathic towards the animals who are in her care. Otherwise the situation could become very disturbing and raise many questions, some possibly even about the very nature of this practice itself. It also seems likely that the fact Weiss is a woman plays some part in his attitude, women supposedly being thought of as more emotional and less rational than men. Emotion, it appears, is understood as weakness and a functional disability.

Jerom is knocked down for more tests and Weiss raises her concerns about Jerom's mental health with the veterinarian who is carrying out the knockdown. She is worried Jerom might be getting dementia, but the vet dismisses this concern as he does the opportunity for an X-ray on the anaesthetised Jerom. In order to gather observations to be presented in a research publication, Jerom is simply being observed day after day as his health steadily deteriorates. The scientific goals, the goals of the researchers and the institution, are the only priority. Weiss stands alone, as if seeing things that do not even exist for other members of staff.

Jerom's behaviour alters; he seems to try to control everything and becomes frustrated and even gets obsessed about the boots of the care workers. By December 1995 he is becoming evermore frantic and violent, desperately trying to break down the division between his and Buster's cell. Weiss describes in detail these changes, including his developing the practice of regurgitation and reingestion, or r + r as it is known, where a chimpanzee will vomit and then re-ingest his vomit from the floor or from his hand. Jerom was even re-ingesting foul vomit and:

> [t]he tension Jerom was experiencing got even worse, until he was "painting" with feces
> on the wall of his cell, and pacing with an irregular, abnormal gait around his cage.[37]

Through all of this, Weiss touchingly records her intimate observations of Jerom; his funny, quirky habits, his fear and frustration and the effects his isolation and disease have on him. Doing this is something only an empathic, feeling, engaged individual can do – attempting to understand, however imperfectly, the world of a fellow being undergoing life-ending trauma and isolation from his peers.

Jerom no longer seems to be of any real interest to the experimenters and is simply existing in his cell because it has been decided that this is his life now. Weiss meanwhile also cares for and interacts with all the other chimpanzees, doing what she can for them physically and psychologically, and getting to know each of them more closely with every passing day, which they spend together away from natural light and fresh air.

But it is Jerom who weighs most heavily on her mind and she becomes evermore desperate to ease his pain and isolation:

> If he sat in the front right corner with his face pressed up against the bars, he could see
> the anteroom door and out the double doors which I often, illegally, opened. If he sat
> toward the front left side of his cage he could see all of the chimpanzees across from
> him. Often I would sit near him, and in the mornings, if he wanted company, he'd hold
> out the back of his hand in greeting. If he wanted me to groom he'd turn his shoulder
> and back toward the bars.[38]

Weiss describes how once, in a desperate attempt to offer the chimpanzees some stimulation, a TV was brought in and they were shown *People of the Forest: The Chimps of Gombe,* a documentary co-written by Jane Goodall and Hugo van Lawick and narrated by Donald Sutherland. Imprisoned chimpanzees who are experimented on being shown free living chimpanzees on a TV screen. It would not be the last time this was done in a desperate attempt to help them mentally "escape the dungeon". An act of genuine compassion was, inevitably, in such a place, transformed into yet another form of torment. As Weiss says today, "There was no way to do right by them."[39]

## Final days

Jerom's health fluctuates as it has done over the years, but by the end of January it starts to deteriorate seriously, just when – with Yerkes' announcement that he is infected with a retrovirus – he is becoming "famous". However, he becomes more aggressive towards Weiss and she feels his illness is affecting him more badly than ever. At one point the heating in the facility cannot cope with the cold weather and Jerom sits shivering in his bleak cell enduring the cold; his pale anaemic gums exposed when he yawns.

Although desperately ill, he is knocked down repeatedly, and on 6 February he is knocked down yet again so that the vet can take a blood sample. This time Jerom takes a long time to wake up and then he collapses and there is blood in his mouth and he has bitten his tongue. His young life is ebbing away.

> When I returned to CID after I had a quick lunch, Jerom was sitting on the bed board with no expression on his face. It looked as if none of the muscles of facial expression were working properly. When I sprayed down the cages that afternoon he curled up on his bed board and stayed that way for a long time.[40]

After the laboratory tests come back it is clear that Jerom is extremely ill and the senior vet feels he should be euthanised. But it is not as simple as that. The case for killing Jerom will have be argued for in front of a committee because, ironically, Jerom is "protected":

> There are several criteria that must be met before a member of a threatened species can be killed, and Emory's Institutional Animal Care and Use Committee, a regulatory body, had strict criteria of their own.[41]

Jerom cannot even die in peace, not even when a veterinarian believes it is the right thing to do and that it is in Jerom's best interests. His interests are not seen as important and a committee of those who have been responsible for making him this way must decide if his death is acceptable to them. But there is yet another group which must ponder over the path of Jerom's final days:

> This meant that the PI would call a meeting of all interested parties on the AIDS Project, and this meeting would set a date for Jerom's euthanasia (I will not use the biomedical term "sacrifice" when discussing Jerom's death) when all interested parties could be present. Jerom would die within the next two weeks. I felt very conflicted about this news. Half of me wanted Jerom to die with some shred of dignity intact: quietly in his cage (death by anemia would not be unpleasant). The other part of me wanted to be assured that Jerom's life and death were for a reason – as useful to the research as possible (not because I supported the research, but because that's what Jerom's entire existence was about).[42]

It is taken for granted that the term "all interested parties" naturally excludes Jerom. The interested parties are the scientific researchers and this is all about human goals being achieved at the expense of an abused, dying and lonely chimpanzee.

Jerom lives and has lived in a never-ending hell of utter powerlessness as others used his body for their own purposes. His life is all he has, all he has ever possessed, but those who have painfully violated him for years will eventually be the ones to take it from him where, when and how they see fit. Then he will be disposed of as no longer of any further use.

Jerom's medications are stopped.

Jerom looked terrible. He had huge bags under his eyes, and looked as if he hadn't slept in a week. He let me rub his back for quite a while. I noticed that he'd eaten every single edible thing in his cage over night, and was very anxious to take food from me.[43]

On the 9 February Weiss notes that Jerom seems ravenous and, poignantly, as his death approaches, he spends his time looking through a door at a world of which he has been so cruelly deprived:

I had the doors open and Jerom spent a lot of time looking outside. Like most everybody else in CID, Jerom paid little attention to me when he could see the sky and trees and hear the calls of chimpanzees from the general colony.[44]

Opening the doors is against the rules as this is a level two containment facility. But to see other living beings outside, sense the fresh air and relative freedom only metres away but always out of reach is the only respite Weiss is able to offer Jerom. Her friend is dying and she refuses to withhold her compassion:

The day before Jerom died I spent hours with him, and noted in my journal that I hadn't seen him laugh in weeks. It had been my goal, every day of the previous six months, to make him laugh. Many days I did not succeed, but I always tried.[45]

Her supervisor does something strange on that day, perhaps because of guilt or out of sympathy, we do not know:

In the morning my supervisor sent me to CID with a Coke, a Butterfinger candy-bar, and some powdered donuts. After I'd suited up and said good morning, I put some Coke in a paper cup and held it up to the bars for Jerom to drink.[46]

As I said, I spent virtually my entire day with Jerom. I wanted to be assured that I had done everything I possibly could for him. I saved the powdered donuts for his evening meal. I opened the package and handed them to him one by one. He seemed to know what they were, and after eating one (and getting powdered sugar all over his face) put the others carefully on his bed board. That was Jerom's last day.[47]

Even at this stage Jerom knows what he is doing and he does not eat everything all at once. Desperately sick though he is, he still looks to the future and showing great discipline, carefully saves a few treats for later.

## Jerom's last day

It is the next morning and Jerom's final hours have arrived. He needs droperidol for sedation and would normally not be allowed any food but Weiss ignores the no food ban. And he gets to see his old friend Buster one more time, if only in a mirror:

I came to work very early the next morning. Everyone in CID was quite calm when I came in to say good morning and give them all a banana. The vet had told me that the droperidol I would give Jerom would upset his empty stomach, so he too got a banana, despite the mandatory fast. I decided to let him and Buster see each other one last time.

I had a large square mirror which I held in my lap as I sat several feet in front of the cement wall between the boys' cells. Both Buster and Jerom came to look at themselves, and stared at each other for a long time.[48]

Eventually Jerom is darted but the anaesthetic takes a long time to take effect. Weiss and the vet look at Jerom's still and bloated body as they wait for lab results and final permission from the person in charge to proceed. The permission does not come but they ignore that rule and go ahead anyway:

The vet decided not to wait for the PI's okay, after all. He went to get the gurney. I said good-bye to Jerom. The vet returned with a gurney covered in white sheets – unusual, royal treatment (usually the chimps were slung, unceremoniously, onto the cold steel gurney). I bent down to pick up Jerom's feet, and the vet told me not to: my supervisor came into the chimp room, into Jerom's cell, picked up his feet while the vet picked up his arms. They put him on the sheets and covered him in more sheets. He looked like he was sleeping; everyone else in the building yelled and screamed and jumped up and down. No one had ever left CID before. I kissed Jerom goodbye as they took him away. He died on the table in the necropsy room two hours later.[49]

What we are witnessing are the rigid conventions of animal testing blurring and fraying at the edges; sugary doughnuts and Coke, sheets for the patient, treated like royalty, handled carefully and kissed goodbye. As Jerom leaves the building it is like a death row prison scene as the inmates shout and scream and the condemned individual is taken away to be executed. And executed he was.

## Afterwards

After Jerom's death Weiss wants to help the other chimpanzees, especially Nathan who has been infected. She speaks to the person in charge but is told there will be no treatment for Nathan. Dissatisfied with this, she asks for an appointment with the Director who made very clear to her how these animals are viewed:[50]

He also told me that there were no plans to treat Nathan. I was shocked; he explained to me that it was important to collect HIV infected tissues from Nate, which would be hampered by any virus-inhibiting treatments. He reminded me that Nathan was a laboratory animal, born and bred. He reminded me that Nathan's comfort and well-being were not of primary concern to the research. He admitted that infecting Nathan may have been premature…I left the meeting confused, dismayed, and disgusted.[51]

Nathan is *a laboratory animal* and *his comfort and well-being were not of primary concern*. Weiss went on vacation and then decided to resign. She was surprised to find that the Center seemed shocked and concerned about this and wanted to know why she had chosen this course of action. She asked for an exit interview but found little interest from Yerkes, although the Director himself did attend – something which was very unusual:

The director's presence at my exit interview was an unprecedented event, and this man listened to me, a lowly care-tech, for over an hour. He had to leave before the meeting's

conclusion. He stood up, walked across the small office and, towering over me, shook
my hand, looking me square in the eye. I met his challenging stare and thought that he
looked a bit frightened. I didn't know whether that look meant that I had scared him
because of what I might do with the information I'd learned, or because somewhere
inside him he knew I was right. Whatever its source, it was that look that gave me the
inspiration to write Jerom's story.[52]

This moment between Weiss and the Director captures much of the struggle regarding
animal experimentation. Weiss challenging the power of the institution and the
authority of scientific orthodoxy with its inherent ideology of human elitism and,
in all likelihood, defying the ideology of male superiority as well. It is a tribute to her
courage and determination that during her time at Yerkes she refused to be moulded
into something she is not, that she refused the way of obedience and disengagement and
was not crushed by her experiences. Having shared part of her life with an individual
for whom she cared, and having witnessed him suffer dreadfully and finally have his life
taken away, she made her choices and would never be the same again.

What was it about her actions and words that made an impression on the Director?
Perhaps her honesty had touched some of his own deepest concerns and doubts about
what goes on behind those walls and many others like them.

In the final words of her narrative Weiss writes:

> I am obviously not a likely candidate for objectivity. Nonetheless, I have done my
> utmost to ensure that the telling of this tale remained as forthright and honest as I
> possibly could make it. I did not need to embellish to make this story poignant: the
> truth itself was nightmare enough.
>
> Rachel Weiss, July 1997[53]

She wonders about her objectivity but she has recorded events and descriptions which
would never appear in the records of experimentation. She has had the courage to write
about what is edited out of scientific reports, to fill in the blanks and actually tell the
truth. I know of no such accounts in any of the scientific journals and institutional
reports that have been published.

The experiential worlds of Jerom and Weiss cannot be allowed to exist because this
would expose the exploitive social practice of animal experimentation, along with its
supporting ideology, to the authentic critical examination which they deserve.

Following her resignation, Weiss spent nearly a year in Uganda working at the Semliki
Chimpanzee Project where she was the first Assistant Project Director. Today she says:

> I like to believe that what Jerom and the CID chimps, as well as the chimps of Semliki,
> taught me about who chimpanzees are enabled me to be a better human being. I don't
> think I'll ever be finished repaying them.[54]

I am reminded of a piece of writing by Jane Goodall about some of the primates she has
known. It appears in her introduction to the book, *Rattling the Cage* by Steven M. Wise,
a book which has made a huge contribution to bringing the subject of animals and the
law into the public domain.[55] She writes about Dick, a chimpanzee she met who lived in

a small cage with a cement floor in a zoo and who showed clear signs of stress. Next to the cage was a male gorilla who would continually vomit into his hand and then reingest the vomit.[56] Then there was Jade who was used as entertainment for upmarket birthday parties and other events. All her teeth had been removed. Finally, there was Jojo an adult male whose home was a five foot by five foot cage in a windowless basement of a research laboratory. He was born in Africa but had spent over ten years in the laboratory.

This is Goodall's deeply moving description of these and so many millions of other individuals have had torn away from them by us.

> It will be too late for Jojo, Jade and Dick – they are gone. Yet still I think of them and I feel a deep sense of shame; shame that we, with our more sophisticated intellect, with our greater capacity for understanding and compassion, deprived them of freedom, stole from them the dim greens and browns; the soft gray light of that African forest, the peace of the afternoon; when the sun flecks through the canopy and small creatures rustle and flit and creep among the leaves. Deprived them of the freedom to choose each day, how they would spend their time, and where and with whom. Deprived them of the sounds of nature, the gurgling of the streams, murmuring wind in the branches, of chimpanzee calls which ring out so clear, and rise up through the tree tops and drift away in the hills. Deprived them of their comforts, the soft leafy floor of the forest, the springy, leafy branches from which sleeping nests can be made. But it is not too late for hundreds of others who are, as this book goes to press, languishing in manmade prisons.[57]

## All that they have

Our abbreviated and fragmentary journey through the physical, written and spoken texts of our world has shown us that the animal text is everywhere. We are steeped in it and by far the majority of it reinforces and justifies our violent exploitation of our fellow earthlings: These texts continually whisper to us that we are an elite species with permission to use "lower" animals, that these creatures have purposes which are to serve our desires, that they are tools and slaves, willing combatants, gleeful racers, production machines and much more. These are the lies our human minds have created for burying the truth and normalising our incessant cruelty.

We are an army of occupation laying waste to everything in our path, claiming land, water and other living beings as our own, to take and use as we please. In this ongoing conflict we long ago selected our slaves and today we relentlessly exploit them as we have done to generations of their ancestors. And we will continue to do this to their children and their children's children down through the generations unless we are stopped. Unlike us, our fellow earthlings take only what they need from this world, just enough for them and their families to survive, but we take or poison even that.

The Great Karoo in South Africa is a semi desert region of around 400 000 square km and as recently as two hundred years ago it was home to many free-living animals. But with the encroachment of farming, the erection of fences and systematic killing, these residents were annihilated and today they are no more. We find only isolated farms where goats and sheep scorch beneath the hammer of the sun, crowded under a small, twisted acacia or seeking relief in ephemeral shadows from whatever tufts of scrub they can find. For the most part this is now a vast empty landscape just like so many other places all over the world. The animals who, for hundreds of thousands of years, occupied it as their ancestral home are gone because of us. Only their ghosts haunt these beautiful plains and the small kopjes which turn amber as the light of day fades. This and all those other emptied landscapes on the globe, and there are so many of them, are texts speaking of immense loss and unremitting violence. Are we willing to read the texts of our culpability and to make reparations to the scattered kin of those whose land we have stolen and whose ancestors we have murdered in their millions? Are we willing to restore the land to the descendants of its original occupants as justice surely demands?

## Walking towards liberation

Following the Peterloo Massacre in 1819 in Manchester when cavalry, with swords drawn, charged a peaceful meeting of around 70 000 people who wanted electoral reform, the famous English poet and vegetarian, Percy Bysshe Shelly, wrote his epic work *The Masque of Anarchy*. The poem is said to be the first modern statement of non-violent resistance and in it he captures, amongst other things, the powerlessness of the oppressed people of the time, but the words also seem to speak so eloquently of our nonhuman captives as well:

> 'Tis to be a slave in soul
> And to hold no strong control
> Over your own wills, but be
> All that others make of ye.

So how can we bring about change for our fellow earthlings? There are multiple ways and so many people doing wonderful work, but one thing I think we need to do is read and interpret those ubiquitous animal texts etched into this landscape of the damned, in order to expose their ideologies sanctioning our abuse. Time and again, the industries and institutions which use such ideologies to justify their actions are allowed to deflect interrogation elsewhere, to economics, scientific methods, culture or wherever. We need to stay with the old Quaker's question and demand, "By what right do you do this?" and follow that question relentlessly until we reach the core ideology being used and expose it for critical examination. Bring it into the light and let those who support it account for it.

Second, if we are alert to the conditions which facilitate moral disengagement, we can learn to disrupt and disable them. We saw how this happened as a natural process as the story of Pheonix unfolded and to some extent it was there during the foot-and-mouth epidemic generally and certainly in the creation of the Watchtree Nature Reserve.

As we learn to recognise and disable the mechanisms of moral disengagement, we are better able to comprehend their omnipresence and their ceaseless manipulating assault upon our perceptions. They swirl around us all the time in multiple contexts. Being able to disable them also offers us the opportunity to have more effective, accurate and open communication with people who carry out or support animal oppression.

An example of a simple way to highlight and disrupt some of these mechanisms is by changing the language we ourselves use such as refusing to employ terms like zoo animals, layers, pack animals, race horses, animal models or dairy cows, but instead saying plainly what is really happening to these exploited beings. This can lead to some very interesting conversations although we should not forget that a refusal to be a party to violent oppression, can often offend.

We must bring animals back into our consciousness and truly see them as fellow beings, as individuals who are alive in this world with us and who have shared our collective journey of millions of years of evolution. And we must recognise that the psychological distance which has been created between us and them is a tool of moral disengagement. We need to see them, in Henry Benson's words as "...other nations, caught with ourselves in the net of life and time, fellow prisoners of the splendour and travail of the earth."[58]

We can act in constructive ways and employ discourses of compassion, care, diversity, equality, unity and justice and recognise how the struggle for the liberation of nonhuman animals is intimately connected with other struggles such as those against sexism, racism, economic exploitation, slavery and so on. And crucially we can produce our own texts. A letter to a newspaper, a silent demonstration, a march, a religious service, asking for a vegan meal, singing an anthem together (every revolution needs a good anthem!), commemorating activists who have died or who have been imprisoned, writing pamphlets, speaking to groups, putting up a plaque of commemoration or a statue, using paintings and photography to tell the story and so on. There are so many things we can do and while some may seem quite minor and insignificant, we should not be deceived because even the smallest of actions or perhaps a few words, can possess immense semiotic power for someone. There are no small victories.

Well over a hundred years after those clashes in Battersea, the Brown Dog still tells his story every single day in England's capital city. He has not been silenced. Will Jerom and the many other victims of our abuse have their memorials one day as well? Will we have empty zoos turned into flower and herb gardens with space for free-living animals, disused slaughterhouses as museums to animal farming, services of remembrance of our violence against our fellow earthlings, wild areas set aside only for the benefit of their free living inhabitants, and so much more?

Ultimately transformation comes from changing ourselves and we need to construct the "barricades of peace" in our minds, in our children's minds and in the minds of those occupying our institutions, because our minds are where our violence originates and from here it bleeds into the world causing misery and death. It does not have to be like this.

I hope this book will help you to look at some part of your everyday world and read it for the first time; read in it the story of oppression it records, read the animal text written, scratched, worn, built and riven into this landscape of the damned, recording the pain and suffering of its billions of victims.

Confident of our collective journey towards liberation, I will leave the final words of a future of hope to Shelley with these lines, which although from separate poems seem particularly appropriate together here:

Hope is strong; Justice and Truth their winged child have found...
...Let a great assembly be, of the fearless, of the free.

# Endnotes

## Introduction
1. Desmond Tutu in Alex Perry, "Retiring from Public Life, Desmond Tutu Reflects on Good and Evil", *Time*, 7 October 2010.

## Chapter 1
2. Du Fu or Tu Fu cited in Guy Gavriel Kay, *Under Heaven* (New York: Ace, 2011).

## Chapter 2
1. Title Not Known, *Sunday Herald Sun*, 13 January 2003.
2. Norman Fairclough, *Language and Power.*, 2nd ed. (Harlow: Pearson Education, 2001), 2.
3. Bourdieu cited in Fairclough, 76.
4. Sayer cited in B Danermark et al., *Explaining Society: Critical Realism in the Social Sciences.* (London: Routledge, 2002), 37.
5. Fairclough, *Language and Power.*, 27.
6. Teun A. van Dijk, "Principles of Critical Discourse Analysis," *Discourse & Society* 4, no. 2 (April 1993): 255, https://doi.org/10.1177/0957926593004002006.
7. "Brief History of Barbed Wire," accessed February 21, 2016, http://www.rushcounty.org/barbedwiremuseum/bwhistory.htm; Alan Krell, *The Devil's Rope: A Cultural History of Barbed Wire* (London: Reaktion Books, 2002).
8. "Brief History of Barbed Wire."
9. David Nibert A, *Animal Opression and Human Violence: Domesecration, Capitalism and Global Conflict* (New York: Colombia Univeristy Press, 2013).
10. "Farmer and the Cowman Lyrics – Oklahoma Musical," accessed February 2, 2018, https://www.allmusicals.com/lyrics/oklahoma/farmerandthecowman.htm.
11. Nibert, *Animal Opression and Human Violence: Domesecration, Capitalism and Global Conflict.*
12. "Brief History of Barbed Wire."
13. Jason Hribal, "'Animals Are Part of the Working Class': A Challenge to Labor History," *Labor History* 44, no. 4 (November 2003): 447, https://doi.org/10.1080/0023656032000170069.
14. J.M. Coetzee, *The Lives of Animals* (London: Profile Books Ltd, 2000), 22.

## Chapter 3
1. Speech Philip K. Dick, "How To Build A Universe That Doesn't Fall Apart Two Days Later", (1978), https://urbigenous.net/library/how_to_build.html.
2. Norman Fairclough, *Language and Power*, 2nd ed. (Harlow: Pearson Education, 2001). 87.
3. Vol 5 Truth and Reconciliation Commission, "Truth and Reconciliation Commission of South Africa Report," October 29, 1998, 294, http://www.justice.gov.za/trc/report/finalreport/Volume5.pdf.
4. Teun A. Van Dijk, "Critical Discourse Analysis," in *The Handbook of Discourse Analysis*, ed. Deborah Schiffrin, Deborah Tannen, and Heidi E. Hamilton (Oxford: Blackwell, 2001), 352.
5. Teun A. Van Dijk, "Critical Discourse Analysis," *The Handbook of Discourse Analysis*, 2001, 349–371.
6. Fairclough, *Language and Power.*
7. Many of these are drawn from Fairclough.

8. A McKee, *Textual Analysis: A Beginners Guide.* (London: Sage, 2003).

9. Paul Starkey and Pascal Kaumbutho, eds., *Meeting the Challenges of Animal Traction: A Resource Book of the Animal Traction Network for Eastern and Southern Africa*, ATNESA Publication (Harare: ATNESA, 1999), 2.

10. Elizabeth Atwood Lawrence, "Conflicting Ideologies: Views of Animal Rights Advocates and Their Opponents.," *Society & Animals* 2, no. 2 (1994): 183. https://doi.org/10.1163/156853094X00199.

11. Vol 5 Truth and Reconciliation Commission, "Truth and Reconciliation Commission of South Africa Report," 297.

## Chapter 4

1. J.M. Coetzee, The Lives of Animals (London: Profile Books Ltd, 2000).

2. Joan Dunayer, *Animal Equality: Language and Liberation* (Derwood, Maryland: Ryce Publishing, 2001), 1.

3. Lisa A. Kemmerer, "Verbal Activism: 'Anymal'," *Society and Animals* 14, no. 1 (2006): 9, https://doi.org/10.1163/156853006776137186..

4. Andrew Linzey, *Creatures of the Same God, Explorations of Animal Theology* (Winchester: Winchester University Press, 2007), xi.

5. Institute for Security Studies, "Murder and Robbery Overview of the Official Statistics: 2014/15," September 2015, https://issafrica.s3.amazonaws.com/site/uploads/SA-Crime-Stats%E2%80%932015-Murder-and-robbery-fact-sheetV2.pdf.

6. "FACTSHEET: South Africa's Crime Statistics for 2016/17," Africa Check, accessed May 8, 2018, https://africacheck.org/factsheets/south-africas-crime-statistics-201617/.

7. Arran Stibbe, "As Charming as a Pig: The Discursive Construction of the Relationship between Pigs and Humans," *Society & Animals* 11, no. 4 (2003): 375–392, https://doi.org/10.1163/156853003322796091

8. cited in Stibbe.

9. Stibbe.

10. Stibbe, 378–79.

11. Sigmund Freud, "A Difficulty in the Path of Psychoanalysis," 1917, In *The Standard Edition of the complete psychological works of Sigmund Freud* vol 3. (London: Hogarth Press, 1953).

12. "Etymology – Origin of the Phrase, 'There's More than One Way to Skin a Cat.' – English Language & Usage Stack Exchange," accessed March 5, 2016, http://english.stackexchange.com/questions/32123/origin-of-the-phrase-theres-more-than-one-way-to-skin-a-cat.

13. Cited in "Etymology – Origin of the Phrase, 'There's More than One Way to Skin a Cat.' – English Language & Usage Stack Exchange."

14. cited in "Etymology – Origin of the Phrase, 'There's More than One Way to Skin a Cat.' – English Language & Usage Stack Exchange."

15. "Handle with Kid Gloves – Meaning and Origin.," accessed March 12, 2016, http://www.phrases.org.uk/meanings/handle-with-kid-gloves.html.

16. "Handle with Kid Gloves – Meaning and Origin."

17. "Handle with Kid Gloves – Meaning and Origin."

18. Cited in "Handle with Kid Gloves – Meaning and Origin."

19. Christina Hardyment, "Breast, Bottle or Goat's Udder?," the Guardian, November 17, 2007, http://www.theguardian.com/lifeandstyle/2007/nov/17/familyandrelationships.family2.

20. "Definition of Chamois," accessed March 12, 2016, http://www.merriam-webster.com/dictionary/chamois.

21. "The Shambles York | Inside York," accessed March 5, 2016, http://www.insideyork.co.uk/what-to-see/shambles.html.
22. "The Shambles York | Inside York."
23. "The Shambles York | Inside York."
24. "The Historical Gazetteer of England's Place-Names," accessed March 5, 2016, http://placenames.org.uk/browse/mads/epns-deep-28-fd-mappedname-000563.
25. "The Historical Gazetteer of England's Place-Names,"
26. "Online Etymology Dictionary," accessed March 7, 2016, http://www.etymonline.com/index.php?term=rendering.
27. "2.Slaughterhouses," accessed March 7, 2016, http://www.fao.org/wairdocs/lead/x6114e/x6114e04.htm.
28. David Meeker, "North American Rendering: Processing High Quality Protein and Fats for Feed," *Revista Brasileira de Zootecnia* 8(SPE) (2009): 432-440, https://doi.org/10.1590/S1516-35982009001300043
29. "Render Magazine," accessed March 31, 2016, http://www.rendermagazine.com/.
30. "About | National Renderers Association," accessed December 18, 2017, http://www.nationalrenderers.org/about/.
31. "Events – 82nd NRA Annual Convention," accessed March 31, 2016, http://convention.nationalrenderers.org/events-tours/.
32. "By Name – Attendees – 82nd NRA Annual Convention," accessed March 31, 2016, http://convention.nationalrenderers.org/attendees/name/.
33. National Geographic Society, "Domestication," National Geographic Society, January 21, 2011, http://www.nationalgeographic.org/encyclopedia/domestication/.
34. Smith cited in Nibert, *Animal Opression and Human Violence: Domesecration, Capitalism and GlobalConflict* (New York: Colombia University Press, 2013).
35. Charles Patterson, *Eternal Treblinka* (New York: Lantern Books, 2001).
36. Bamber Gasgoine, "History of the Domestication of Animals," accessed March 15, 2016, http://www.historyworld.net/wrldhis/PlainTextHistories.asp?historyid=ab57.
37. Spencer, *The Heretic's Feast.*
38. "'Cattle' Online Etymology Dictionary," accessed March 15, 2016, http://www.etymonline.com/index.php?term=cattle.
39. "'Chattel' Online Etymology Dictionary," accessed March 15, 2016, http://www.etymonline.com/index.php?term=chattel.
40. "'Capital' Online Etymology Dictionary," accessed March 15, 2016, http://www.etymonline.com/index.php?term=capital.
41. Linda Kalof, "The Multi-Layered Discourses of Animal Concern.," in *Social Discourse and Environmental Policy: An Application of Q Methodology*, ed. A Helen and J Proops (Cheltenham: Edward Elgar, 2000), 4.
42. Kalof, 5.
43. J. Mason, "The Animal Question: Uncovering the Roots of Our Domination of Nature and Each Other.," in *Igniting a Revolution: Voices in Defense of the Earth*, ed. S. Best and A. Nocella J. (Edinburgh: AK Press, 2006), 181.
44. Abdela cited in A McKee, *Textual Analysis: A Beginners Guide* (London: Sage, 2003), 44.
45. C. Merchant, *The Death of Nature.* (San Francisco: Harper Row, 1980), 127.
46. Merchant, 165.
47. Merchant, 168, 169.
48. Carol J. Adams, *The Sexual Politics of Meat: A Feminist-Vegetarian Critical Theory* (London: Continuum, 2000).

49. Carol J. Adams, "The Book — Carol J. Adams," accessed March 25, 2018, http://caroljadams.com/spom-the-book/.
50. Adams, *The Sexual Politics of Meat: A Feminist-Vegetarian Critical Theory*.
51. T Duckworth, "Dictionary of English Slang and Colloquialisms of the UK," accessed March 26, 2018, http://www.peevish.co.uk/slang/index.htm.
52. Duckworth.
53. Duckworth.
54. N. Fiddes, *Meat: A Natural Symbol*. (London: Routledge, 1991), 148–51.
55. Fiddes, 148–51.
56. Fiddes, 148–51.
57. Fiddes, 154.

## Chapter 5

1. Cormac Cullinan, *Wild Law* (Claremont, South Africa: Siber Ink, 2002).
2. Sean Nee, "The Great Chain of Being," *Nature* 435, no. 26 (May 2005). https://doi.org/10.1038/435429a,
3. Steven Wise M, *Rattling the Cage. Towards Legal Rights for Animals* (Cambridge Massachusetts: Perseus Publishing, 2000).
4. Aristotle, "Politics," accessed March 20, 2016, http://classics.mit.edu/Aristotle/politics.1.one.html part V.
5. Aristotle part VIII.
6. Aristotle part V.
7. Preece, "Thoughts out of Season on the History of Animal Ethics." *Society and Animals* 15, no. 4 (2007): 365–378. https://doi.org/10.1163/156853007x235537.
8. Wise, *Rattling the Cage. Towards Legal Rights for Animals*.
9. Cicero, "De Natura Deorum," accessed March 21, 2016, http://penelope.uchicago.edu/Thayer/E/Roman/Texts/Cicero/de_Natura_Deorum/2A*.html.
10. Wise, *Rattling the Cage. Towards Legal Rights for Animals*.
11. "Summa Theologica – Christian Classics Ethereal Library," accessed April 4, 2016, http://www.ccel.org/ccel/aquinas/summa.FP_Q96_A1.html.
12. Rod Preece and David Fraser, "The Status of Animals in Biblical and Christian Thought:A Study in Colliding Values," *Society and Animals* 8, no. 3 (2000): 245–263. https://doi.org/10.1163/156853000511113.
13. "XXVI. Prometheus; Or the State of Man. Bacon, Francis. Of the Wisdom of the Ancients. 1857," accessed April 6, 2016, http://www.bartleby.com/82/26.html.
14. "Petrus Camper (1722–1789)," accessed April 7, 2016, http://petruscamper.com/camper.htm.
15. "Petrus Camper (1722–1789)."
16. Martin Kemp, "Slanted Evidence," *Nature* 402, no. 6763 (1999): 727–727, https://doi.org/10.1038/45392.
17. Kemp.
18. Kemp, 727.
19. Kemp, 727.
20. Marjorie Spiegel, *The Dreaded Comparison. Human and Animal Slavery* (New York: Mirror Books, 1996), 21.
21. S. Gould J, *Wonderful Life* (London: Huchinson, 1989).
22. Gould, 28.

23. S. Gould J, *Bully for Brontosaurus. Essays in Natural History* (London: Huchinson, 1991), 181.

24. Nee, "The Great Chain of Being," 429.

25. David Baltimore, "50,000 Genes, and We Know Them All (Almost)," *The New York Times*, June 25, 2000, sec. Opinion, http://www.nytimes.com/2000/06/25/opinion/50000-genes-and-we-know-them-all-almost.html.

26. Alok Jha and science correspondent, "Gorilla Genome Analysis Reveals New Human Links," *The Guardian*, March 7, 2012, sec. Science, https://www.theguardian.com/science/2012/mar/07/gorilla-genome-analysis-new-human-link.with close parallels in sensory perception and hearing"

27. Kay Prüfer et al., "The Bonobo Genome Compared with the Chimpanzee and Human Genomes," *Nature* 486, no. 7404 (June 28, 2012): 527–31, https://doi.org/10.1038/nature11128.27; C. Adams J, "The War on Compassion," *Antennae Issue 14: 5-11*, no. 14 (2010): 7.

## Chapter 6

1. Jacob Bronowski, "The Disestablishment of Science," *Encounter*, July 1971.

2. E Carlson, "EugenicsArchive.Org: Image Archive on American Eugenics Movement Scientific Origins of Eugenics," accessed January 18, 2017, http://www.eugenicsarchive.org/eugenics/list3.pl.

3. S. Selden, "EugenicsArchive.Org: Image Archive on American Eugenics Movement Popularization of Eugenics," accessed January 18, 2017, http://www.eugenicsarchive.org/eugenics/list3.pl.

4. Carlson, "EugenicsArchive.Org: Image Archive on American Eugenics Movement Scientific Origins of Eugenics."

5. Charles Patterson, *Eternal Treblinka* (New York: Lantern Books, 2001),

6. Carlson, "EugenicsArchive.Org: Image Archive on American Eugenics Movement Scientific Origins of Eugenics," 2.

7. Carlson, "EugenicsArchive.Org: Image Archive on American Eugenics Movement Scientific Origins of Eugenics."

8. Patterson, *Eternal Treblinka*, 87.

9. Patterson, 82,83.

10. Selden, "EugenicsArchive.Org: Image Archive on American Eugenics Movement Popularization of Eugenics," 2.

11. Carlson, "EugenicsArchive.Org: Image Archive on American Eugenics Movement Scientific Origins of Eugenics," 4.

12. Carlson, 4.

13. Selden, "EugenicsArchive.Org: Image Archive on American Eugenics Movement Popularization of Eugenics."

14. Degler cited in Patterson, *Eternal Treblinka*, 88.

15. Patterson, 81–90.

16. Kuhl cited in Patterson, 98.

17. Les Mitchell, "Nonhumans and the Ideology of Purpose," *Anthrozoös* 25, no. 4 (2012): 491–502. https://doi.org/10.2752/175303712X13479798785931.

18. G. Miles, "Supertaler Causes Rift between Breed Societies," *Farmer's Weekly*, February 2005, 36.

19. McMaster, "Quest for Excellent Dohnes.," *Farmer's Weekly*, December 10, 2004, 33.

20. R. Billet, "Getting to Grips with Poultry Terms.," *Farmer's Weekly*, December 17, 2004, 44.

21. Mitchell, "Nonhumans and the Ideology of Purpose."

22. Mitchell, 500.

23. Ufrieda Ho, "One Nguni Cow Turned into 400 Plates of Food to Teach Responsible Eating," Sunday Times, accessed September 22, 2016, http://www.timeslive.co.za/sundaytimes/lifestyle/2016/09/18/One-Nguni-cow-turned-into-400-plates-of-food-to-teach-responsible-eating.

## Chapter 7

1. "Sympathy" in Paul Laurance Dunbar, *The Complete Poems of Paul Laurence Dunbar.* (New York: Dodd, Mead and Company, 1925).
2. Marjorie Spiegel, *The Dreaded Comparison.: Human and Animal Slavery* (New York: Mirror Books, 1997).
3. P. E Lovejoy, "Slavery in the Context of Ideology.," in *The Ideology of Slavery in Africa.*, ed. P. E Lovejoy (Beverly Hills: Sage, 1981), 11.
4. Hutereau cited in Keima. A. C, "Women in Slavery among the Mangbetu.," in *Women and Slavery in Africa*, ed. C. C Robertson and M. A Klien (Portsmouth: Heinemann, 1997), 148.
5. C Meillassoux, "Female Slavery.," in *Women and Slavery in Africa*, ed. C. C Robertson and M. A Klien (Portsmouth: Heinemann, 1997), 53.
6. J. O De Sardan, "The Songhay-Zarma Female Slave: Relations of Production and Ideological Status.," in *Women and Slavery in Africa*, ed. C. C Robertson and M. A Klien (Portsmouth: Heinemann, 1997), 139.
7. Allen cited in D Northrop, "The Ideological Context of Slavery in Southeastern Nigeria in the 19th Century.," in *The Ideology of Slavery in Africa*, ed. P. E Lovejoy (Beverly Hills: Sage, 1981), 110.
8. Retel-Laurentin in Meillassoux, "Female Slavery.," 53.
9. J Walvin, *Black Ivory.* (London: Harper, 1992), 206.
10. J Walvin, *Questioning Slavery.* (London: Routledge, 1996), 101.
11. Beckford cited in Walvin, 55.
12. Spiegel, *The Dreaded Comparison. Human and Animal Slavery*, 38.
13. Walvin, *Black Ivory.*, 54.
14. Spiegel, *The Dreaded Comparison. Human and Animal Slavery*, 56.
15. Walvin, *Black Ivory.*, 198.
16. Albert Taylor Bledsoe et al., *Cotton Is King, and pro-Slavery Arguments: Comprising the Writings of Hammond, Harper, Christy, Stringfellow, Hodge, Bledsoe, and Cartwright, on This Important Subject*, vol. 3 (Pritchard, Abbott & Loomis, 1860), vii.
17. Bledsoe et al., 3:ix.
18. Bledsoe et al., 3:xiii.
19. M Midgley, "Persons and Non-Persons.," in *In Defence of Animals*, ed. P Singer (Oxford: Blackwell, 1985), 54.
20. "Aristotle, Politics, Book 1, Section 1253b," accessed January 25, 2017, http://www.perseus.tufts.edu/hopper/text?doc=Aristot.%20Pol.%201.1253b&lang=original.
21. R. Nash F., *The Rights of Nature.* (Madison: University of Wisconsin Press, 1989), 118.

## Chapter 8

1. "The Slaughterer" in Isaac Bashevis Singer, *The Collected Stories of Isaac Bashevis Singer* (English and Yiddish Edition) (New York: Farrar Straus & Giroux, 1982).
2. "Fears over Tactics Used by Vegan Activists at Abattoirs and Restaurants," accessed April 1, 2017, http://news.sky.com/story/fears-over-tactics-used-by-vegan-activists-at-abbatoirs-and-restaurants-10820168.
3. Hribal, "'Animals Are Part of the Working Class,'" 435.
4. "About Us," South African Feedlot Association, October 3, 2016, http://safeedlot.co.za/about-us/.

5. Les Mitchell, "Animals and the Discourse of Farming in Southern Africa," *Society & Animals* 14, no. 1 (2006): 39–59, https://doi.org/10.1163/156853006776137122; Les Mitchell, "Farming: Animals or Machines?," *Southern African Linguistics and Applied Language Studies* 31, no. 3 (September 2013): 299–309, https://doi.org/10.2989/16073614.2013.837606; Les Mitchell, "Moral Disengagement and Support for Nonhuman Animal Farming," *Society & Animals*, 19, no.3 (2011), https://doi.org/10.1163/156853011X545529.
6. C. Gittens, "Good Grass; Better Cattle.," *Farmer's Weekly*, April 29, 2005, 40.
7. "Neil DeGrasse Tyson on Twitter," Twitter, accessed August 10, 2017, https://twitter.com/neiltyson/status/894689139853012992.
8. C Nel, "A Quest for the Ultimate Bush-Suited Steer.," *Farmers Weekly*, November 26, 2004, 36.
9. "Beefmaster SA | About the Breed," accessed May 24, 2016, http://www.beefmastersa.co.za/p2/about-the-breed/about-the-beefmaster-breed.html.
10. The South African Livestock and Stud Book Association in Mitchell, "Animals and the Discourse of Farming in Southern Africa," 43,44.
11. Nel, "A Quest for the Ultimate Bush-Suited Steer.," 37.
12. C. Gittens, "Ensuring the Best in Pig Genetics.," February 18, 2005, 43.
13. W. Flowers L., "Semen Quality Assurance" (Forty-ninth Annual North Carolina Pork Conference, Greenville, NC, 2005), https://projects.ncsu.edu/project/swine_extension/ncporkconf/2005/sessions/flowers.htm.
14. "Strict Selection Is Key, Says Top Dohne Breeder," *Farmer's Weekly* (blog), April 11, 2014, http://www.farmersweekly.co.za/animals/cattle/strict-selection-is-key-says-top-dohne-breeder/.
15. Denene Erasmus, "Farmer's Weekly | Strict Selection Is Key, Says Top Dohne Breeder," accessed August 30, 2016, http://www.farmersweekly.co.za/article.aspx?id=56231&h=Rearing-pigs-on-acorns.
16. "Beefmaster SA | About the Breed."
17. "Beefmaster SA | About the Breed."
18. "American Sheep Industry | Productivity of Ewes on Range," accessed January 17, 2017, https://www.sheepusa.org/ResearchEducation_OtherResearch_ProductivityOfEwesOnRange.
19. "Breeds – Belgian Blue," The Cattle Site, accessed September 7, 2016, http://www.thecattlesite.com/breeds/beef/8/belgian-blue/.
20. Michael Moss, "Animal Welfare at Risk in Experiments for Meat Industry," January 19, 2015, https://www.nytimes.com/2015/01/20/dining/animal-welfare-at-risk-in-experiments-for-meat-industry.html.
21. "Research Programs and Projects at This Location: USDA ARS," accessed December 28, 2017, https://www.ars.usda.gov/research/programs-projects/?modeCode=30-40-05-00.
22. Moss, "Animal Welfare at Risk in Experiments for Meat Industry."
23. Moss.
24. https://www.facebook.com/caitlin.dewey, "Wounded Pigs and Dehydrated Ducks: Questions Arise about How the Agriculture Department Treats Its Animals," Washington Post, accessed May 15, 2018, https://www.washingtonpost.com/news/wonk/wp/2018/05/14/usda-animal-research/.
25. https://www.facebook.com/karin.jacobsonbrulliard, "USDA Abruptly Purges Animal Welfare Information from Its Website," Washington Post, accessed May 15, 2018, https://www.washingtonpost.com/news/animalia/wp/2017/02/03/the-usda-abruptly-removes-animal-welfare-information-from-its-website/.

## Chapter 9

1. Plutarch, "Essays and Miscellanies", accessed 8 August 2019, https://ebooks.adelaide.edu.au/p/plutarch/essays/.
2. "Horse Meat – Questions and Answers – Food Safety – European Commission," Food Safety, accessed December 12, 2016, https://ec.europa.eu/food/safety/official_controls/food_fraud/horse_meat/qanda_en.
3. David Nibert A, *Animal Opression and Human Violence: Domesecration, Capitalism and Global Conflict* (New York: Colombia Univeristy Press, 2013).
4. Jason Hribal, "'Animals Are Part of the Working Class': A Challenge to Labor History," *Labor History* 44, no. 4 (November 2003): 447, https://doi.org/10.1080/0023656032000170069.
5. Citing The Animal World, September 1918 "Welsh Colliery Horses," National Museum Wales, accessed July 4, 2017, https://museum.wales/articles/2007-06-12/Welsh-colliery-horses/.
6. B. Coombes L and B. Jones, *These Poor Hands. The Autobiogrpahy of a Miner Working in South Wales* (Cardiff: Univeristy of Wales Press, 2002).
7. Coombes and Jones.
8. Hribal, "'Animals Are Part of the Working Class.'"
9. Hribal, 445.
10. "Waiting: The Monument to the Liverpool Working Horse, Land Transport," accessed January 24, 2019, http://www.liverpoolmuseums.org.uk/mol/collections/transport/item.aspx?id=468559.2019,
11. "Hack | Origin and Meaning of Hack by Online Etymology Dictionary," accessed December 18, 2018, https://www.etymonline.com/word/hack.
12. "Hack | Origin and Meaning of Hack by Online Etymology Dictionary."
13. Hribal, "'Animals Are Part of the Working Class,'" 446,447.
14. "Animals In War Memorial – The Animals In War Memorial – Park Lane, London," accessed May 6, 2016, http://www.animalsinwar.org.uk/index.cfm?asset_id=1373.
15. Don Gwilliam and Angela Curran, "In Memoriam: Two Accounts of the Memorial Service for Animals in London," The Ark, Spring 2010, http://www.all-creatures.org/ca/ark-214-3.html.
16. "Horse Memorial, Port Elizabeth," Guide to South Africa, accessed May 6, 2016, http://www.southafrica.net/za/en/articles/entry/article-southafrica.net-the-horse-memorial-port-elizabeth.
17. "Equestrian Statistics | British Horse Society," accessed May 3, 2016, http://www.bhs.org.uk/our-charity/press-centre/equestrian-statistics citing the British Equestrian Trade Association survey.2016,
18. "Equestrian Statistics | British Horse Society."
19. Mark Roodhouse, "Break the Taboo on Horsemeat – or Food Fraud Will Continue," February 11, 2013, http://www.historyandpolicy.org/opinion-articles/articles/break-the-taboo-on-horsemeat-or-food-fraud-will-continue.
20. "Horse Meat – Susanna Forrest," accessed February 21, 2018, https://susannaforrest.wordpress.com/category/horse-meat/.
21. "Horse Meat – Susanna Forrest."
22. Roodhouse, "Break the Taboo on Horsemeat – or Food Fraud Will Continue."
23. Roodhouse.
24. Roodhouse.
25. "Why Are the British Revolted by the Idea of Horsemeat?," BBC News, accessed May 6, 2016, http://www.bbc.com/news/magazine-21043368.

26. "Why Are the British Revolted by the Idea of Horsemeat?"

27. "Why Are the British Revolted by the Idea of Horsemeat?"

28. "Why Are the British Revolted by the Idea of Horsemeat?"

29. "UK Newspapers Ranked by Total Readership (Print and Online) | Press Gazette," accessed May 9, 2016, http://www.pressgazette.co.uk/uk-newspapers-ranked-total-readership-print-and-online.

30. "TimesLive | Times Media Group," Business, accessed May 3, 2016, http://www.timesmedia.co.za/businesses/media/3429-2/timeslive/.

31. "Scandal – Definition of Scandal in English | Oxford Dictionaries," Oxford Dictionaries | English, accessed December 14, 2016, https://en.oxforddictionaries.com/definition/scandal.

32. Darren Hamilton, "'I Loved Horsemeat so Much, I'll Treat the Family'," *The Sun* (blog), February 18, 2013, https://www.thesun.co.uk/archives/news/512768/i-loved-horsemeat-so-much-ill-treat-the-family/.

33. "Goat Found in 5% of Supermarket Ready Meals Labelled Lamb," *The Sun* (blog), May 12, 2013, https://www.thesun.co.uk/archives/news/725454/bleatin-disgrace/.

34. Sapa, "Horsemeat Found in Nestle Products as Scandal Grows," accessed December 16, 2016, http://www.timeslive.co.za/lifestyle/2013/02/19/Horsemeat-found-in-Nestle-products-as-scandal-grows1?service=print.

35. Andrew Chamberlain, "Horse Meat Scandal – Now DNA Found in School Dinners and Many Pub Meals," *The Sun*, February 15, 2013, https://www.thesun.co.uk/archives/news/507230/horse-meat-scandal-now-dna-found-in-school-dinners-and-many-pub-meals/.

36. Sapa-AFP, "Horsemeat in 29 out of 2 501 Beef Products in Britain: Tests," Times LIVE, accessed December 16, 2016, http://www.timeslive.co.za/lifestyle/2013/02/16/Horsemeat-in-29-out-of-2-501-beef-products-in-Britain-tests.

## Chapter 10

1. William Orville Douglas, *The Douglas Letters: Selections from the Private Papers of Justice William O. Douglas* (Adler & Adler, 1987).

2. "Normalising the Unthinkable: The Ethics of Using Animals in Research" (Oxford Centre For Animal Ethics, 2015), http://eprints.port.ac.uk/17079/1/Normalising_the_Unthinkable_Report.pdf.

3. "Normalising the Unthinkable."

4. Joan Dunayer, *Animal Equality: Language and Liberation* (Derwood, Maryland: Ryce Publishing, 2001), 104.

5. "Normalising the Unthinkable," 8.

6. Great Britain and Home Office, *Guidance on the Operation of the Animals (Scientific Procedures) Act 1986.*, 2014, 9.

7. Great Britain and Home Office, 14.

8. Great Britain and Home Office, 14.

9. Great Britain and Home Office, 112.

10. Council for International Organizations of Medical Sciences and World Health Organization, eds., *International Ethical Guidelines for Biomedical Research Involving Human Subjects* (Geneva: CIOMS, 2002).

11. Council for International Organizations of Medical Sciences and World Health Organization, 17.

12. Council for International Organizations of Medical Sciences and World Health Organization, 17.

13. Council for International Organizations of Medical Sciences and World Health Organization, 17.

14. Council for International Organizations of Medical Sciences and World Health Organization, 17,18.

15. Council for International Organizations of Medical Sciences and World Health Organization, 18.
16. Valerie Pedlar, "Experimentation or Exploitation? The Investigations of David Ferrier, Dr Benjulia, and Dr Seward," *Interdisciplinary Science Reviews* 28, no. 3 (September 2003): 90, https://doi.org/10.1179/030801803225005201.
17. "Select Committee – 2002 – Select Committee on Animals in Scientific Procedur.Pdf," n.d. (House of Lords, July 16, 2002), 15, https://publications.parliament.uk/pa/ld20102/ldselect/ldanimal/150/150.pdf.
18. "Select Committee – 2002 – Select Committee on Animals in Scientific Procedur.Pdf," 15.
19. "Select Committee – 2002 – Select Committee on Animals in Scientific Procedur.Pdf," 15.
20. Chapter XVII, note 122 Jeremy Bentham, *An Introduction to the Principles of Morals and Legislation, Chapter XVII | Library of Economics and Liberty*, reprint of 1832 (Oxford: Clarendon Press, 1907), http://www.econlib.org/library/Bentham/bnthPML18.html.
21. Chapter XVII, note 122 Bentham.
22. "Select Committee – 2002 – Select Committee on Animals in Scientific Procedur.Pdf," 15.
23. T Regan, *The Case for Animal Rights.*, 2nd ed. (London: Routledge, 1988).
24. "Select Committee – 2002 – Select Committee on Animals in Scientific Procedur.Pdf," 15.
25. "Select Committee – 2002 – Select Committee on Animals in Scientific Procedur.Pdf," 15.
26. "Select Committee – 2002 – Select Committee on Animals in Scientific Procedur.Pdf," 15.
27. "Select Committee – 2002 – Select Committee on animals in Scientific Procedur.Pdf," 15.
28. "Corpse," TheFreeDictionary.com, accessed October 26, 2016, http://legal-dictionary.thefreedictionary.com/corpse.
29. "Corpse."
30. "Customary IHL – Rule 113. Treatment of the Dead," accessed October 15, 2016, https://ihl-databases.icrc.org/customary-ihl/eng/docs/v1_cha_chapter35_rule113.
31. "Customary IHL – Rule 113. Treatment of the Dead."
32. "Customary IHL – Rule 113. Treatment of the Dead."
33. "Customary IHL – Rule 90. Torture and Cruel, Inhuman or Degrading Treatment," accessed January 31, 2017, https://ihl-databases.icrc.org/customary-ihl/eng/docs/v1_rul_rule90.
34. Human Tissue Authority, "Code_of_practice_5_-_Disposal_of_human_tissue.Pdf," 2014, https://www.hta.gov.uk/hta-codes-practice-and-standards-0 n.d., 6.
35. Human Tissue Authority, "Code_of_practice_5_-_Disposal_of_human_tissue.Pdf," 16.
36. Elliott T. Ash, "Cannibalism," LII / Legal Information Institute, May 1, 2010, https://www.law.cornell.edu/wex/cannibalism.
37. Nick Baines, "I Ate My Wife's Placenta Raw in a Smoothie and Cooked in a Taco," the Guardian, April 30, 2014, http://www.theguardian.com/lifeandstyle/2014/apr/30/i-ate-wifes-placenta-smoothie-taco-afterbirth.
38. Homa Khaleeli, "Eating People Is Wrong, but Is It against the Law?," the Guardian, December 16, 2015, http://www.theguardian.com/law/shortcuts/2015/dec/16/eating-people-is-wrong-but-is-it-against-the-law.
39. "Performance Art," accessed February 26, 2018, https://www.rickgibson.net/perform.html.

## Chapter 11

1. Noam Chomsky, *Imperial Ambitions* (New York: Metropolitan Books, 2005).
2. M. A. K Halliday, "Writing Science: Literacy and Discursive Power," in *The Language of Science*, ed. J. J. Webster (London: Continuum, 2004), 199–225.

3. Adem Can et al., "The Mouse Forced Swim Test," *Journal of Visualized Experiments: JoVE*, no. 59 (2012): abstract, https://doi.org/10.3791/3638.

4. "About the OECD – OECD," accessed November 4, 2016, http://www.oecd.org/about/.

5. OECD, "OECD Guideline for the Testing of Chemicals. Acute Inhalation Toxicity," n.d., https://doi.org/10.1787/9789264070608-en

6. OECD, 1.

7. OECD, 2.

8. OECD, 2.

9. OECD, 3.

10. S. Parasuraman, "Toxicological Screening," *Journal of Pharmacology & Pharmacotherapeutics* 2, no. 2 (June 2011): 74, https://doi.org/10.4103/0976-500X.81895.

11. Parasuraman.

12. Dunayer, *Animal Equality: Language and Liberation*, 111,112.

13. Maja Djurendic-Brenesel et al., "Regional Distribution of Opiate Alkaloids in Experimental Animals' Brain Tissue and Blood," *Acta Veterinaria* 62, no. 2–3 (2012): 140, https://doi.org/10.2298/AVB1203137D.

14. "Wistar Rat | Charles River," accessed February 3, 2017, http://www.criver.com/products-services/basic-research/find-a-model/wistar-rat.

15. Djurendic-Brenesel et al., "Regional Distribution of Opiate Alkaloids in Experimental Animals' Brain Tissue and Blood," 140.

16. Alberto Lázaro et al., "Beneficial Effect of Short Pretransplant Period of Hypothermic Pulsatile Perfusion of the Warm-Ischemic Kidney after Cold Storage: Experimental Study," *BioMed Research International* 2016 (2016): 1, https://doi.org/10.1155/2016/2518626.

17. Lázaro et al., 1.

18. Nigman Lukmanovich Khabilov et al., "The Study of Structural Changes in Bone Tissue of Alveolar Process of Jaws in Experimental Animals after Implantation of a New Construction of Dental Implant from Titanium Bt-1.00 Developed in Uzbekistan," *European Medical, Health and Pharmaceutical Journal* 8, no. 1 (2015): 21, https://doi.org/10.12955/emhpj.v8i1.538.

19. Nigman Lukmanovich Khabilov et al.

## Chapter 12

1. Cesar Chavez, "Accepting a Lifetime Achievement Award from In Defense of Animals", (1992).

2. "Envigo Opens Its Doors For Business On 21 September," accessed November 16, 2016, http://www.clinicalleader.com/doc/envigo-opens-its-doors-for-business-on-september-0001.

3. "Envigo Opens Its Doors For Business On 21 September."

4. "Huntingdon and Harlan Becomes Envigo," Contract Pharma, accessed November 16, 2016, http://www.contractpharma.com/contents/view_breaking-news/2015-06-25/huntingdon-and-harlan-becomes-envigo/.

5. "CRL 2015 Annual Report_ FINAL (Low Res).Pdf," 2015, 2.

6. "CRL 2015 Annual Report_ FINAL (Low Res).Pdf," i.

7. Carolyn Brown, "Patenting Life: Genetically Altered Mice an Invention, Court Declares," *CMAJ: Canadian Medical Association Journal* 163, no. 7 (October 3, 2000): 867, https://www.ncbi.nlm.nih.gov/pmc/articles/PMC80518/.

8. "Huntingdon Life Sciences And Harlan Laboratories Announce The Launch Of The SHrN Novel Hairless NODSCID Model At AACR 2015," accessed November 16, 2016, http://www.clinicalleader.com/doc/huntingdon-laboratories-shrn-novel-hairless-nod-scid-model-aacr-0001.

9. "SHrN® Hairless NOD.SCID Mouse | Envigo," accessed September 27, 2017, http://www.envigo.com/products-services/research-models-services/models/research-models/mice/mutant/shrn-hairless-nod.scid-mouse/.

10. "Huntingdon Life Sciences And Harlan Laboratories Announce The Launch Of The SHrN Novel Hairless NOÐSCID Model At AACR 2015."

11. "Research Animal Models | Charles River," accessed November 18, 2016, http://www.criver.com/find-a-model.

12. "Our Name Envigo | Envigo," accessed November 16, 2016, http://www.envigo.com/about-envigo/our-name-envigo/.

13. "General Toxicology Studies | Safety Assessment | Covance," accessed November 16, 2016, http://www.covance.com/industry-solutions/drug-development/services/safety-assessment/general-toxicology.html.

14. "General Toxicology Studies | Safety Assessment | Covance."

15. "General Toxicology Studies | Safety Assessment | Covance," accessed February 28, 2018

16. "Core Toxicology Services | Covance," accessed February 6, 2017, http://www.covance.com/industry-solutions/drug-development/services/safety-assessment/general-toxicology/core-toxicology-services.html.

17. "General Toxicology Studies | Safety Assessment | Covance."

18. "General Toxicology Studies | Safety Assessment | Covance."

19. "General Toxicology Studies | Safety Assessment | Covance."

20. "Gavage – Definition of Gavage by The Free Dictionary," accessed November 18, 2016, http://www.thefreedictionary.com/gavage.

21. "Online Etymology Dictionary," accessed November 18, 2016, http://www.etymonline.com/index.php?term=gavage.

22. "Ocular Development Services | Covance," accessed February 6, 2017, http://www.covance.com/industry-solutions/drug-development/services/safety-assessment/general-toxicology/ocular-development-services.html.

23. "Ocular Development Services | Covance."

24. "Specialty Toxicology Testing Services | Charles River," accessed November 16, 2016, http://www.criver.com/products-services/safety-assessment/toxicology/specialty.

25. "Specialty Toxicology Testing Services | Charles River."

26. "Model of Retinal Degeneration and Neuroprotection | Charles River," accessed March 27, 2018, https://www.criver.com/products-services/discovery-services/vivo-pharmacology/ocular-disease-pharmacology-models/model-retinal-degeneration-neuroprotection?region=3701.

27. "Blue Light Exposure Model of Retinal Degeneration and Neuroprotection" | Charles River," https://www.criver.com/products-services/discovery-services/vivo-pharmacology/ocular-disease-pharmacology-models/model-retinal-degeneration-neuroprotection?region=3696

28. "Blue Light Exposure Model of Retinal Degeneration and Neuroprotection | Charles River,"

29. "Micro Drill for Surgical Applications," accessed November 16, 2016, https://www.wpiinc.com/product-listers/micro-drill-for-surgical-applications/.

30. "Lab Animal Buyers' Guide," accessed November 20, 2016, http://guide.labanimal.com/.

## Chapter 13

1. T Regan, *The Case for Animal Rights.*, 2nd ed. (London: Routledge, 1988)

2. Nuno Franco, "Animal Experiments in Biomedical Research: A Historical Perspective," *Animals* 3, no. 1 (March 19, 2013): 239, https://doi.org/10.3390/ani3010238.

3. Franco, "Animal Experiments in Biomedical Research," 239, 240.

4. Franco, 240.

5. Franco, 241.

6. Franco, 242.

7. citing Tubbs, R.S.; Loukas, M.; Shoja, M.M.; Shokouhi, G.; Oakes, W.J. Franco, 249.

8. Franco, 249.

9. JTH Conner, "Cruel Knives Vivisection and Biomedical Research in Victorian English Canada," *Canadian Bulletin of Medical History* 14 (1997): 37–64.

10. Nelson cited in Conner, 39.

11. Conner, 39.

12. Conner, 39.

13. Nelson cited in Conner, 39.

14. Nelson cited in Conner, 39,40.

15. Conner, 40.

16. Conner, 42.

17. D Tacium, "A History of Antivivisection (1) from the 1800s to the Present: Part I (Mid-1800s to 1914)," *The Black Ewe* (blog), June 10, 2009, https://brebisnoire.wordpress.com/a-history-of-antivivisection-from-the-1800s-to-the-present-part-i-mid-1800s-to-1914/.

18. C Bernard cited in Tacium.

19. Davis cited in Franco, "Animal Experiments in Biomedical Research," 250.

20. Franco, 250.

21. C. Lansbury, *The Old Brown Dog* (University of Wisconsin Press, 1985).

22. "Remember Kinder Scout – Give Back Britain's Common Land | Peter Lazenby | Opinion | The Guardian," accessed October 26, 2018, https://www.theguardian.com/commentisfree/2012/apr/30/remember-kinder-scout-britain-common-land.

23. Citing work by K Cahill in "Who owns Britiain? "Remember Kinder Scout – Give Back Britain's Common Land | Peter Lazenby | Opinion | The Guardian.""

24. David Edwards, "Victorian Liverpool: Some Facts and Figures – David Edwards P3-13," *The Bulletin of the Liverpool Medical History Society*, 3–13, accessed September 4, 2017, http://www.evolve360.co.uk/Data/10/Docs/Wives/WivesEdwards.pdf; Mike Dash, "Quite Likely the Worst Job Ever," Smithsonian, accessed October 3, 2017, http://www.smithsonianmag.com/history/quite-likely-the-worst-job-ever-319843/.

25. Edwards, "Victorian Liverpool: Some Facts and Figures – David Edwards 3–13," 12.

26. Edwards, 4.

27. Edwards, 11,12.

28. Spencer, *The Heretic's Feast*, 295.

29. Spencer, 295.

30. Edwards, "Victorian Liverpool: Some Facts and Figures – David Edwards 3–13," 4.

31. Paget cited in C. Lansbury, "Gynaecology, Pornography and the Antivivisection Movement.," *Victorian Studies* 28, no. 3 (Spring 1985): 416.

32. Frances Power Cobbe (1881), The Medical Profession and Its Morality, The Modern Review, 2, p. 311 cited in Anne L. Scott, "Physical Purity Feminism and State Medicine in Late Nineteenth-Century England," *Women's History Review* 8, no. 4 (December 1999): 629, https://doi.org/10.1080/09612029900200220.

33. Kingsford cited in Lansbury, "Gynaecology, Pornography and the Antivivisection Movement.," 417.

34. Kingsford cited in Lansbury, 416.

35. Blackwell cited in Lansbury, 419.

36. Maugham Lansbury, 417.
37.  Maudsley Pozzi cited in Lansbury, 417.
38. Lansbury, 417.
39. Kathryn Hughes, "Gender Roles in the 19th Century," The British Library, accessed September 4, 2017, https://www.bl.uk/romantics-and-victorians/articles/gender-roles-in-the-19th-century.
40. Sir Mathew Hale cited in "Rape, Marriage, and Rights," openDemocracy, accessed October 4, 2017, http://www.opendemocracy.net/5050/sasha-hart/rape-marriage-and-rights.
41. Lawson Tait (1889) Diseases of Women and Abdominal Surgery, vol. 1, p. 31 (Leicester) cited in Scott, "Physical Purity Feminism and State Medicine in Late Nineteenth-Century England," 629.
42. Lansbury, "Gynaecology, Pornography and the Antivivisection Movement.," 421.
43. Lansbury, 421.
44. "Ruth Padel, "Saddled with Ginger: Women, men and horses", Encounter, November 1980, 47–54, accessed September 4, 2017, https://www.unz.com/print/Encounter-1980nov-00047/.
45. Tacium, "A History of Antivivisection from the 1800s to the Present."
46. Tacium.
47. Padel, "Saddled with Ginger: Women, men and horses", 48.
48. Padel, 48, 50.
49. Anna Sewell, Black Beauty. The Autobiography of a Horse, Gutenberg e-book, 2006, 15
50. Padel, "Saddled with Ginger: Women, men and horses", 48.
51. Lansbury, "Gynaecology, Pornography and the Antivivisection Movement.," 423.

## Chapter 14

1. Isabel Allende, 'Tales of Passion' (March 2007), http://www.isabelallende.com/en/words/tales_of_passion.
2. Nuno Franco, "Animal Experiments in Biomedical Research: A Historical Perspective," Animals 3, no. 1 (March 19, 2013): 245, https://doi.org/10.3390/ani3010238.
3. D Tacium, "A History of Antivivisection (1) from the 1800s to the Present: Part I (Mid-1800s to 1914)," The Black Ewe (blog), June 10, 2009, https://brebisnoire.wordpress.com/a-history-of-antivivisection-from-the-1800s-to-the-present-part-i-mid-1800s-to-1914/.
4. Bernard cited in Percy M. (Percy Millard) Dawson, A Biography of François Magendie (Brooklyn-New York: A.J. Huntington, 1908), 54, http://archive.org/details/biographyfrancoi00daws.
5. Bernard cited in Dawson, 55.
6. Hayley Rose Glaholt, "Vivisection as War: The 'Moral Diseases' of Animal Experimentation and Slavery in British Victorian Quaker Pacifist Ethics," Society & Animals 20, no. 2 (January 1, 2012): 154, https://doi.org/10.1163/156853012X631360.
7. Bernard cited in Dawson, A Biography of François Magendie, 55.
8. Tacium, "A History of Antivivisection from the 1800s to the Present."
9. Franco, "Animal Experiments in Biomedical Research," 251.
10. "Frances Power Cobbe," Spartacus Educational, accessed March 1, 2018, http://spartacus-educational.com/Wcobbe.htm.
11. C. Lansbury, "Gynaecology, Pornography and the Antivivisection Movement," Victorian Studies 28, no. 3 (Spring 1985): 414.
12. Richet cited in Michael R. Finn, "Dogs and Females: Vivisection, Feminists and the Novelist Rachilde," French Cultural Studies 23, no. 3 (2012): 192, http://doi.org/10.1177/0957155812443180.
13. C. Lansbury, "Gynaecology, Pornography and the Antivivisection Movement," 416.
14. French cited in Finn, "Dogs and Females," 193.

15. Finn, 193.
16. Finn, 194,195.
17. Finn, 196.
18. Finn, 196.
19. "The Hystrical Female," Restoring Perspective: Life & Treatment at London's Asylum, accessed September 11, 2017, https://www.lib.uwo.ca/archives/virtualexhibits/londonasylum/hysteria.html.
20. John Studd, "Ovariotomy for Menstrual Madness and Premenstrual Syndrome – 19th Century History and Lessons for Current Practice'. *Gynecological Endocrinology*: 22, no. 8 (August 2006): 411–415. https://doi.org/10.1080/09513590600881503.
21. "Brown – 1866 – On the Curability of Certain Forms of Insanity, Ep.Pdf," n.d.; Helen King, "The Rise and Fall of FGM in Victorian London," The Conversation, accessed January 9, 2018, http://theconversation.com/the-rise-and-fall-of-fgm-in-victorian-london-38327.
22. King, "The Rise and Fall of FGM in Victorian London."
23. "Brown – 1866 – On the Curability of Certain Forms of Insanity, Ep.Pdf."
24. King, "The Rise and Fall of FGM in Victorian London."
25. John Duffy, "Clitoridectomy: A Nineteenth Century Answer to Masturbation," accessed January 9, 2018, http://www.nocirc.org/symposia/first/duffy.html.
26. "Hysteria Online Etymology Dictionary," accessed May 4, 2017, http://www.etymonline.com/index.php?term=hysteria.
27. Henry Maudsley (1874) Sex in Mind and Education, in Fortnightly Review, 15, pp. 466–483 cited in Scott, "Physical Purity Feminism and State Medicine in Late Nineteenth-Century England," 636.
28. Marvin, *The Philosophy of Spiritualism*, pp. 47–48 cited in Scott, 636, 637.
29. Craig Buettinger, "Antivivisection and the Charge of Zoophil-Psychosis in the Early Twentieth Century". *The Historian* 55, no. 2 (1993): 277–88.
30. Buettinger, "Antivivisection and the Charge of Zoophil-Psychosis in the Early Twentieth Century"; L. Kelly D, "Commentary: Academic Medicine," *Journal of the Association of American Medical Colleges* 77, no. 6 (June 2002): 532, http://journals.lww.com/academicmedicine/Fulltext/2002/06000/Commentary.9.aspx.
31. Buettinger, "Antivivisection and the Charge of Zoophil-Psychosis in the Early Twentieth Century".
32. Buettinger, "Antivivisection and the Charge of Zoophil-Psychosis in the Early Twentieth Century".
33. Kelly, "Commentary."
34. Kelly.
35. Finn, "Dogs and Females," 194.
36. Finn, 195.
37. Buettinger, "Antivivisection and the Charge of Zoophil-Psychosis in the Early Twentieth Century".
38. Finn, "Dogs and Females," 197.
39. Lansbury, *The Old Brown Dog*, 9.
40. Lansbury, 9.
41. Tacium, "A History of Antivivisection from the 1800s to the Present."
42. C. Lansbury, *The Old Brown Dog* (University of Wisconsin Press, 1985), 10.
43. "Brown Dog Affair – Wikipedia," accessed September 8, 2017, https://en.wikipedia.org/wiki/Brown_Dog_affair#cite_note-FOOTNOTEKean199525-14.

44. Lansbury, *The Old Brown Dog*, 12.

45. "Brown Dog Affair – Wikipedia."

46. Lansbury, *The Old Brown Dog*, 10,11.

47. "Brown Dog Affair – Wikipedia."

48. Lansbury, *The Old Brown Dog*, 14.

49. "Bright Light 67. Ring the Bells of Mercy – Hymnary.Org," accessed April 28, 2017, http:// hymnary.org/hymn/BL1893/67.

50. "The Brown Dog Affair – Advocacy for Animals," accessed May 2, 2017, http://advocacy. britannica.com/blog/advocacy/2010/01/the-brown-dog-affair/.

51. Lansbury, *The Old Brown Dog*, 16.

52. Lansbury, 16.

53. Lansbury, 16.

54. "Brown Dog Affair – Wikipedia."

55. Lansbury, *The Old Brown Dog*, 16.

56. Lansbury, *The Old Brown Dog*.

57. "The Brown Dog Affair – Advocacy for Animals."

58. Lansbury, *The Old Brown Dog*, 17.

59. Lansbury, 18.

60. Mike Phillips, "John Archer (1863–1932) Black Europeans," British library Online, accessed September 18, 2017, https://www.bl.uk/onlinegallery/features/blackeuro/pdf/archer.pdf.

61. Phillips

62. Phillips

63. Phillips

64. Lansbury, *The Old Brown Dog*, 19, 20.

65. Lansbury, 21.

66. Lansbury, *The Old Brown Dog*.

67. "The Brown Dog and His Friends," *British Medical Journal*, March 5, 1910, 588.

68. "The Brown Dog and His Friends," 588,589.

69. Physiological Society, "The Physiologists vs. the Antivivisectionists: The Brown Dog Affair," n.d., http://www.physoc.org/sites/default/files/page/Info_Sheet_Brown_Dog_Affair.pdf.

70. "The Society Dog | Physiological Society," accessed September 12, 2017, http://www.physoc.org/ society-dog.

71. "The Brown Dog Affair – Advocacy for Animals."

72. "NAVS: About Us: History: The Little Brown Dog," National Anti-Vivisection Society -- campaigning against the use of animals in research, accessed May 3, 2017, https://www.navs. org.uk/about_us/24/0/286/.

73. "Bands of Mercy," *Be Kind: A Visual History of Humane Education* (blog), February 26, 2012, https://bekindexhibit.org/exhibition/bands-of-mercy/.

74. "Bands of Mercy."

75. "Bands of Mercy."

76. "Bands of Mercy."

77. Lansbury, *The Old Brown Dog*, 40.

78. Lansbury, 40.

79. Ravindra B. Ghooi, "The Nuremberg Code–A Critique". *Perspectives in Clinical Research* 2, no. 2 (2011): 72–76. https://doi.org/10.4103/2229-3485.80371.

## Chapter 15

1. George Orwell, *1984* (Signet Classic, 1961).
2. "Select Committee – 2002 – Select Committee on Animals in Scientific Procedur.Pdf," 16. (House of Lords, July 16, 2002), 16, https://publications.parliament.uk/pa/ld20102/ldselect/ldanimal/150/150.pdf.
3. "Human Radiation Experiments," Atomic Heritage Foundation, accessed August 9, 2017, http://www.atomicheritage.org/history/human-radiation-experiments; U.S. Department of Energy, "Human Radiation Experiments Associated with the U.S. Department of Energy and Its Predecessors," July 1995, https://www.osti.gov/opennet/servlets/purl/16141769/16141769.pdf.
4. "Unethical Human Experimentation – Wikipedia," accessed January 16, 2018, https://en.wikipedia.org/wiki/Unethical_human_experimentation#Guatemala.
5. Nicholas D. Kristof, "Unmasking Horror  - A Special Report.; Japan Confronting Gruesome War Atrocity," accessed August 8, 2017, http://www.nytimes.com/1995/03/17/world/unmasking-horror-a-special-report-japan-confronting-gruesome-war-atrocity.html.
6. Kristof.
7. Takashi Tsuchiya, "Why Japanese Doctors Performed Human Experiments in China 1933-1945," *Eubios Journal of Asian and International Bioethics* 10 (2000): 179–80, http://www.eubios.info/EJ106/EJ106C.htm.
8. "The Trial of Unit 731," The Japan Times, June 5, 2001, http://www.japantimes.co.jp/opinion/2001/06/05/commentary/world-commentary/the-trial-of-unit-731/.
9. "The Trial of Unit 731."
10. Kristof, "Unmasking Horror  - A Special Report.; Japan Confronting Gruesome War Atrocity."
11. Kristof.
12. Kristof.
13. Kristof.
14. "The Trial of Unit 731."
15. "The Trial of Unit 731."
16. Tsuchiya, "Why Japanese Doctors Performed Human Experiments in China 1933-1945."
17. "Nazi Medical Experiments," United States Holocaust Memorial Museum, accessed February 7, 2017, https://www.ushmm.org/wlc/en/article.php?ModuleId=10005168.
18. "The Ladies Depart," accessed March 7, 2018, http://www.friendsjournal.org/wp-content/uploads/emember/downloads/1959/HC12-50201.pdf.
19. "After Hitler's Pal Died, Nazis Recreated His Injuries in a Sick Experiment | New York Post," accessed March 7, 2018, https://nypost.com/2016/05/08/the-women-tortured-by-nazi-doctors-and-the-american-heiress-who-saved-them/.
20. "After Hitler's Pal Died, Nazis Recreated His Injuries in a Sick Experiment | New York Post."
21. "After Hitler's Pal Died, Nazis Recreated His Injuries in a Sick Experiment | New York Post."
22. "After Hitler's Pal Died, Nazis Recreated His Injuries in a Sick Experiment | New York Post."
23. Nsdap #5 et al., "Josef Mengele – Wikipedia," accessed February 26, 2019, https://en.wikipedia.org/wiki/Josef_Mengele.
24. "Josef Mengele," United States Holocaust Memorial Museum, accessed February 7, 2017, https://www.ushmm.org/wlc/en/article.php?ModuleId=10007060.
25. "The Nuremberg Code–A Critique," accessed January 14, 2018, https://www.ncbi.nlm.nih.gov/pmc/articles/PMC3121268/#sec1-2title.

## Chapter 16

1. Antonio Gramsci in Alistair Davidson, *Antonio Gramsci: Towards an Intellectual Biography.*

London: Merlin Press (London: Merlin Press, 1977).

2. Mark Sweney, "Mail Online Close to 100m Users," the Guardian, February 23, 2012, http://www.theguardian.com/media/2012/feb/23/mail-online-close-to-100m-users.

3. Sweney.

4. By Danny Penman for MailOnline, "Caged and Bound for Britain: Factory-Farmed Monkeys Are Being Shipped in Their Thousands to UK Laboratories," Mail Online, November 26, 2010, http://www.dailymail.co.uk/news/article-1333156/Factory-farmed-monkeys-shipped-thousands-UK-laboratories.html.

5. "Test Driven | World News | The Guardian," accessed February 22, 2017, https://www.theguardian.com/uk/2006/mar/04/animalwelfare.highereducation.

6. Royal Society, "The Use of Non-Human Animals in Research: A Guide for Scientists," February 2004.

7. Royal Society, 1.

8. Royal Society, 1.

9. Royal Society, 10.

10. Royal Society, 10.

11. Royal Society, 10.

12. By Danny Penman for MailOnline, "Caged and Bound for Britain: Factory-Farmed Monkeys Are Being Shipped in Their Thousands to UK Laboratories".

13. By Tom Rawstorne for The Mail on Sunday, "Is It Really Right to Blow up Pigs Even If It Saves Our Soldiers' Lives?," Mail Online, May 28, 2010, http://www.dailymail.co.uk/news/article-1282357/Is-really-right-blow-pigs-saves-soldiers-lives.html.

14. Robin McKie, "Scientists Fear for Animal Testing as Norman Baker Joins Home Office," the Guardian, November 17, 2013, http://www.theguardian.com/science/2013/nov/17/scientists-fear-for-animal-testing.

15. Hannah Devlin and Stuart Clark, "Rosetta Probe Lands on Comet 67P Ending 12-Year Mission," the Guardian, September 30, 2016, http://www.theguardian.com/science/2016/sep/30/rosetta-probe-lands-on-comet-67p-ending-12-year-mission.

16. Guy Gugliotta, "Rosetta the Comet Chaser," Air & Space Magazine, accessed November 29, 2016, http://www.airspacemag.com/space/rosetta-comet-chaser-180950138/.

17. Ian Kennedy, "Unmasking Medicine: The New Magicians," 1980 The Reith Lectures, November 12, 1980.

18. Kennedy.

19. By Michael Hanlon for the Daily Mail, "Vivisection Is Right, but It Is Nasty – and We Must Be Brave Enough to Admit This," Mail Online, July 24, 2012, http://www.dailymail.co.uk/debate/article-2178249/Vivisection-right-nasty--brave-admit-this.html.

20. By Fiona Macrae Science Correspondent, "GM Research Sends Animal Testing to a 30-Year High as Nearly 4m Are Subject to Scientific Experiments," Mail Online, July 11, 2012, http://www.dailymail.co.uk/news/article-2171787/GM-research-sends-animal-testing-30-year-high.html.

21. Bibi van der Zee, "Animal Testing – It's Time to Talk about It Again | Bibi van Der Zee," the Guardian, July 18, 2013, http://www.theguardian.com/commentisfree/2013/jul/18/animal-testing-talk-about-medical-research.

22. "Lords Again Affirm Support for Animal Research | Understanding Animal Research," accessed November 28, 2016, http://www.understandinganimalresearch.org.uk/news/policy-issues/lords-again-affirm-support-for-animal-research/.

23. R. Sharpe, The Cruel Deception (Wellingborough: Thorsons, 1988), 25.

24. E. P Thompson, The Making of the English Working Class, 1980 (London: Penguin, 1963), 365.

25. Sharpe, *The Cruel Deception*.

26. Sharpe, 21–40.

27. Sharpe, 24.

28. Sharpe, 24.

29. John B. McKinlay and Sonja M. Mckinlay, "The Questionable Contribution of Medical Measures to the Decline of Mortality in the United States in the Twentieth Century.," *The Milbank Memorial Fund Quarterly. Health and Society* 55, no. 3 (Summer 1977): 425. https://doi.org/10.2307/3349539.

30. "UNICEF – Goal: Reduce Child Mortality," accessed February 21, 2017, https://www.unicef.org/mdg/childmortality.html.

31. "WHO | Diarrhoeal Disease," WHO, accessed June 2, 2017, http://www.who.int/mediacentre/factsheets/fs330/en/.

32. "WHO | 2. Background," WHO, accessed February 21, 2017, http://www.who.int/nutrition/topics/2_background/en/.

33. "WHO | 2. Background."

34. "WHO | Obesity and Overweight," WHO, accessed October 11, 2017, http://www.who.int/mediacentre/factsheets/fs311/en/.

## Chapter 17

1. Arundhati Roy, "The 2004 Sydney Peace Prize Lecture (*Sydney Morning Herald*)", 2004, https://www.smh.com.au/national/roys-full-speech-20041104-gdk1qn.html.

2. "Animal Research Is Brave, Not Cruel, Science | Fiona Fox | Opinion | The Guardian," accessed August 14, 2017, https://www.theguardian.com/commentisfree/2012/sep/28/animal-research-brave-not-cruel-science.

3. Staff and agencies, "Masked Attackers Beat Huntingdon Boss," the Guardian, February 23, 2001, http://www.theguardian.com/uk/2001/feb/23/animalwelfare.world.

4. Leader, "Leader: Animal Testing," the Guardian, February 27, 2006, http://www.theguardian.com/news/2006/feb/27/leadersandreply.mainsection.

5. "Former Soldier Debbie Vincent Jailed for Terror Campaign against Animal Testing Company | Daily Mail Online," accessed August 14, 2017, http://www.dailymail.co.uk/news/article-2606974/Former-soldier-animal-rights-commander-jailed-six-years-campaign-terror-against-animal-testing-company.html.

6. Steven Morris, "Animal Rights Campaigner Convicted of Huntingdon Life Sciences Conspiracy," the Guardian, March 28, 2014, http://www.theguardian.com/world/2014/mar/28/animal-rights-campaigner-huntingdon-life-sciences-debbie-vincent.

7. "About Us Overview | AnimalRightsExtremism.Info," AnimalRightsExtremism.Info, accessed May 22, 2018, http://www.animalrightsextremism.info/about-us/about-us-overview/.

8. "ARE Incident Map | AnimalRightsExtremism.Info," AnimalRightsExtremism.Info, accessed May 22, 2018, http://www.animalrightsextremism.info/are-incident-map/.

9. "ARE Incident Map | AnimalRightsExtremism.Info."

10. David Adam and Duncan Campbell, "Changing Perspectives on Vivisection Battleground," the Guardian, August 27, 2005, http://www.theguardian.com/uk/2005/aug/27/animalwelfare.businessofresearch.

11. "Diaries of Despair Report: Xenotransplantation Exposed," accessed November 21, 2016, http://www.xenodiaries.org/overview.htm.

12. Stuart Jeffries, "Test Driven," the Guardian, March 4, 2006, http://www.theguardian.com/uk/2006/mar/04/animalwelfare.highereducation.

13. "Animal Research Is Brave, Not Cruel, Science | Fiona Fox | Opinion | The Guardian."
14. "Animal Rights and Wrongs," *Nature* 470, no. 7335 (February 24, 2011): 435–435, https://doi.org/10.1038/470435a.
15. Daniel Cressey and others, "Battle Scars," *Nature* 470, no. 24 (2011): 452–453, https://doi.org/10.1038/470452a.
16. Cressey, "Battle Scars"
17. Cressey, 453.
18. "Standing up to Bullies; Editorial," *Nature Immunology* 5, no. 4 (April 2004): 345. https://doi.org/10.1038/ni0404-345.
19. "Standing up to Bullies; Editorial."
20. "Center for Consumer Freedom – SourceWatch," accessed December 6, 2016, http://www.sourcewatch.org/index.php/Center_for_Consumer_Freedom.
21. Dario Martinelli, *A Critical Companion to Zoosemiotics:*, vol. 5, Biosemiotics (Dordrecht: Springer Netherlands, 2010), 1, http://link.springer.com/10.1007/978-90-481-9249-6.
22. Frans de Waal, "Opinion | What I Learned From Tickling Apes," accessed June 12, 2017, https://www.nytimes.com/2016/04/10/opinion/sunday/what-i-learned-from-tickling-apes.html.
23. Waal.

## Chapter 18

1. Tôm Segev, *Soldiers of Evil: The Commandants of the Nazi Concentration Camps* (Grafton Books (Original, the University of Michigan), 1988).
2. Philip Zimbardo, "A Situationist Perspective on the Psychology of Evil: Understanding How Good People Are Transformed into Perpetrators.," in *The Social Psychology of Good and Evil*, ed. A. Miller G (New York: Guilford Press, 2004), 23, http://pdf.prisonexp.org/evil.pdf.
3. Z. Bauman, *Modernity and the Holocaust.* (Cambridge: Polity Press, 1989), 12.
4. Charles Patterson, *Eternal Treblinka* (New York: Lantern Books, 2001).
5. L Chorbajian, "Introduction.," in *Studies in Comparative Genocide in the Twentieth Century*, ed. L. Chorbajian and G. Shirinian (Houndmills, UK: Macmillan, 1999), xv–xxxv.
6. R. W. Smith, "State Power and Genocidal Intent: On the Uses of Genocide in the Twentieth Century". In *Studies in Comparative Genocide in the Twentieth Century.*, ed. L Chorbajian and G. Shirinian (Houndmills, UK: Macmillan, 1999), 3.
7. Les Mitchell, "Animals and the Discourse of Farming in Southern Africa," *Society & Animals* 14, no. 1 (2006): 39–59, https://doi.org/10.1163/156853006776137122. Les Mitchell, "Moral Disengagement and Support for Nonhuman Animal Farming," *Society & Animals*, 19, no.3 (2011), https://doi.org/10.1163/156853011X545529. Les Mitchell, "Nonhumans and the Ideology of Purpose," *Anthrozoös* 25, no. 4 (2012): 491–502 https://doi.org/10.2752/175303712X13479798785931..
8. Smith, "State Power and Genocidal Intent", 4.
9. Smith, "State Power and Genocidal Intent", 7.
10. Des Forges cited in P. Verwimp, "Peasant Ideology and Genocide in Rwanda under Habyarimana.," in *Genocide in Cambodia and Rwanda: New Perspectives.*, ed. S. Cook E. (New Brunswick: Transaction, 2006), 29.
11. JM Glass, *Life Unworthy of Life: Racial Phobia and Mass Murder in Hitler's Germany.* (New York: Basic Books, 1997), 86.
12. J. Weiss, *Ideology of Death: Why the Holocaust Happened in Germany.* (Chicago: Ivan R Dee, 1996), 342.
13. Feingold cited in Bauman, *Modernity and the Holocaust.*, 8.

14. Weiss, *Ideology of Death: Why the Holocaust Happened in Germany.*, 349.
15. Patterson, *Eternal Treblinka*, 132.
16. Glass, *Life Unworthy of Life: Racial Phobia and Mass Murder in Hitler's Germany.*, 27.
17. Stillman & Pfaff cited in Bauman, *Modernity and the Holocaust.*, 9.
18. Patterson, *Eternal Treblinka*, 113.
19. Bauman, *Modernity and the Holocaust.*, 159.
20. Smith, "State Power and Genocidal Intent", 9, 10.
21. Weiss, *Ideology of Death: Why the Holocaust Happened in Germany.*, 333, 334.
22. Weiss, 333.
23. Weiss, 333, 334.
24. "Enabling Act of 1933 – Wikipedia," accessed October 23, 2017, https://en.wikipedia.org/wiki/Enabling_Act_of_1933.
25. I. Horowitz L, "Science, Modernity and Authorized Terror: Reconsidering the Genocidal State.," in *Studies in Comparative Genocide.*, ed. L Chorbajian and G. Shirinian (Houndmills, UK: Macmillan, 1999), 26.
26. Weiss, *Ideology of Death: Why the Holocaust Happened in Germany.*, 339.
27. Weiss, 339.
28. Mironko cited in S. Cook E., "Introduction," in *Genocide in Cambodia and Rwanda: New Perspectives* (New Brunswick: Transaction, 2006), ix.
29. H. C Kelman and V. L Hamilton, *Crimes of Obedience* (New Haven: Yale University Press, 1989).
30. Kelman and Hamilton, 12.
31. Cook, "Introduction," x.
32. M. Schnurer, "At the Gates of Hell: The ALF and the Legacy of Holocaust Resistance.," in *Terrorists or Freedom Fighters?: Reflections on the Liberation of Animals.*, ed. S. Best and A. Nocella J. (New York: Lantern Books, 2004), 117.
33. Glass, *Life Unworthy of Life: Racial Phobia and Mass Murder in Hitler's Germany.*, 17.
34. Glass, 28, 29.
35. P. Haidu, "The Dialectics of Unspeakability: Language, Silence and the Narratives of Desubjectification.," in *Probing the Limits of Representation: Nazism and the "Final Solution".*, ed. S. Friedlander, (Cambridge: Harvard University Press, 1992), 287, 289.
36. Ophir cited in M. Biagioli, "Science, Modernity and the 'Final Solution,'" in *Probing the Limits of Representation: Nazism and the "Final Solution,"* ed. S. Friedlander, (Cambridge: Harvard University Press, 1992), 201, 202.
37. Glass, *Life Unworthy of Life: Racial Phobia and Mass Murder in Hitler's Germany.*, 31–33.
38. Glass, 33.
39. Proctor cited in Biagioli, "Science, Modernity and the 'Final Solution,'" 193.
40. Lang cited in Glass, *Life Unworthy of Life: Racial Phobia and Mass Murder in Hitler's Germany.*, 29.
41. Haidu, "The Dialectics of Unspeakability: Language, Silence and the Narratives of Desubjectification." 291.
42. Smith, "Smith, R., W. (1999). State Power and Genocidal Intent: On the Uses of Genocide in the Twentieth Century. In L. Chorbajian, & G. Shirinian (Eds.), Studies in Comparative Genocide. (Pp. 3-14). Houndmills: Macmillan.," 4.
43. Dower cited in Patterson, *Eternal Treblinka*, 39.
44. Patterson, 43.
45. CK Mironko, "Ibitero: Means and Motive in the Rwandan Genocide.," in *Genocide in Cambodia and Rwanda: New Perspectives*, ed. S. Cook E. (New Brunswick: Transaction, 2006), 177–82.
46. Mironko, 180.

47. Mironko, 180.

48. K. Mam, "The Endurance of the Cambodian Family under the Khmer Rouge Regime: An Oral History.," in *Genocide in Cambodia and Rwanda: New Perspectives*, ed. S. Cook E. (New Brunswick: Transaction, 2006), 135.

49. Isaac Singer Beshevis, *Enemies, A Love Story* (New York: Farrar, Straus & Giroux, 1972), 257.

50. Smith, "State Power and Genocidal Intent", 4.

## Chapter 19

1. Albert Camus, *Notebooks Vol 1* (Knopf (Original, Univerisity of Michigan), 1963).

2. Philip Zimbardo, "A Situationist Perspective on the Psychology of Evil: Understanding How Good People Are Transformed into Perpetrators.," in *The Social Psychology of Good and Evil*, ed. A. Miller G. (New York, 2004), 21.

3. Zimbardo, 21.

4. Zimbardo, 25.

5. Lee, Zimbardo and Berthoff cited in Zimbardo, 24.

6. Lee, Zimbardo and Berthoff cited in Zimbardo, 24.

7. Lee, Zimbardo and Berthoff cited in Zimbardo, 24.

8. S. Milgram, *Obedience to Authority: An Experimental View* (London: Tavistock, 1974).

9. Milgram, 3.

10. Milgram, 3.

11. Milgram, 20.

12. "The Man Who Shocked The World," Psychology Today, accessed February 27, 2017, http://www.psychologytoday.com/articles/200203/the-man-who-shocked-the-world.

13. Milgram, *Obedience to Authority: An Experimental View*, 21.

14. Milgram, 22.

15. Milgram, 23.

16. Milgram, 36.

17. Milgram, 142.

18. Milgram, 142.

19. Milgram, 145, 146.

20. Milgram, 5.

21. Zimbardo, "A Situationist Perspective on the Psychology of Evil: Understanding How Good People Are Transformed into Perpetrators.," 2004, 27, 28.

22. Zimbardo, 29.

23. Zimbardo, 29.

24. Zimbardo, 38.

25. Zimbardo, 39.

26. Philip Zimbardo, "Stanford Prison Experiment," accessed March 21, 2018, http://www.prisonexp.org/.

27. Zimbardo.

28. Zimbardo, "A Situationist Perspective on the Psychology of Evil: Understanding How Good People Are Transformed into Perpetrators.," 2004, 37, 38.

29. Zimbardo, "Stanford Prison Experiment."

30. Zimbardo, "A Situationist Perspective on the Psychology of Evil: Understanding How Good People Are Transformed into Perpetrators.," 2004, 40.

31. Zimbardo, "Stanford Prison Experiment."

32. Zimbardo, "A Situationist Perspective on the Psychology of Evil: Understanding How Good People Are Transformed into Perpetrators.," 2004, 40.

33. Zimbardo, 40.

34. Zimbardo, 33.

35. Zimbardo, 39.

36. J Rehm, M. Steinleitner, and W. Lilli, "Wearing Uniforms and Aggression – a Field Experiment.," *European Journal of Social Psychology* 17 (1987): 357–60. https://doi.org/10.1002/ejsp.2420170310.

37. A. Silke, "Deindividuation, Anonymity and Violence; Findings from Northern Ireland.," *The Journal of Social Psychology* 143, no. 4 (2003): 493–99. https://doi.org/10.1080/00224540309598458.

38. R. Watson I., "Investigation into Deindividuation Using a Cross-Cultural Technique.," *Journal of Personality and Social Psychology* 25, no. 3 (1973): 342–45. https://doi.org/10.1037/h0034218.

39. Bandura et al cited in Zimbardo, "A Situationist Perspective on the Psychology of Evil: Understanding How Good People Are Transformed into Perpetrators.," 2004, 31, 32.

40. Bandura et al cited in Zimbardo, 31, 32.

41. Albert Bandura, "Moral Disengagement in the Perpetration of Inhumanities.," *Personality & Social Psychology Review* 3, no. 3 (1999): 193–209. https://doi.org/10.1207/s15327957pspr0303_3.

42. Albert Bandura, "Selective Moral Disengagement in the Exercise of Moral Agency," *Journal of Moral Education* 31, no. 2 (June 2002): 101–19, https://doi.org/10.1080/0305724022014322.

43. Bandura, 103–10.

44. Bandura, 109.

45. Les Mitchell, "Discourse and the Oppression of Nonhuman Animals: A Critical Realist Account." PhD thesis, (Rhodes University: South Africa, 2007).

46. Les Mitchell, "Moral Disengagement and Support for Nonhuman Animal Farming," *Society & Animals*, 19, no.3 (2011), https://doi.org/10.1163/156853011X545529.

47. Les Mitchell, "Nonhumans and the Ideology of Purpose." *Anthrozoös* 25, no. 4 (2012): 491–502 https://doi.org/10.2752/175303712X13479798785931.

48. Personal communication N. Van Rensberg, 2017.

## Chapter 20

1. Thomas Berry, *Evening Thoughts* (San Francisco: Sierra Club Books, 2006).

2. Rod Preece, *Brute Souls, Happy Beasts, and Evolution: The Historical Status of Animals* (Vancouver: University of British Columbia Press, 2005).

3. Augustine cited in Preece, 8.

4. St Athanasius cited in Preece, 9.

5. St Athanasius cited in Preece, 9.

6. Preece, 9.

7. Waddell cited in Preece, 9.

8. Preece, 10.

9. I. Bradley, *The Celtic Way* (London: Darton, Longman and Todd, 1993), 32, 33.

10. Bradley, 55.

11. Bradley, 55.

12. Brendan Lehane, *Early Celtic Christianity* (London: Constable and Company Limited, 1968), 64.

13. Lehane, 65.

14. Flower cited in Lehane, 65.

15. Cambrensis cited in Lehane, 66.

16. Flower cited in Lehane, 66.

17. Adamnan cited in Lehane, 136.
18. Adamnan cited in Bradley, *The Celtic Way*, 56.
19. Adamnan cited in Lehane, *Early Celtic Christianity*, 136.
20. St Isaac the Syrian cited in Linzey, *Creatures of the Same God, Explorations of Animal Theology*, 1.
21. The Food and Environment Research Agency webmaster@csl gov uk Department for Environment Food and Rural Affairs (Defra), "Defra, UK – Foot and Mouth Disease – Information Page," accessed January 30, 2018, http://footandmouth.fera.defra.gov.uk/ citing the Royal Society.
22. Anthony Browne, "The Observer Profile: Phoenix the Calf," the Guardian, April 29, 2001, http://www.theguardian.com/news/2001/apr/29/politics.footandmouth.
23. Browne.
24. Browne.
25. Browne.
26. Browne.
27. Browne.
28. Rachel Weiss, "Jerom" (Unpublished, 2001), http://www.faunafoundation.org/wp-content/uploads/2014/02/jerom.pdf
29. Weiss, 5.
30. Weiss, 4.
31. Weiss, 5.
32. Weiss, 10.
33. Weiss, 10.
34. Weiss, 10.
35. Weiss, 12.
36. Weiss 13.
37. Weiss 16.
38. Weiss 21.
39. Rachel Weiss, "Jerom," January 31, 2018, personal communication
40. Weiss "Jerom", 28.
41. Weiss, 29.
42. Weiss, 29.
43. Weiss, 29.
44. Weiss, 30.
45. Weiss, 30.
46. Weiss, 30,31.
47. Weiss, 31.
48. Weiss, 31.
49. Weiss, 32.
50. Weiss, 33.
51. Weiss, 33.
52. Weiss, 34.
53. Weiss, 2.
54. Weiss, "Jerom," January 31, 2018, personal communication.
55. Wise, *Rattling the Cage. Towards Legal Rights for Animals*.
56. Wise, "Jerom", x, xi.
57. Wise, "Jerom", xii.
58. Henry Beston, *The Outeremost House* (New York: Henry Holt and Company, 1988), 25.

# Appendix: Physical texts

Here are six photographs of physical texts which you might be interested in considering from the perspective of those whose lives have or had, little or no power.

It is the processes of enquiry and reflection which are essential here; they sensitise us and take us into a deeper understanding of the meanings existing all around us in our everyday world.

I have provided a little background and a few considerations in each case.

## Text 1

This shows the "towpath" of a section of the Leeds to Liverpool canal which is 204 km long and was completed in 1816. Various goods were carried along it including stone and at one time, over a million tons of coal a year. The large, heavy boats were pulled by horses and the coal dug from the mines by the efforts of exploited workers and the terribly abused animals known as "pit ponies". These exploitive practices used the bodies of powerless individuals to create wealth for a few people. The overarching ideology would have been some form of hierarchical view of the world amalgamated to the engine of capitalism.

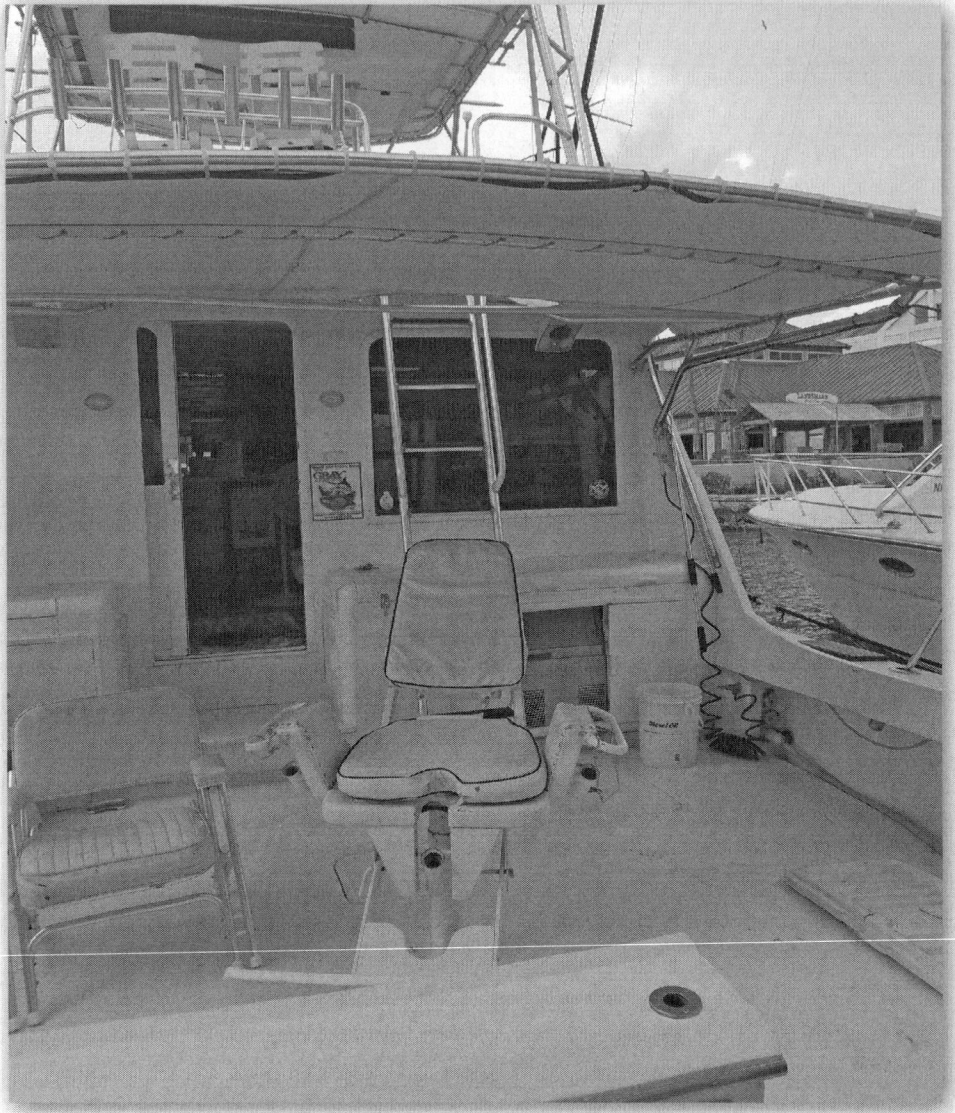

This is a *Fighting Chair* used by a fisherman to catch large fish. There are various fittings on the chair to enable the person doing this to support the equipment in use and secure themselves against the pulling of the fish who is trying to escape being killed. The fish has a hook or hooks in some part of its body and these are attached to a line which is held by the person fishing. This boat is based in the Bahamas and is hired out for this practice.

Power is everywhere, from the physical power of the chair and the boat itself to the social and economic power of those who use it. The animals who are attacked and killed in this way have no power. The ideology in use condones the killing of free living animals by humans and describes this particular activity as sport, as in "sport fishing".

## Text 3

This is a "sheep farm" near Ingleton, Yorkshire in the UK. It is the type of scene we might feel represents the countryside, the natural world, Nature. Apart from the few oaks, probably serving as a wind break or marker, the hills are devoid of trees although a few will be found in the narrow gorges of river valleys. The area was once forested but over many years the trees were removed by human activity in order to make open grassland for farming and also to obtain timber. All of the nonhuman occupants of the forests lost their homes. Some might have found shelter in the remaining scraps of forest, others would have starved and many would have been hunted and killed.

The stone walls, of which there are thousands of kilometres, are ancient and designed to confine captive nonhuman animals, especially cattle, pigs and sheep used for farming. The farming of animals dates back thousands of years and in the Middle Ages the Cistercians ran a large sheep breeding enterprise because wool was a much sort after commodity.[1] Following the devastating effects of the black death, labour was in short supply and rearing sheep was a good way to use humans efficiently and so a great wool industry developed even exporting wool and woollen cloth to mainland Europe. The monasteries were later dissolved but Yorkshire continued to prosper and wool became a major product during the industrial revolution.[2]

Large amounts of money were, and still are, made from the bodies of these captives. The sheep in the picture are a particular breed, having been genetically selected over many years. They are a monetary investment and an ongoing form of revenue stream with many people living off their bodies in some way or other.

In summary: over time the land was cleared, the original inhabitants wiped out and walls constructed to incarcerate the animals who were being exploited in farming. Animal farming is an oppressive social practice with a justifying ideology which is often based in some way on a hierarchy of beings.

**Text 4**

This is a photograph of part of the gardening section of a hardware shop in South Africa. It shows chemicals for killing ants, cockroaches, insects generally, snails, mice and rats. The merchandise on offer has snappy brand names and the packaging refers to the poisons in use. Behind these products are huge chemical plants where the constituents are manufactured with scientific expertise, a complex supply chain, organisation, administration and legislation. Research has been carried out into the effects of these poisons on many different living beings as well as those being "targeted". The global pesticide industry is valued at over sixty-five billion dollars. Here is a social practice of killing those beings whom we decide should not be present in "our" environment and these are some of the tools for that practice. An ideology supports and justifies these actions and is probably based on some form of human elitism amalgamated with capitalism.

**Text 5**

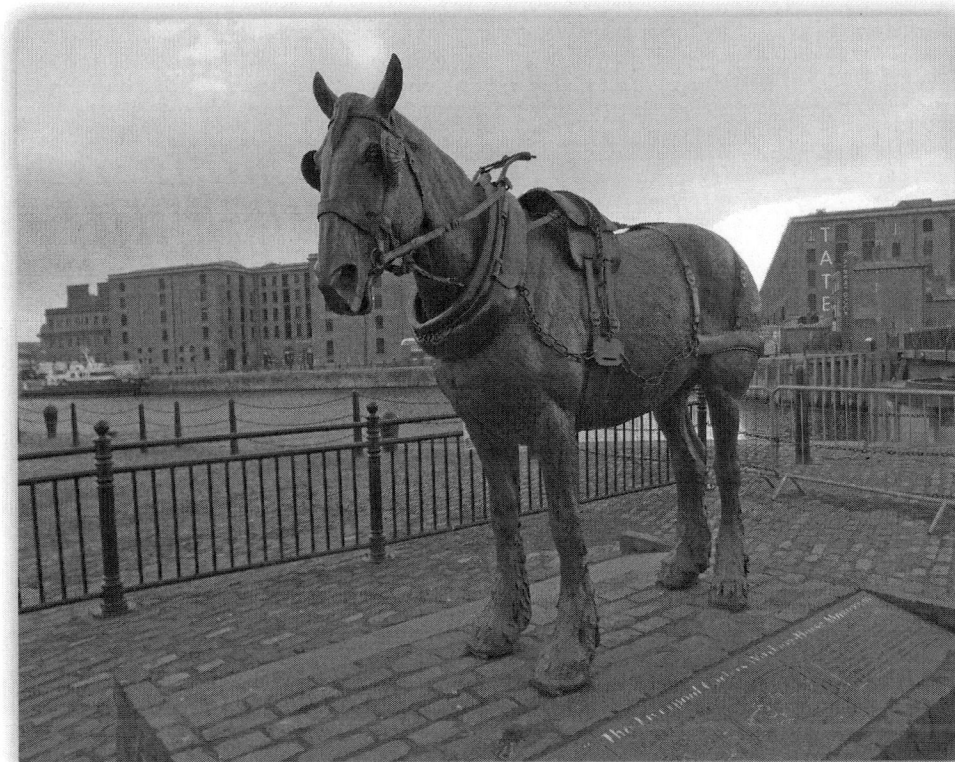

This monument titled "Waiting", was created by Judy Boyt to commemorate horses who were forced to work in all sorts of ways in the city of Liverpool. Many thousands were used daily, in all weathers and conditions, as industrialisation increased in the country. In the background are just a few of the many, large, old warehouses around the docks which speak of a thriving city, but while a few were getting rich most of its human inhabitants lived in dire poverty, and lived short lives.

The port was heavily involved in the slave trade and nearby, just out of shot of this photograph, is the International Slavery Museum. Ships took on goods here which would be sold in Africa in exchange for slaves who would then be transported to the southern states of America or perhaps other places.

These large horses were the victims of terrible mistreatment as were the working people of the city and the slaves taken from their homes in Africa. All were victims of exploitive social practices, each with its own ideological justification although I would suggest that all three were very similar.

**Text 6**

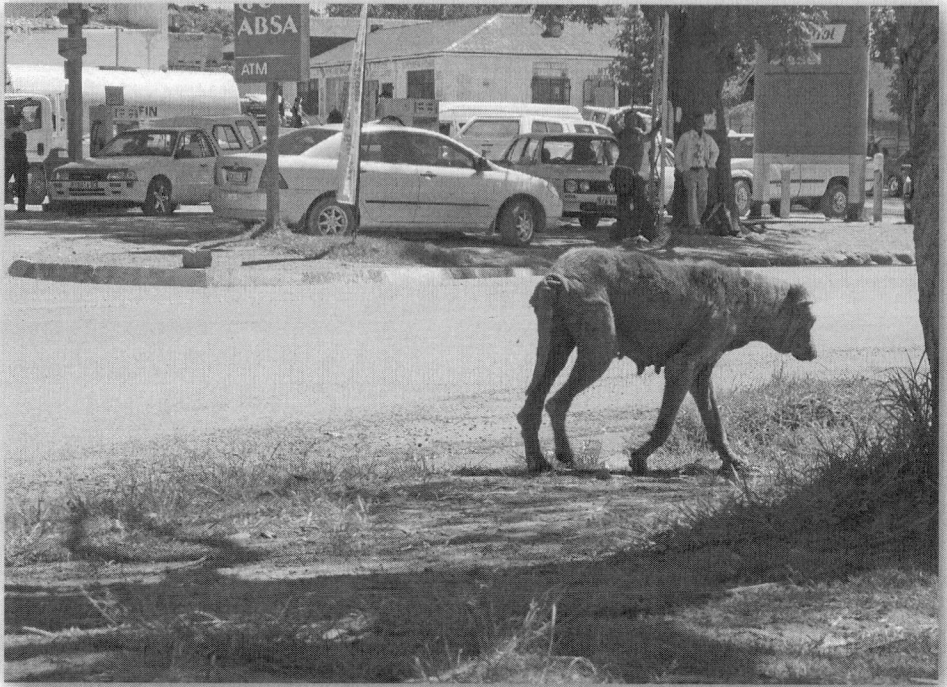

Here is a female dog in a small town in the Eastern Cape of South Africa. She is suffering from severe mange. It is likely she is a stray, possibly having been abandoned because of her condition and it is unlikely she will receive help. Behind her in this photograph stands the human occupied land of this place, the petrol station and shops and the roads carrying vehicles which are a threat to her life. She will look for food and water wherever she can find them and risk assault from humans in the process. She is an outsider, an outcast, no longer of any use and she has no home.

We make a practice of "keeping animals" for many uses and disposing of them at our convenience. In many, if not most, cases these are exploitive relationships but our ideological explanations about normality, purpose and hierarchy justify and excuse our actions.

### Endnotes

1   Simon Bell and Gemma Bell, "Introduction and history of sheep farming in the UK", The CANEPAL Project (Estonia: Estonian University of Life Sciences, November 2011).
2   Bell and Bell.

# Errata

*Reading the animal text in the landscape of the damned*

**Page 194: Endnotes to Chapter 1**

## Chapter 1

1. Du Fu or Tu Fu cited in Guy Gavriel Kay, *Under Heaven* (New York: Ace, 2011).
2. "History," Watchtree (blog), accessed February 2, 2016, http://www.watchtree.co.uk/reserve/history/.
3. BBC, "Makeover Miracle," accessed February 2, 2016, http://www.bbc.co.uk/cumbria/content/articles/2007/10/08/nob_watchtree_feature.shtml; Angelique Chrisafis, "The Killing Field of Cumbria," *The Guardian*, March 27, 2001, sec. UK news, http://www.theguardian.com/uk/2001/mar/27/footandmouth.angeliquechrisafis; "History."
4. M. Mort, "Psychosocial Effects of the 2001 UK Foot and Mouth Disease Epidemic in a Rural Population: Qualitative Diary Based Study," *BMJ* 331, no. 7527 (November 26, 2005): 1234–0, https://doi.org/10.1136/bmj.38603.375856.68.
5. "Foot and Mouth Disease in Cumbria – 2001," Visit Cumbria (blog), accessed March 20, 2018, https://www.visitcumbria.com/foot-and-mouth-disease-in-cumbria/; Angelique Chrisafis, "Foot and Mouth: The Killing Field of Cumbria," *The Guardian*, March 27, 2001, http://www.theguardian.com/uk/2001/mar/27/footandmouth.angeliquechrisafis.
6. David Campbell and Robert Lee, "Culling by Numbers Blackboard Economics and Foot and Mouth Disease Control, " http://www.fmd.brass.cf.ac.uk/culling.pdf, n.d.; National Audit Office, "The 2001 Outbreak of Foot and Mouth Disease," NAO Report (HC 939 2001-2002), https://www.nao.org.uk/wp-content/uploads/2002/06/0102939.pdf, 2002; Department for Environment Food and Rural Affairs (Defra), "UK – Foot and Mouth Disease – Information Page," accessed February 2, 2016, http://footandmouth.fera.defra.gov.uk/.
7. Solway Shore-Walker, "From 'Killing Field' to Wetland and Woods: Watchtree Nature Reserve, Cumbria," Solway Shore-Walker (blog), February 17, 2016, https://solwayshorewalker.wordpress.com/2016/02/17/from-killing-field-to-wetland-and-woods-watchtree-nature-reserve-cumbria/.
8. European Union, "Attitudes of EU Citizens towards Animal Welfare," *Special Eurobarometer* 270, 2007.
9. European Union, "Social Values, Science and Technology," *Special Eurobarometer* 225, 2005.
10. American Veterinary Medical Association, "U.S. Pet Ownership & Demographics Sourcebook (2012)," accessed February 10, 2016, https://www.avma.org/KB/Resources/Statistics/Pages/Market-research-statistics-US-Pet-Ownership-Demographics-Sourcebook.aspx?
11. George Dickinson, "Household Pet Euthanasia and Companion Animal Last Rites," *Phi Kappa Phi Forum* 94, no. 2 (Summer 2014): 4–6.
12. Kevin M. Donohue, "Pet Loss: Implications for Social Work Practice," *Social Work* 50, no. 2 (April 2005): 187–90, https://doi.org/10.1093/sw/50.2.187; Tamina Toray, "The Human-Animal Bond and Loss: Providing Support for Grieving Clients," *Journal of Mental Health Counseling* 26, no. 3 (July 2004): 244–59, https://doi.org/10.17744/mehc.26.3.udj040fw2gj75lqp.
13. Donohue, "Pet Loss: Implications for Social Work Practice."
14. Alastair Jamieson, "Owners Pay to Be Buried with Their Pets," *The Telegraph*, January 23, 2010, sec. News, http://www.telegraph.co.uk/news/health/pets-health/7061716/Owners-pay-to-be-buried-with-their-pets.html; "New Bill Would Allow Owners to Have Deceased Pets Buried with

Them," Life With Dogs (blog), accessed February 11, 2016, http://www.lifewithdogs.tv/2015/07/new-bill-would-allow-owners-to-have-deceased-pets-buried-with-them/.

15. Dickinson, "Household Pet Euthanasia and Companion Animal Last Rites."

16. Rod Preece, "Thoughts out of Season on the History of Animal Ethics," *Society & Animals* 15, no. 4 (October 1, 2007): 368, https://doi.org/10.1163/156853007X235537.

17. Andrew Linzey, *Creatures of the Same God: Explorations in Animal Theology* (New York: Lantern Books, 2009); Andrew Linzey, ed., *The Global Guide to Animal Protection*, (Urbana, Illinois: University of Illinois Press, 2013); Colin Spencer, *The Heretic's Feast: A History of Vegetarianism*, (Hanover, NH: UPNE, 1995).

18. C.J.C. Phillips, Principles of Cattle Production. (Wallingford: CABI Publishing., 2001).

19. Steven M. Wise, "Animal Rights One Step at a Time," in Animal Rights: Current Debates and New Perspectives, ed. Cass R Sunstein and Martha Nussbaum C (Oxford: Oxford University Press, 2004), 10.

20. Andrew Linzey, The Global Guide to Animal Protection, First (Urbana: University of Illionois Press, 2013).

21. Lisa Johnson, *Power Knowledge and Animals* (Houndmills, UK: Palgrave Macmillan, 2012).

22. "Ohio Revised Code – 959.13 Cruelty to Animals (1977).," accessed February 4, 2016, http://codes.ohio.gov/orc/959.13.

23. RSA (Republic of South Africa), "Animals Protection Act No.71 of 1962.' *Government Gazette Extraordinary*, 22 June 1962.

24. Karen Davis, *Prisoned Chickens Poisoned Eggs*, 2nd ed. (Summertown: Book Publishing Company, 2009), 179.

25. Les Mitchell, "Moral Disengagement and Support for Nonhuman Animal Farming," *Society & Animals* 19, no. 1 (January 1, 2011): 38–58, https://doi.org/10.1163/156853011X545529; Les Mitchell, "Discourse and the Oppression of Nonhuman Animals: A Critical Realist Account." PhD thesis, (Rhodes University: South Africa, 2007).

26. Robert Agnew, "The Causes of Animal Abuse: A Social-Psychological Analysis," *Theoretical Criminology* 2, no. 2 (1998): 179.

27. FAO, "FAOSTAT," 2014, http://www.fao.org/faostat/en/#data/QL

28. Upton Sinclair, *The Jungle*, Literary Touchstone Edition (Clayton, Delaware: Prestwick House, 2005), 41.